Tools, Tips, and Techniques for Enhancing
Your Internet Activities

1999

Canadian Internet
Handbook

NATIONAL NO. 1 BESTSELLER

Jim Carroll / Rick Broadhead

Canada's Bestselling Internet Authors

**Foreword by John Cleghorn,
Chairman and CEO, Royal Bank of Canada**

Prentice Hall Canada Inc.
Scarborough, Ontario

Canadian Cataloguing in Publication Data

Annual.
1994–
Compiled 1994– by Jim Carroll and Rick Broadhead.
ISSN 1204-9034
ISBN 0-13-974940-3 (1999)

1. Internet (Computer network) – Handbooks, manuals, etc. I. Carroll, Jim, 1959–
II. Broadhead, Rick

TK5105.875.I57C37   004.6'7 C96-900997-6

 © 1998 J.A. Carroll and Rick Broadhead
Prentice Hall Canada Inc.
Scarborough, Ontario
A Division of Simon & Schuster/A Viacom Company

Prentice-Hall, Inc., Upper Saddle River, New Jersey
Prentice-Hall International (UK) Limited, London
Prentice-Hall of Australia, Pty. Limited, Sydney
Prentice-Hall Hispanoamericana, S.A., Mexico City
Prentice-Hall of India Private Limited, New Delhi
Prentice-Hall of Japan, Inc., Tokyo
Simon & Schuster Southeast Asia Private Limited, Singapore
Editora Prentice-Hall do Brasil, Ltda., Rio de Janeiro

ISBN 0-13-974940-3

Director, Trade Group: Robert Harris
Editor: Betty Robinson
Assistant Editor: Joan Whitman
Production Coordinator: Shannon Potts
Art Direction: Mary Opper
Cover and Interior Design: Sputnik
Cover Photograph: William Huber/Photonica
Page Layout: Anne Goodes/Hermia Chung

1 2 3 4 5 W 02 01 00 99 98

Printed and bound in Canada

Visit the Prentice Hall Canada Web site! Send us your comments, browse our catalogues,
and more. **www.phcanada.com**

Every reasonable effort has been made to obtain permissions for all articles and data used in this
edition. If errors or omissions have occurred, they will be corrected in future editions provided
written notification has been received by the publisher.

Accolades for Previous Editions of the Canadian Internet Handbook

One of the best things about the book is its consistently Canadian perspective in a medium saturated with American opinions.

The Vancouver Sun, April 25, 1998

Jim Carroll and Rick Broadhead are a publishing powerhouse to be reckoned with when it comes to books on the Canadian Internet. With almost 20 best-selling titles to their credit, and several hundreds of thousands of copies of their books sold, there are few wired Canadian households that do not contain a copy of at least one of their books. This new edition represents a major step forward for Carroll and Broadhead, who have just written what should be considered the definitive book on the state of the Net in Canada.

Keith Schengili-Roberts, *The Computer Paper*, January 1998

What started out as an introduction to the Internet has wisely evolved into an encyclopedia of social, economic and political issues all Canadians must understand about cyberspace.

Jack Kapica, *The Globe and Mail*, December 12, 1997

Authors Jim Carroll and Rick Broadhead have just come out with the latest edition of their annual look at Canada's cyberspace, and once again it's informative, enlightening, and damning—sometimes all at the same time. Regardless of whether you're a web-slinging pro or a hopeless novice, there is simply nothing else that compares to this volume when it comes to taking the chaos and trying to figure out what it all means...Carroll and Broadhead's book is a rarity in the field of computer publishing; it makes the Net matter to ordinary people, and shows us why we should care about what will happen next.

Mitchell Brown, *CNET Canada*, October 27, 1997

Condensed, focused and relevant to the issues Internet users face today, the 1998 edition is a must-have for anyone currently online. Even if you feel you are an informed, experienced Internet user, the 1998 Handbook will offer you new insights into areas of the online world you may not have noticed before.

Andrew Robulack, *Yukon News*, November 12, 1997

Internet handbooks, typically thousand-page compendia of everything you would ever want to know about the Net, typically suffer from instant obsolescence. The 1997 *Canadian Internet Handbook* is one of the few of the genre that bucks the trend.

Matthew Friedman, *The Montreal Gazette*, December 11, 1996

The *Handbook* is almost an annual "year in review" for Canadians online. And this, to me, is its greatest charm.

K.K. Campbell, *The Toronto Star*, December 12, 1996

If you're at all serious about taming the Net, you won't want to venture into the cyber frontier without the *1996 Canadian Internet Handbook*. If there is something you want to know about the Internet in Canada that is not in this book, my guess is the only place you'll find it is on the Net.

Gerry Blackwell, January 6, 1996

If you are to buy only one Internet reference book this year, get the 1996 edition of the Canadian Internet Handbook by Jim Carroll and Rick Broadhead.

Marg Meikle, *Canadian Living*, December 31, 1995

I highly recommend this book to both new and experienced Internet users. The *Canadian Internet Handbook* has joined Newton's Telecom Dictionary as a key reference which I keep right beside my computer.

Ian Angus, *TELEMANAGEMENT Magazine*, The Angus Report on Communications Systems, Services, and Strategies, February 1995

Contents

Foreword

by John Cleghorn

E-economy and the New Business Realities

When Guglielmo Marconi transmitted the first transatlantic radio signal from Newfoundland to Cornwall, England, nearly 100 years ago, he may not have imagined the full impact that technological innovations like his would have on Western economies. He may not have guessed that by 1930 the agrarian economy would be overshadowed by industry, and that it would plummet to only 10% of the U.S. GDP, from 60% in 1890.

The winners at the turn of the last century were those nations and enterprises who foresaw, welcomed, and adapted to the transformation from an agrarian to an industrial economy. The same is likely to happen with the current shift to an electronic economy (e-economy), with knowledge replacing labour and with capital as the key value driver. Amid the shifting tides, threats and opportunities abound. Enterprising nations and organizations stand to benefit a great deal, but failure to adapt can also entail great loss. How Canada fares will depend largely on the ability of our businesses and governments to anticipate the outcome of the epic changes we are witnessing.

Our governments realize the importance of embracing this new reality. In fact, Prime Minister Jean Chrétien sees developing world-class computer and information technology as the new national dream for a new millennium as vital to Canada's future as was the construction of roads, bridges, and buildings during this century. Finance Minister Paul Martin believes that although natural resources remain an important part of the Canadian economy, our future success will be determined by our expertise in meeting the challenges of the new modern silicon economy.

The Canadian financial services sector has so far played a leading role in developing and using information technology. Besides delivering the obvious consumer benefits of greater access and convenience, bank investments in technology have helped put Canada on the map in terms of the e-economy and knowledge-based employment.

No longer is the front door of the local branch the main access point for bank clients. Only five years ago, computer banking, telephone banking, smart cards, and Internet banking were virtually unknown to Canadian consumers. Today, bank customers serve themselves, check account balances, make transfers and loan payments, fill out credit card, loan and membership applications, pay bills, buy and sell securities, and download transaction information to personal finance software, all from the comfort of their own homes.

The players and the marketplace are also changing. As globalization erases borders and increases our market opportunities, competition increases as well. All competitors have one thing in common: they are taking advantage of Internet technology to deliver financial intermediary products to Canadians. They also have very deep financial pockets.

Banks from around the world have recognized that they can use the Internet as another delivery network. In fact, Internet-only banks such as American Finance & Investment, Atlanta Internet Bank, Busey e-bank, and Compubank are emerging. With no branch office overhead, Internet-only banks can offer customers loans and other services at a lower cost and savings accounts at higher interest rates, all at a higher profit.

The Internet enables banks to diversify in ways we never could before. We can expand our services to serve broader markets or streamline them to reach more targeted groups with a focus on specifics such as mutual funds or lending.

This all adds up to convenience and choice for consumers and fiercer-than-ever competition for Canadian banks. Royal Bank is responding to the new competitive realities by innovating, investing further in technology, and expanding into new markets. We have been providing Internet banking for several years and have expanded our reach to the United States through The Security First Network Bank of Atlanta, the world's first Internet bank. This acquisition gives Royal Bank as well as Canada a head start in a business that will likely dominate banking in the 21st century.

In order for Canada to compete in the Information Age, governments, businesses, and ordinary citizens need to make choices conducive to increasing the knowledge-based sector. As things stand, Canadian banks play a major, but largely unacknowledged, role in enhancing our country's knowledge-based sector.

We need to challenge, encourage, and provide incentives for our future workforce to make them realize the potential they have. We also need to keep stimulating jobs in Canada and stop the exodus of some of our best minds to companies south of the border.

The rapid and transformational nature of change will continue to place new demands on the workforce. We need to value our workforce and provide the training and opportunities to succeed.

As knowledge-based work increases in the financial services industry, so will the opportunities for employees with higher education. Currently, Royal Bank has 93% of its jobs in Canada. Our intention is to achieve a scale that would support and grow high-quality, knowledge-based jobs in Canada, through both direct hirings and increased business to knowledge-based suppliers.

The Internet offers us many opportunities as individuals and as a country. It has already changed our lives and will continue to do so. If we manage our resources well and take advantage of what the Internet offers us, Canada will become a global leader, creating and maintaining wealth in a knowledge-based economy.

Some critics of the Internet say that it removes the human connection. While some see this as a real risk, we see it as an opportunity; we complement our online services with a continued focus on relationship banking. While you may not see your banker for your everyday transactions, your business encounters with us will consist of higher-quality relationships built on offering financial advice and counsel.

The Internet presents exciting opportunities. As it evolves, we all play a role in how it will shape our future. Just as Marconi's radio connected two continents almost a century ago, the Internet will connect Canada to the world and the business opportunities it holds.

About the Authors

Jim Carroll, **CA**, is an internationally recognized Internet expert, popular media authority, and business consultant. He is author of the critically acclaimed book *Surviving the Information Age*, a motivational work that encourages people to cope with the future, and is a popular contributor to many leading Canadian publications. He has been recognized by the *Financial Post* as one of Canada's leading keynote speakers, providing motivating and challenging presentations for tens of thousands of North Americans at annual conferences, meetings, corporate events, and seminars. Clients include the Business Development Bank of Canada, the American Marketing Association, the Canadian Life and Health Assurance Association, the National Association of Fleet Administrators, Nortel, IBM, Remax, the Canadian Institute of Mortgage Brokers and Lenders, the CIBC, Montreal Trust, Great West Life, Scotia McLeod, the Royal Bank of Canada, Canada Trust, and many others. With his consulting practice, Mr. Carroll is noted for his ability to help organizations think strategically about the opportunity afforded by the Internet. Mr. Carroll is represented in Canada by the National Speakers Bureau of Vancouver, B.C., an organization that represents Canada's leading speakers and thinkers. He is also represented in the United States by Leading Authorities, a speakers bureau that represents many of the world's most widely recognized and popular political, entertainment, business, and technology personalities. He can be reached online by e-mail at **jcarroll@jimcarroll.com** or through his Web site, **www.jimcarroll.com**.

Rick Broadhead, **MBA**, is one of Canada's foremost Internet experts, industry observers, and a leading consultant and commentator on the Internet and the fast-growing field of electronic commerce. Mr. Broadhead has been retained as a keynote speaker, workshop facilitator, and consultant by businesses and associations across North America to help them understand how the latest electronic commerce trends will affect their industries. Rick also teaches at York University's Division of Executive Development in Toronto, where he has advised managers and senior executives from hundreds of leading North American firms and helped them integrate the Internet into all facets of their businesses. In his consulting practice, Mr. Broadhead assists organizations in formulating and implementing their Internet strategies. His expertise has been sought by Fortune 500 firms and many Canadian and North American industry leaders, including McDonald's, Microsoft Corporation, the Royal Bank of Canada, Sprint, VISA International, Imperial Oil, PolyGram, EMI Music, Manulife Financial, and Mackenzie Financial Services. He can be reached by e-mail at **rickb@sympatico.ca**, or visit his World Wide Web site at **www.rickbroadhead.com**.

Acknowledgments

We would like to thank the entire editorial, sales, marketing, and production team at Prentice Hall Canada for their efforts on this book.

A special thanks to Robert Harris for skillfully and professionally managing all of our book projects. We would also like to acknowledge Karen Alliston, Judy Bunting, Hart Hillman, and Joan Whitman for their editorial assistance; Andrea Aris, Michael Bubna, Trina Milnes, and Linda Voticky for their sales and marketing support; and Jan Coughtrey, Kelly Dickson, David Jolliffe, and Erich Volk for their production assistance.

To Betty Robinson, our editor: our hectic world is made all the more manageable and bearable through your hard efforts! A huge thanks!

A very warm thank you to Mike Quinn of IBM Canada for arranging the ThinkPad 770 on which much of this book was prepared. At last, a laptop computer that has the capacity, power, screen resolution, and other features that make it a true partner to the creative process!

We are grateful to Internet Light and Power, Internet Direct, iSTAR Internet, Rogers WAVE, Sympatico, and Netcom Canada for the provision of Internet accounts and Web hosting services.

We would like to thank all the Canadian Webmasters who took the time to respond to our Canadian Webmaster survey: Ellen Agger, Virginia Brailey, Jean Pierre Burdett, Wayne Carrigan, Addy Ching, Simon Cohen, Tom Dawson, Thomas Hader, Mike Hyttinen, Theresa Jobateh, John Pullam, Paul Schwartz, Hart Steinfeld, Sandy Wills, Jenny Winterbottom, the General Motors of Canada Internet Marketing Organization, and the Webmaster at Alliance Video Store.

Additional thanks go to Tibor Shanto at Dow Jones Interactive Publishing in Toronto and Ian Barker at Infomart for arranging the guest accounts that we used while writing portions of this book.

The CD-ROM at the back of this book wouldn't have been possible without the assistance and support of Doug MacDonald at TUCOWS and John Nemanic at Internet Direct in Toronto. Thank you both!

Thanks also to Leslie Ray at Northern Light for working with us to develop the special offer at the front of this book.

We are also grateful to our families. Rick would like to thank his family for their continuing support. Jim would like to give his heartfelt thanks and appreciation to his wife, Christa, for effort above and beyond the call, and to Thomas and Willie for cheering daddy on to get the book done.

We appreciate the ongoing support of our readers and fans and the millions of Internet users across Canada. This book would not be possible without you!

Finally, a lasting tribute to a true friend, althepal, who for many years shared with one of the authors—his son—many warm and encouraging e-mail messages. With his determination and enthusiasm to master the Internet, he demonstrated that technology is much more than a tool.

Contacting Us

We are always interested in hearing from our readers. We welcome your comments, criticisms, and suggestions, and we will use your feedback to improve future editions of this book. We do try to respond to all e-mail sent to us.

We are also very interested in tracking Canadian Internet "success stories." If you have found the Internet helpful for either business or leisure activities, drop us a line. We might use your experience in a future case study. Similarly, if you are aware of a Canadian organization that is using the Internet in an innovative or significant way, please let us know.

Contacting the Authors Directly

Here is how to contact us on the Internet:

To reach	Send e-mail to
Both authors	authors@handbook.com
Jim Carroll	jcarroll@jimcarroll.com
Rick Broadhead	rickb@sympatico.ca

Automatic E-mail Information

You can easily obtain current information about this book or any of our other books by sending a message to **info@handbook.com**. You will be sent back a message that provides details on our books, our online resources, ordering instructions, and other relevant information.

Our World Wide Web Sites

The World Wide Web site for all our books is **www.handbook.com**. There you will find information about all of our publications, including press releases, reviews from the media, and ordering instructions.

Jim Carroll maintains a World Wide Web site at **www.jimcarroll.com**, where he provides background with respect to his consulting and speaking activities, and where he regularly posts the articles he has written for various publications. In addition, the site includes the video that is discussed in the chapter about adding audio and video to your Web site.

Rick Broadhead maintains a World Wide Web site at **www.rickbroadhead.com** with information about his work, his clients, and pointers to World Wide Web sites from his articles, presentations, and seminars about the Internet and electronic commerce.

Conventions Used in This Book

Throughout this book, we provide pointers to sites or discussion groups that can be found on the Internet—for example, World Wide Web sites or USENET newsgroups. These addresses are bolded as follows:

www...

for example, **www.handbook.com**.

We have made every effort to ensure that the Internet addresses contained in this book are accurate. All the addresses were verified at the time of editing. But because the Internet is constantly changing, inevitably some resources will have changed their location or just disappeared. If you find an address that doesn't work, please let us know about it by sending an e-mail to **authors@handbook.com**. We will update the entry in subsequent editions of this book.

This is the sixth annual edition of the *Canadian Internet Handbook*. The first four editions, beginning in 1994, focused on helping Canadians learn how to use the Internet. Last year the 1998 edition took a dramatic turn. Instead of focusing on "how to," we examined the impact of the Internet on our daily lives, our society, and our culture and looked at ways that Canadians could use the Internet more effectively and more proactively.

It was that last issue that seemed to strike a chord with our many loyal readers. So with this year's edition we are focusing on tools, tips, and techniques for enhancing your Internet activities.

Regardless of how much time you spend on the Internet, we think you will agree that there are always new tools to discover, new tips to learn, and new techniques to make the Web less frustrating, more productive, and more efficient. We are in the fortunate position that our careers are defined by the Internet. The result is that we are constantly learning about new technologies, services, and software programs that will enhance your online activities. And since we love to share it all with you, this year's edition of the *Canadian Internet Handbook* focuses on practical information that will help you to improve all aspects of your Internet use.

We have divided this book into four themes:

• Assessing the Effectiveness of Your Web Site

• Protecting Yourself Online

• Improving Your Productivity on the Internet

• Enhancing Your Web Site

In the first theme we examine a variety of innovative techniques and tools that you can use to assess the effectiveness of your Web site. How confident are you that your Web site isn't disappointing or frustrating your users? Are your Web pages taking horrendously long periods of time to download? Are old Web pages from your site still showing up on search engines? How easily can customers find you on the Web? How accessible is your Web site to visually impaired users? To help you evaluate the design and usability of your site and fix any problems, we have prepared a comprehensive checklist that every Canadian Web site owner should review. We are also excited to pass on to you the personal insights of some of Canada's most progressive Webmasters. Our panel of 17 Canadian Webmasters has given their opinions on everything from Internet strategy to Web site design; we have summarized their responses to our questions in an easy-to-reference format.

In the second theme we focus on giving you the tools and information you need to adequately protect yourself online. We are becoming increasingly concerned with the many risks now on the Internet: viruses, privacy, security, and data loss. We thoroughly review each issue and recommend steps to take to safeguard your assets and your personal information.

We have devoted our third theme to helping you improve your productivity online. One problem with the Internet is that the longer you use it, the more likely you will fall into a routine. And it is likely that your routine may not be the most productive. We think you will be pleasantly surprised by the wide range of software programs that are available to help you solve some of the most frustrating problems associated with the Internet. In addition to reviewing productivity applications for the Web, we show you how to improve the speed of your Internet connection, archive your e-mail messages, search the Internet faster, set up electronic newsclipping services, and use remote communication and videoconferencing software.

In the final theme we discuss how you can add audio and video capabilities to your Web pages, and we show how easy it is to process credit card transactions on your Web site. Thanks to a new type of company called an "e-commerce service provider," setting up a retail presence on the Internet is easier than ever before. Both multimedia and e-commerce technologies are maturing rapidly. We will show you what is involved in integrating these technologies into your existing Web site.

Finally, we close the book with our observations on where we think the Internet is headed. We have chosen to focus our comments on the impact of the Linux operating system and what is known as open source software. We think that the Internet is about to undergo a significant change as a result of these technologies. This is an important chapter for anyone who is interested in the future of the Internet.

Perhaps best of all, we have prepared a CD-ROM containing trial versions of virtually all the tools and software programs that we have illustrated and recommended throughout the book. As soon as you finish a chapter, you can begin experimenting with the programs immediately. The CD-ROM also contains many of the programs that were recommended by our panel of Canadian Webmasters. You'll find the CD-ROM in a pouch at the back of the book.

Whether you're an experienced Internet user or a novice, we are confident that in this book you will find tools, tips, and techniques that you never knew before. Let's get started!

Assessing the Effectiveness of Your Web Site

If, like many users of the Internet, you have had a Web site for several years, it is probably time that you gave it a good, hard, critical look. That is why in this section we take a look at tools, tips, and techniques that you can use to enhance the effectiveness of your Web site.

In Chapter 1, "Evaluating the Design and Reliability of Your Web Site," we walk you through the process of assessing your site in terms of how well it works and how well it does its job. We have visited far too many Web sites that feature broken links, massive graphics that take too long to download, and other design flaws. There are lots of useful and innovative programs available to help you assess your own site, in addition to a number of practical tips. Read this chapter, and you will be able to fine-tune your site to maximum effect.

And then there are the great Web sites that nobody can visit because we can't find them! We don't know how many times we have gone looking for a Canadian company or Web site and haven't been able to find it. We are amazed at the number of Canadian Web sites whose creators have not taken the time to ensure that they are listed on major search engines and directories, as well as listing themselves elsewhere on the Internet. In Chapter 2, "How to Improve Your Web Site's Visibility on the Internet?" we take a look at what you should be doing to ensure that people can find you online. We give guidance on where you should be listing your site and what you should do to ensure that you appear near the top of the list when people do a search online.

Finally, for the best tips and guidance on ensuring the effectiveness of your Web site, we contacted the Webmasters of many of Canada's leading Web sites. Their observations are in Chapter 3, "Tips From Canadian Webmasters." You will find their comments to be particularly useful and relevant for fine-tuning your Web site.

chapter one

Evaluating the Design and Reliability of Your Web Site

...it's a good time to do an assessment of your Web site from a business perspective and get a handle on how it is affecting your bottom line.

Brooks Talley and Lori Mitchell, "Web Site Analysis: Controlling Your Web Site," *InfoWorld*, July 27, 1998, Vol. 20, Issue 30

Highlights

1. Regularly audit your Web site to check for orphan Web pages, to verify that all the links are working, and to ensure that old Web pages are not showing up on search engines.

2. Make sure that your Web site can be viewed by users with disabilities as well as by users with different browsers. Consider translating important sections of your Web site into different languages to encourage non-English-speaking visitors.

3. Consider using a market research firm to survey visitors to your Web site. Examples of such firms include SurveySite and TestNow.

4. Your site should be easy for users to navigate. Use intuitive names for all the links on your site, consider implementing a dropdown menu on your homepage, and make sure that a consistent set of navigation buttons appears on all pages of your site.

5. Regularly test the speed of pages in your Web site to ensure that they don't take too long to download. Consider using a service like NetMechanic's Server Check Pro to assess the reliability and performance of the computer that is hosting your Web site.

If you have had a Web site for a few years, or even if you have set up a new site in the last little while, we think that it is useful to assess how effective your Web site is in terms of its content, layout, and design. There are a lot of useful tools available that help you determine if your site is technically in tip-top shape. There are also many practical things that you can do to ensure that the Web site avoids some of the more common pitfalls that cause much frustration to visitors.

In this chapter we look at tools, tips, and techniques for undertaking an assessment of the overall design and reliability of your Web site.

Web Site Checklist

1. Is it easy for people to locate you through your Web site?

This is probably the biggest beef that we have with many Web sites. Quite often, we find that it is very difficult to locate information about how to contact someone affiliated with a particular Web site, or to find an e-mail address, phone number, or fax number associated with a particular person or department. There are simply too many Web sites that still do not list basic contact information.

You should ensure that you have a section, found directly on your homepage, that provides detailed contact information. Make all of it available in one place; don't scatter it throughout your site, forcing the user to look for it. Include basic information that is appropriate to your Web site, such as names, phone numbers, e-mail addresses, fax numbers, street address, and other information.

It seems like a simple thing to do, but there are a lot of sites that don't do it.

2. Is there a consistent set of navigation buttons in the site?

The second common fault we find with many Canadian Web sites is that it isn't easy to navigate throughout the site.

Most Web developers have come to the decision that a Web site should have a consistent set of navigation buttons that are located on all pages of the site. Wherever you are in the Web site, you will be presented with this list of buttons. This helps you in navigating to the major sections located within the site.

A good example is GlobeFund (**globefund.theglobeandmail.com**), a mutual fund service from *The Globe and Mail*. Visit any page within the Web site, and you will notice that the top of the screen always lists a series of buttons that you can use to easily travel anywhere within the site:

You don't have to be a sophisticated Web developer to include this capability, nor do you have to use what are known as "frames," which can be quite complicated to implement on a Web site. You simply need to ensure that the same set of buttons is included on each and every page, regardless of the content on that page.

3. Are your pages very slow to retrieve?

It is very easy to go overboard in designing a Web page, loading it up with all kinds of graphics and images that make it extremely pleasing to view. But these images can be very, very slow to retrieve, particularly for someone who isn't using a very fast modem.

This is why you should use a program that checks your Web site and prepares a report on how long it could take to view particular pages for different speeds of connecting to the Internet. Two such programs are Linkbot, from a Canadian company called Tetranet Software (**www.tetranetsoftware.com/linkbot-info.htm**), and SiteSweeper (**www.sitetech.com**) from Site Technologies Inc. Both provide a report that tells you whether you have potential problems with the size of the images that you use in your site, in terms of how long it will take someone to retrieve the page. They do this by accessing every page in your Web site, reviewing the size of each page including the images on the page, and then calculating an average download time for each page.

Linkbot summarizes this information in a report detailing "slow pages," which says how long it could take for someone to retrieve certain pages on your Web site if a 28.8 Kbps modem is used or if an ISDN or dedicated T1 connection to the Internet is used:

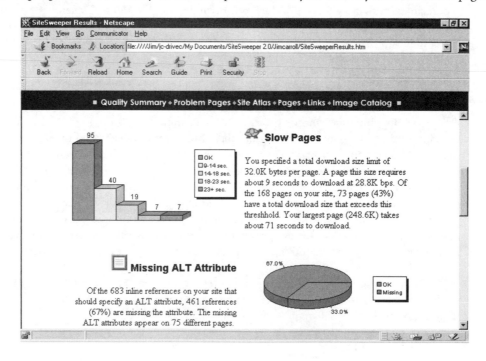

SiteSweeper provides a summary of the basic problems that your site may have with slow pages:

It then provides a report identifying the problem pages:

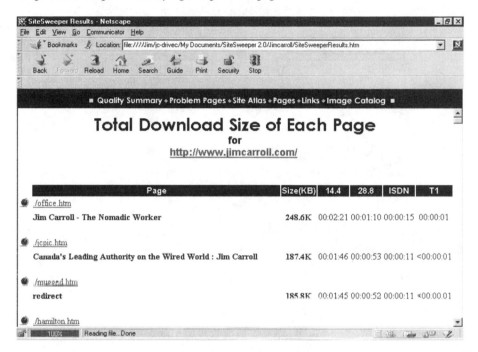

It can be very easy to overlook the potential for a problem with your pages in terms of size, particularly as your site becomes more complicated.

We admit that in analyzing one of our sites using SiteSweeper, we realized we had a pretty serious problem. While writing this chapter we found that because of the excessive size of one particular image that we had uploaded, many of our pages were now 185 KB in size. This meant that it would take visitors with a 14.4 or 28.8 Kbps modem anywhere from 50 seconds to a minute and a half to retrieve any one of the problem pages.

Clearly, we had to reduce the size of that image, a photo that we had taken with a digital camera. What did we do? We used a program called Paint Shop Pro (**www.jasc.com**) to reduce the size of the file substantially, from 185 KB to 65 KB, without any noticeable loss of quality. We strongly recommend that you learn how to reduce the size of image files on your Web site using a program like Paint Shop Pro. You can obtain a demo version of Paint Shop Pro and many other image manipulation programs at TUCOWS (**www.tucows.com**).

There are also some online services to help you deal with manipulating the size of your images. We visited the NetMechanic site (**www.netmechanic.com**), an online service that provides a number of useful utilities to help you with your Web site.

NetMechanic includes a free service called GIFbot, which takes an image from your site and alters it using different levels of image quality. Simply provide it with the Web address of the image or a Web page containing a number of images, and GIFbot will build you a new page that shows the image as it will appear when altered.

You can choose to keep any of the altered images and use them in your Web site, thus reducing the time it takes for people to download that page from your Web site. In our situation, we found that we could reduce our image to about 15,000 bytes and still have a good quality picture:

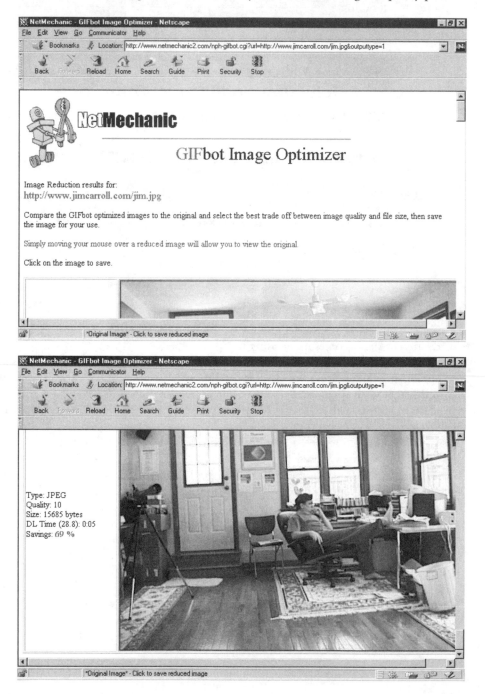

Another service worth checking out is GIFWizard (**www.gifwizard.com**), which does the same type of thing. For a fee of U.S. $1, you can have a trial of the service for one day. You can then have it check pages one by one, throughout your site. GIFWizard will then advise you how it can compress images throughout the site, thereby improving on the length of time it takes to access certain pages. If you find the service useful, you can sign up for one year for U.S. $79. The service is technically more complex than NetMechanic's GIFbot, but it is worth looking into.

With GIFWizard you can also see how your site stacks up against 250 other sites in terms of the page size. GIFWizard will examine the first 10 pages of your site, and then let you know where you stand:

tip Tune Up Your Web Site

GIF Lube (**www.giflube.com**) is a popular commercial service that will optimize the graphics on your Web site.

4. Have you included the ability for visitors to search your site?

As your Web site becomes larger and larger, it might become more difficult for people to find information, even if you include a consistent set of navigation buttons throughout your site.

Enter search engines. You can add a search engine so that visitors to your Web site can easily and quickly find what they want. This feature is on many Web sites, but you may not have thought about adding it to your own site. There are a couple of options here. The first is to check with your Internet service provider to see if they have any tools that you can use to add a search engine to your Web site. Many Internet service providers include instructions on their Web sites to help customers set up search capabilities on their Web sites.

For example, the Web site for our books is located on the Web servers of Internet Direct (**www.idirect.com**), a Toronto-based Internet service provider. In their Help section under "Do-It-Yourself Web" they provide a set of pages that gives advice to their customers on how to establish and maintain a Web site on Internet Direct. Included in this section is a page that details how customers can add a search engine to their Web sites:

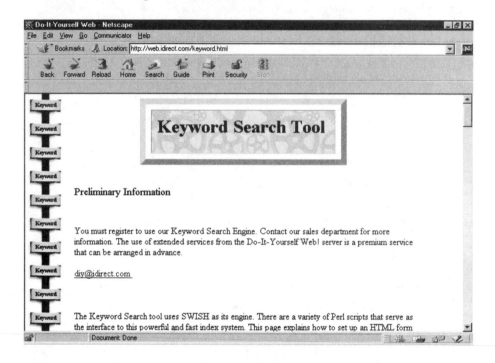

Check with your Internet service provider to find out if they have a similar help file available on their Web site. If they do, adding search capability to your Web site will be as easy as following the instructions that your Internet service provider gives you. If you don't see this type of information on your Internet service provider's Web site, call and ask for assistance. They should be able to provide you with additional guidance or build the search engine for you for a small fee.

Another alternative is to use one of the software programs that allow you to quickly and easily create a search function for your Web site—without any programming or technical knowledge. It used to be the case that if you wanted to set up a search engine on your Web site, you had to get access to your Web server (the computer hosting your Web site) and do some heavy-duty programming. Fortunately, this is no longer the case.

One example is Wisebot (available from **www.tetranetsoftware.com**). Wisebot will scan your Web site and create a site map, search engine, master index, and "What's New" page for your Web site.

For example, here's the alphabetical index that Wisebot created for the Web site belonging to one of the authors of this book:

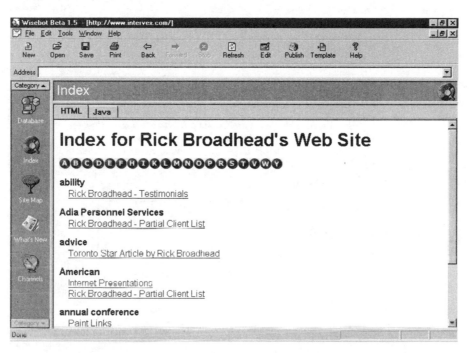

Wisebot creates the index by extracting keywords from all your Web pages and then organizing them in an alphabetical index. Once the index has been created, Wisebot makes it easy to edit the index. For example, you can create your own title for the page and pick the keywords that you want to associate with certain Web pages:

Edit Index

Keywords URLs Options

Page Title	URL
☑ Internet Presentations	http://www.intervex.com/present.htm
☑ Municipal Information Systems ...	http://www.intervex.com/misa4.htm
☑ Paint Links	http://www.intervex.com/paint.htm
☑ Rick Broadhead - Consulting S...	http://www.intervex.com/consult.htm
☑ Rick Broadhead - Partial Client ...	http://www.intervex.com/clients.htm
☑ Rick Broadhead - Testimonials	http://www.intervex.com/quotes.htm
☑ Rick Broadhead, Internet Spea...	http://www.intervex.com/
☑ RRSP Article by Rick Broadhead	http://www.intervex.com/star2.htm
☑ Toronto Star Article by Rick Bro...	http://www.intervex.com/star1.htm

Keywords	Source
☑ bank	Extractor
☑ Canada Trust	User
☑ mutual fund	Extractor
☑ on-line	Extractor
☑ resources	Extractor
☑ retirement	Extractor
☑ RRSP	Extractor
☑ RRSP contribution	Extractor

☐ Hide deleted keywords

[Add Keyword...]

[OK]   [Cancel]   [Help]

Add Keyword

Add keyword for the selected URL:

| Canada Trust |

[OK]   [Cancel]

And you can easily delete keywords completely or delete them only for selected Web pages on your site:

Once you have finished editing your index, Wisebot makes it easy to upload the files to your Web site:

Simply create a link to the index from the homepage of your Web site, and visitors to your site can use it to browse the contents of your Web site:

Assessing the Effectiveness
of Your Web Site

Protecting Yourself Online

Improving Your Productivity
on the Internet

Enhancing Your Web Site

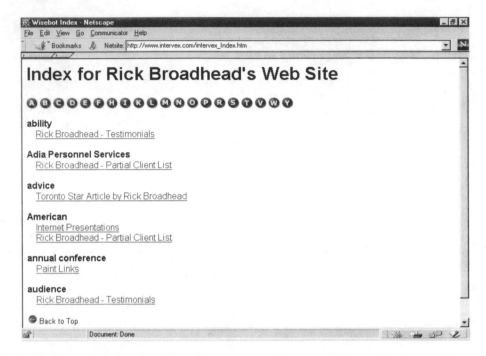

This whole process took less than five minutes and required very little technical knowledge on the part of the user.

You can also use Wisebot to create a Java-based search engine on your site. The search engine contains the same information about your Web site as the master index shown above. The major difference is that users can search your Web site by keyword rather than having to browse an index alphabetically. Visitors can enter the words they are looking for in the search box, and a list of matching Web pages will automatically appear in the lower box:

They can then highlight the page they want to see, click the "Display" button, and Wisebot will automatically connect them to the selected Web page:

Another powerful tool is DocFather Applet Edition from SFS Software (**www.sfs-software.com**). Like Wisebot, DocFather will index all the documents on your Web site and create an alphabetical index, search engine, and site map for your Web site:

Since both Wisebot and DocFather use the Java programming language, they will work on any Java-enabled Web browser (Netscape version 2 or later; Microsoft Internet Explorer 3 or later). Using either program, you will have a fully functional search engine for your Web site in no time.

5. Does your Web site work for visitors with small resolution computer screens, that is, 640×480?

Many of us have been fortunate enough to purchase computers that have come with 17″ screens, and we have discovered the joys of working with large displays. We have been working in what is known as a resolution of 1024×768, or perhaps even higher values. Hence within our Web browser, we can see a lot of information on the screen.

But when designing our Web pages on such a system, it is all too easy to forget that there are still many users of the Internet who are accessing Web pages through 14″ or 15″ monitors, which can only display a resolution of 640×480. The result? These users do not see a lot of the information that you may have included in your site. This is the case particularly if you have set up your Web site such that a lot of your information is on the right-hand side of the screen.

The best way to understand this is to look at an example, the American Mock Trial Association (**www.collegemocktrial.org**). The page looks fine when it is viewed on a high resolution screen:

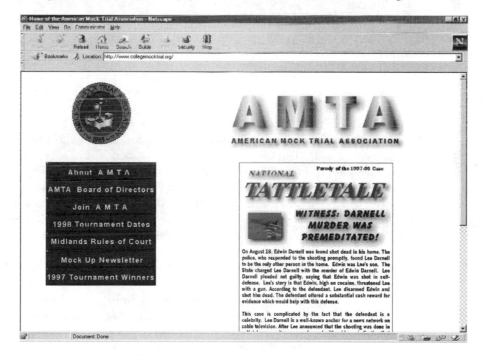

But resize the screen to 640×480, and the site has a real problem:

Assessing the Effectiveness
of Your Web Site

Protecting Yourself Online

Improving Your Productivity
on the Internet

Enhancing Your Web Site

The problem comes about when you insert graphics on a page but do not set them up so that they resize according to the size of the screen of the visitor, or when using tables that are of a fixed size.

How can you figure out if you have a problem with your own Web site? Easy. Change the configuration of your computer so that your large computer screen is showing material at the very low 640×480 resolution. You can do this within Windows by choosing "Settings" from the "Start" menu, then "Control Panel," "Display," and then choose "Settings." Change the "Desktop Area" by sliding it to the left until it is on 640×480. You may need to restart your computer.

You should also check into the Tweak UI utility for Windows 95/98 available from Microsoft (**www.microsoft.com/windows95/info/powertoys.htm**). You can also find a copy on the TUCOWS site (**www.tucows.com**) under "General Tools/Shell Enhancements." Among the many useful utilities found in this package is one that lets you instantly change the resolution of your screen without having to restart Windows.

On a Macintosh you can change the screen resolution within the Control Panel. Choose the Monitors and Sound item.

Once you have switched to a 640×480 resolution, load your browser, and take a look at your Web site. Do you see any problems, such as information that is not in view unless you scroll to the right? If so, consider editing the problem pages while working within a 640×480 screen.

tip Tune Up Your Web Site

A crucial question for marketers and Web site designers is this: what factors make users revisit a site? It is generally agreed that good content is vital to produce visitor satisfaction and a high repeat visit rate. However, what other Web site design features and experiences satisfy visitors and make them return to a site? Alternatively, what design features/experiences are undesirable and make visitors decide not to return?

SurveySite (**www.surveysite.com**) examined this important topic by conducting one of the most comprehensive Web site satisfaction studies ever undertaken on the Web. Visitors to 87 different Web sites were asked to rate the site and evaluate their experience during their visit. Respondents were also asked whether they intended to make a repeat visit to the site. This information allows us to determine which Web site features and/or experiences are most important in determining whether a repeat visit will be made.

SurveySite recruited a total of 87 Web sites in the United States and Canada to participate in this research study. The Web sites included a wide range of topics including Web magazines, software/Internet, news, business directories, entertainment, retail, travel, not-for-profit and health related sites. The results of the survey are shown in the graph below.

What Makes Users Revisit a Web Site?

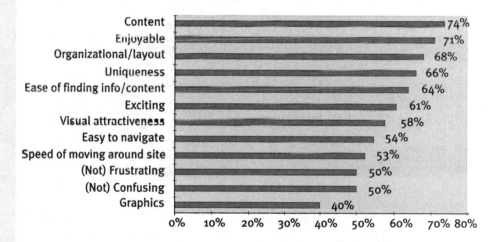

Correlation between attribute and intention to revisit Web site

It was not surprising to find that "Content" correlated most highly (74%) with the likelihood to make a repeat visit to the Web site. Lack of content or "frivolous content" was the main reason given by respondents for why they were not planning on returning to the Web site. These results highlight the fact that Web sites must make "useful or interesting content" their top design priority.

Source: "What Makes Users Revisit a Web Site?" Dr. Marshall Rice, SurveySite (www.surveysite.com).

6. Does your Web site work for visitors using different Web browsers?

It's easy to forget that some people on the Internet are using Netscape's Web browser, others are using Microsoft's Internet Explorer browser or America Online's browser, and still others are using newer browsers like Opera (**www.operasoftware.com**). Why is this important? The way your Web site appears on the screen will depend on the Web browser a person is using. In other words, a person who visits your Web site using Netscape will not necessarily see the same thing as a person who visits your site using Microsoft's Internet Explorer. Usually the differences are subtle, but you should make sure that your site appears more or less the same to Internet users regardless of the browser they are using. Most Internet users use either Netscape or Internet Explorer.

You can use either NetMechanic (**www.netmechanic.com**) or SiteInspector (**www. siteinspector.com**) to determine how well a particular Web page works in terms of handling different browsers. For example, we obtained this report from NetMechanic, which advised of some errors in our pages in terms of features not supported by Internet Explorer:

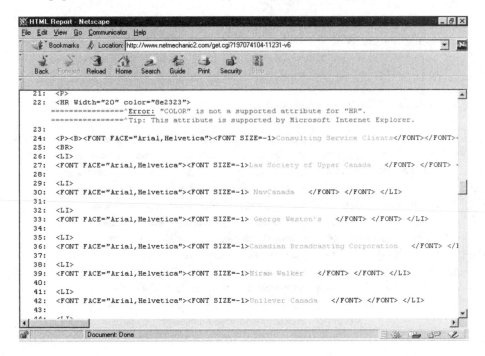

You should also be aware that there are a number of people who access the information found on the Web through a text-based Web browser called Lynx, a tool quite popular in the Unix environment, but available on other computer platforms as well. You can get an idea of how your site looks under Lynx at this Web page put together by Steven Baur, **www.miranova.com/~steve/Lynx-View.html**:

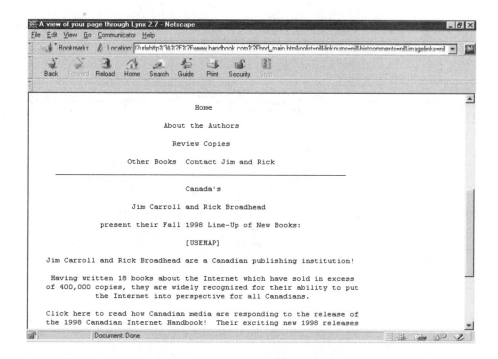

Enter the address of the Web page you wish to check, choose a few of the available options, submit your request, and you will get back the Web page as a Lynx user would see it:

A good page of information about how to ensure that your Web page is accessible by people with different browsers can be found at the Any Browser Pages Web sites **www.anybrowser.org/campaign** and **www.anybrowser.org/campaign/abdesign.shtml**:

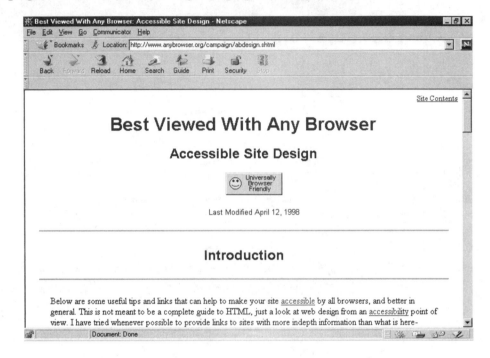

7. Is your Web site accessible to vision-impaired users of the Internet as well as other individuals with disabilities?

There is another issue that many do not address: the problems of surfers who are visually impaired or have some other disability. Many of these people do not "view" the Web in the traditional way, and, as a result, there are many Web pages that they have difficulties with. We admit that in our Web sites we, too, haven't addressed the issue to the extent that we should. Many of these people may use a text-based browser like Lynx and, in particular, an audio interface that would read out the text associated with a particular link on a site.

These types of problems occur when you use a lot of navigation buttons on your Web site and do not use what is known as the "Alt" tag. The Alt tag lets you specify words that should appear in a text-based Web browser that do not display images or are read by an audio interface to the Web browser. You usually enter these words when creating your Web page.

For example, we use Netscape Communicator to edit and maintain our Web pages. When we use an image as a link to another Web page, we can choose to enter the Alt tags that are used by text-based browsers. We do this by choosing the "Alt. Text/LowRes" button on the Image Properties page:

How do you go about determining if you have this problem on your Web site? First, take a good look at the code that was used to build your Web pages, and see if you have used the Alt text capability for many of the buttons and other images used on your Web pages. In Netscape you can do this by selecting "View" from the top menu bar, then "Document Source" or "Page Source." If you are using Microsoft's Internet Explorer, select "View" from the top menu bar, then "Source."

Second, visit "Bobby" (**www.cast.org/bobby**), a site that will assess how accessible your Web pages are for people with disabilities:

Assessing the Effectiveness
of Your Web Site   Protecting Yourself Online   Improving Your Productivity
on the Internet   Enhancing Your Web Site

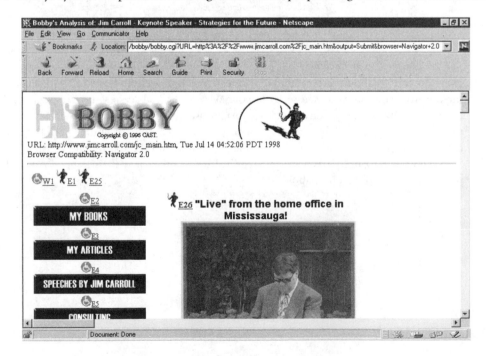

Simply provide Bobby with a Web address, and it will examine that page by retrieving it through the
Internet. It then builds a custom version of that page, flagging each item that it finds on the page that
could cause a problem for vision-impaired or other disabled users of the Internet. It does this by placing a "disability symbol" (the wheelchair on the left side of the screen below) for serious problems,
and a "bobby" symbol for problems that might occur with people using different Web browsers:

Click on any of the flagged items, and you will get an overview of the type of problems that exist:

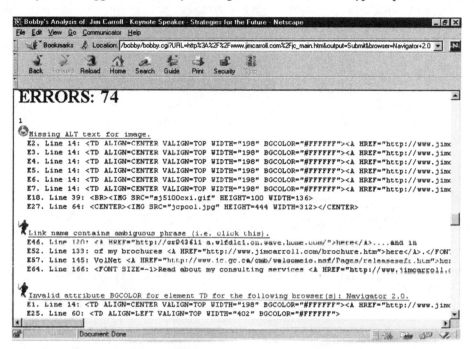

If you want more than an overview, Bobby will give that to you too.

Link name contains ambiguous phrase (i.e. click this)

This hypertext link contains the words "click this", "click here", "this", or "here". All of these phrases are bad choices for link text because they are non descriptive and would be difficult to understand if they were isolated from the surrounding text. Instead, try and use a word or phrase that is related to the purpose of the link. For example, rather than:

`To find out more about global warming click here.`

Try:

`A wealth of information on global warming can be found in the archives.`

Many screen readers for the blind are often able to provide a list of the links in a document extracted from the surrounding text. It is therefore quite important to make link text unique and significant.

By using Bobby, we discovered that when we were using Alt text in our site, it was ambiguous. Without thinking about what we were doing, we often included the phrase "click here" or "click this," which of course would be useless to a vision-impaired person surfing the Web, since it does not describe what a particular link is about.

Using Bobby is a revealing exercise; we highly recommend it.

We also suggest that you take the time to learn about the problems that the vision-impaired and others with disabilities have when using the Web. Through the Bobby site you can also discover a number of useful documents that will help you to ensure that your Web pages are designed with vision-impaired and other disabled users in mind:

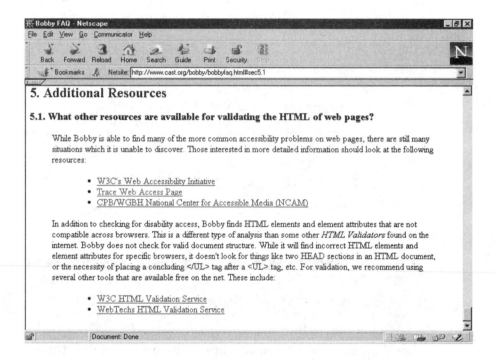

RECOMMENDED DOCUMENTS TO HELP YOU DESIGN MORE ACCESSIBLE WEB PAGES

Yahoo! under Computers & Internet/Information and Documentation/World Wide Web@/Page Design and Layout@/Accessibility	**www.yahoo.com**
Accessible Web Page Design	**www.igs.net/~starling/acc/index.htm**
Designing Access To WWW Pages	**www.ataccess.org/design.html**
Designing More Usable Web Sites	**www.trace.wisc.edu/world/web/index.html**
Web Page Repair	**www1.shore.net/~straub/wpr.htm**

8. Do any of your pages require translating?

Depending on what you do, the purpose of your Web site, and who you are trying to reach, you can also consider translating your Web site into different languages.

In Canada you can find many translation services on the Internet. Simply do a Web search in Yahoo! Canada (**www.yahoo.ca**) for the phrase "translation services," and restrict your search to Canadian services only. You will get a lengthy list of people who are willing to help you:

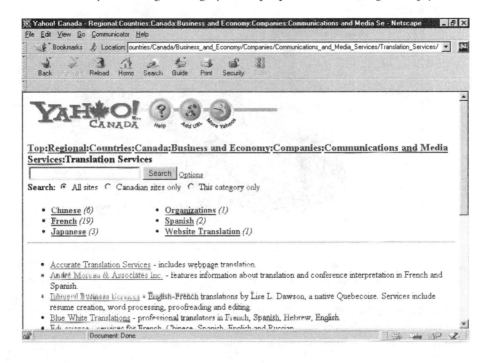

What are you looking at in terms of cost? One fellow told us that "rates vary as a site can be highly technical or of general interest. For the general-interest level, you could have jobs done for CAN$0.10 to $0.15/word. With highly technical, it could reach CAN$0.26/word."

Is it worth it to get your Web site, or at least portions of your site, translated? It can be, particularly if you are trying to reach people from areas of the country or around the world whose primary language is not English. Reach out to them in their language of choice, and you will build a better relationship with them.

You don't necessarily have to translate all the content on your site; quite often, translating key pages will suffice. Consider the City of Brossard (**ville.brossard.qc.ca**), in Quebec, which welcomes visitors with a multilingual page:

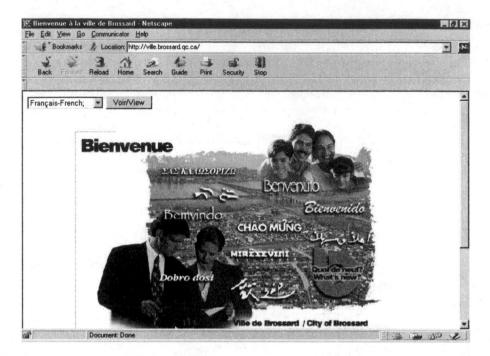

You can easily prepare an estimate of the cost to translate one or more pages in your Web site. Simply copy the material from one of your Web pages into a word processor. Then use the feature within your word processor to count the number of words. Use the per word cost above to get a rough idea of what it would cost you to translate that page, but keep in mind that the actual cost will probably be 10% to 20% higher. (You will be charged for the number of words that are in the resulting translated document, and a French document will probably have 10% to 20% more words than a corresponding English version.)

Here's How to Annoy Your Customers

According to a survey of Internet users by the Georgia Institute of Technology, slow Web pages are the most frequently cited problem associated with using the Internet. Fifty-three percent of respondents reported that they had left a Web site while searching for product information because the site was too slow. The second most frequently cited problem? Broken links on Web pages.

Source: www.gvu.gatech.edu/user_surveys.

9. Are all the links, images, and other files in your Web site valid?

If you have a Web site, then you probably know that it can be challenging to keep it in top-notch operating condition at all times. The bigger it gets, the more complicated it becomes and the more difficult it is to ensure that all the links from a page are still valid. Change a file name on your Web site, and you might forget to change links to that page from some other pages. Or if you are linking to external sites from your Web pages, you may not realize that some of those pages have moved or disappeared, rendering the links on your page invalid.

A "link checker" or "validator" program can work wonders here. Link checkers are available in software form and as a Web-based service. We review each of these alternatives below.

Using a Software Program

There are many software programs that will help you check the links on your Web site. Many are free; others request that you pay a nominal fee if you try out the program and decide to keep it. We regularly use a program called SiteSweeper (**www.sitetech.com**). We simply provide it with the address of our Web site and send it on its way. It reads the entire site, then reports back with lots of useful information, such as a report about the "broken links" that it found on the site. This is a concise summary of instances on our Web site where a link to another Web page either on the site or to an external site isn't working, because that Web page has either disappeared or moved:

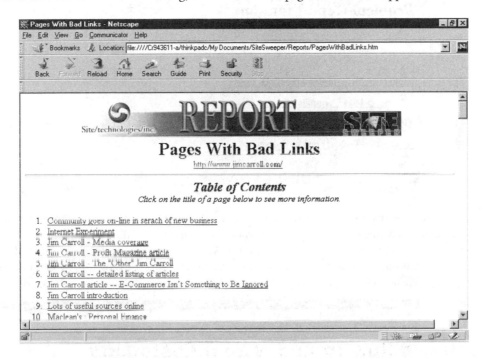

We have also used HTML PowerTools (**www.tali.com**), a set of utilities that provides a number of capabilities, including link checking. But rather than checking an actual Web site online like SiteSweeper, the HTML PowerTools Link Checker program examines a copy of your Web site that you have stored on your computer, thus providing for much faster processing. Keep in mind that the copy of the Web site on your computer has to be an exact match of what you have online for this program to work properly:

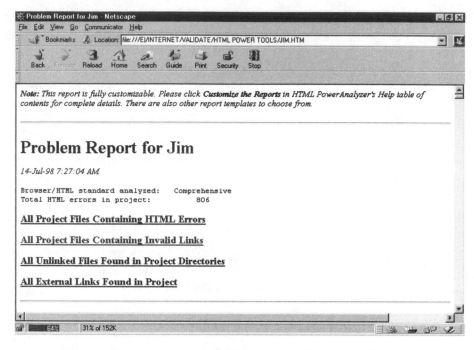

Finally, another program worth checking out is Linkbot, from Tetranet Software (**www.tetranetsoftware.com**). We found it to be one of the most full-featured link-checking programs available. You can have it check a site on the Web or check a copy of a site stored on your computer. In addition, you can view reports either within the Linkbot program, or you can have the program prepare a Web page:

You can also set up a schedule for Linkbot to check your Web site. This allows you to run a daily or weekly review of your Web site to determine if it is in good working order.

There are many other link-checking programs available in addition to the ones we looked at here. Take a look at the TUCOWS Web site (**www.tucows.com**) for information on Macintosh and Windows versions of these programs. Look in the "Validators" category under HTML Tools:

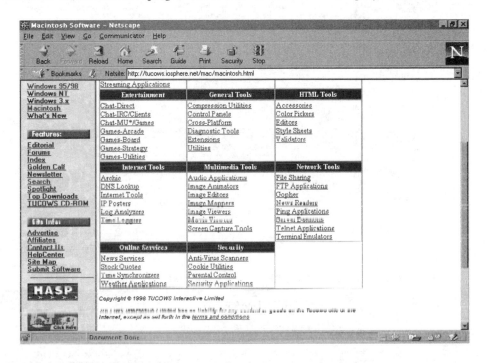

You can also check the Web sites of publications such as *PC Magazine* (**www.pcmagazine.com**), *PC Computing* (**www.pccomputing.com**), *The Computer Paper* (**www.tcp.ca**), and others for information on Web-checking programs. Do a search for "link checker" or "validator" for more information:

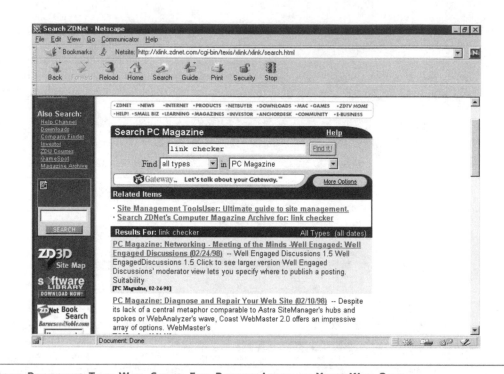

MORE PROGRAMS THAT WILL CHECK FOR BROKEN LINKS ON YOUR WEB SITE

SiteBoss	**www.siteboss.com**
CyberSpyder	**www.cyberspyder.com**
Doctor HTML	**imagiware.com**
InfoLink Checker	**www.biggbyte.com**
CheckWeb	**www.alterego.fr**
LinkSweeper	**www.lss.com.au**

Web-Based Services

In addition to software that does link checking, there are a number of services available online that will do the same thing. Simply visit one of these services on the Web, provide the Web address that you want to check, and you will get a report back a few hours later about broken links on your site, along with some other information. Some of these sites charge for the service.

One of the more popular free services of this type is NetMechanic (**www.netmechanic.com**). On their homepage, choose the "Link Check" service, provide the address of the Web site that you would like to have checked and an e-mail address, and it sets off to do its work. You will receive an e-mail message with a Web address within an hour or two. By accessing the Web address with your Web browser, you will see a report detailing any problems that have been found on your site. Note that you will be limited to 200 pages being checked:

Another service we found worthwhile was WebSiteGarage (**www.websitegarage.com**), although parts of this service are not free. This site offers a number of services related to checking the quality of a Web site, including LinkChecking. Using their free "TuneUp" service, you can check the links on a single Web page or do several pages one by one. Or, for an annual fee of U.S. $59.99, you can sign up to their TuneUp Plus service, which includes link checking of an entire Web site as well as a number of other useful features.

Also worth considering is LinkAlarm (**www.linkalarm.com**). LinkAlarm will regularly check your Web site for any broken links and provide a Web page where you can view a full report summarizing the results. The cost is U.S. $20 for 12 monthly checkups. Each checkup includes the first 200 pages of your Web site. A LinkAlarm report looks like this:

From this page you examine specific error reports, such as this summary of the types of errors that were found on your Web site:

And this report, which shows you which pages on your Web site contained links to Web pages that no longer exist:

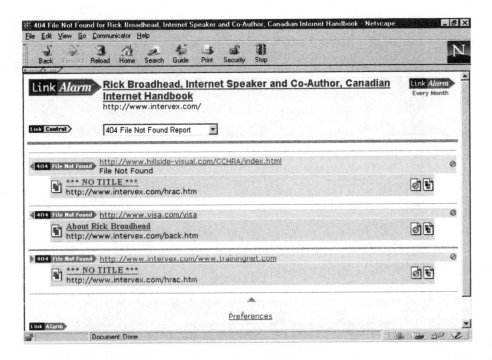

10. Is your Web site performing adequately?

There could be several problems at work here. You could have problems with the reliability of your Web site: the Web server at the company that hosts your Web site might be down frequently, whether for maintenance or due to problems with your Web site. Or traffic to your site could be slow because of congestion on the Internet links at the company that hosts your Web site. You may have a great site that works very well for you, from a business or personal perspective, but it isn't going to help you much if people trying to visit the site walk away because it is simply too slow.

Let's look at the first issue. What if you want to be sure that your Web site is in good working order at all times? That's easy. You can find both software and services that will test a connection to your Web site on a regular basis and report to you if the site seems to be down for an inordinate period of time.

In terms of software, you can find a wide variety of "ping" programs and other software that you can set up to check if a particular Internet site is working. We tried out two: Servers Alive (**www.cmconline.com/salive**) and SuperPing Machine (**members.xoom.com/jupes**). Both took just minutes to install and we could ask both to see if a particular Web site was up.

You can find these two programs, plus lots of others, for both Windows and Macintosh systems at the TUCOWS Web site (**www.tucows.com**). Unfortunately, in order for these programs to work, you need to run them on a computer that is connected to the Internet 24 hours a day.

If you don't want to run such a program on your computer (perhaps because you are not always connected to the Internet), then consider using one of the many online services that can check the status of your Web site on a regular basis. In particular, the NetMechanic site that we looked at earlier offers a service called Server Check Pro. For U.S. $10 per month (or U.S. 33¢ per day), the Server Check Pro service will test your site 24 hours a day, checking its availability, and let you know by e-mail if problems are encountered:

Assessing the Effectiveness of Your Web Site | Protecting Yourself Online | Improving Your Productivity on the Internet | Enhancing Your Web Site

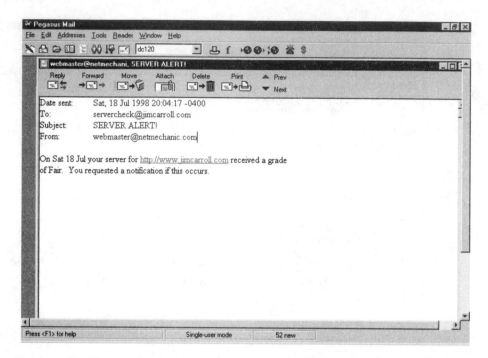

Once you have signed up with Server Check Pro, you can specify that the service should monitor your Web site, 24 hours a day, and report back to you on a variety of issues. You will get a weekly report that provides details about the performance of your site and how it compares to other Web sites on the Internet. This information will help you to assess whether users of your Web site are being plagued by speed problems when accessing your site.

A great feature of Server Check Pro is that you can request to be notified if certain conditions occur (e.g., your Web site does not respond within a defined period of time):

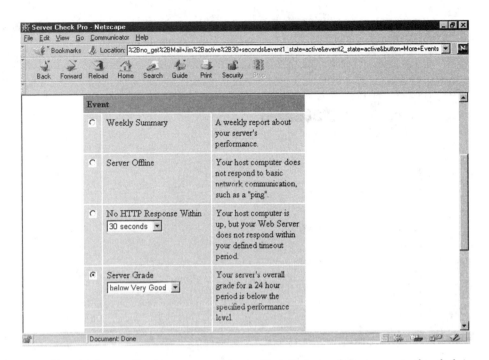

You can specify which e-mail accounts are to be notified for any of these events, thus helping you to alert different people to the status of the site. And you can choose to monitor any other Web site in addition to the one that you established as the primary site, for an additional fee of U.S. 33¢ per day.

Is it worth it? If you are using your Web site as a business tool, you need to ensure that your site is always available to your current and potential customers. Any downtime could result in lost business.

In addition to the commercial version, a free version of Server Check Pro (called Server Check Lite) is available on the NetMechanic Web site (**www.netmechanic.com**). All you need to do is provide the address of the Web site that you want to check and an e-mail address to send the report to, and Server Check Lite will test your site every 15 minutes for the next 8 hours:

Once the testing has concluded, you will receive an e-mail message with a Web address that you can link to in order to retrieve your free report. This report will tell you how your Web site performed in comparison to the last 2,000 Web sites that were tested by the program. You will also be told how fast it took it connect to your Web site on average and how many times the program was unable to access your Web site within a 30-second interval:

Report For: www.intervex.com
Date: Wed 5 Aug
Time: 21:00 - 5:00 USA Eastern Time
Server Type: Netscape-Enterprise/2.0a

Overall Rating: Fair

Performance Summary			
Event	Your Server's Average	NetMechanic Average	Percentile
Host Ping	993.83 millisec	483.34 millisec	13 th
DNS Look Up	0.02 sec	0.09 sec	82 th
Connect Time	1.32 sec	0.86 sec	18 th
Download Time (10k file)	1.53 sec	1.78 sec	32 th
Timeouts	1	-	

This information will tell you whether you have a good, reliable, fast link from your Web site to the rest of the Internet. Server Check Lite is free, so consider using it every week or so to monitor the performance of your Web site.

The major difference between the Lite version and the commercial version is that the commercial version will monitor your Web site 24 hours a day. In addition, as described above, you can request to be notified if certain events occur. The notification service is not available with the free version of the product.

You can learn more about Server Check Pro at the NetMechanic Web site; in particular, take a look at the Server Check Pro FAQ (Frequently Asked Questions) document:

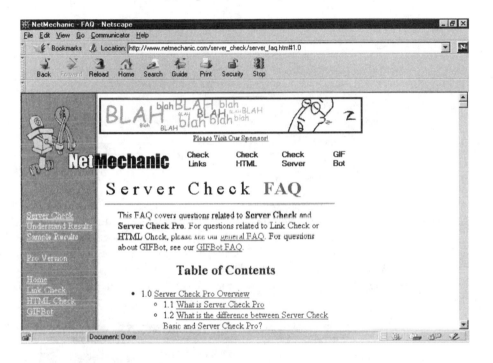

If your Web site is very important to you, then we would definitely recommend Server Check Pro as a worthwhile, low cost, and useful service.

11. Are your visitors happy with your Web site?

Once you have invested in a Web site, you should make an effort to find out whether users are experiencing any problems using it. Consider hiring one of the independent Web usability services that will review your Web site and report back to you with the results. Some of these services, like TestNow (**www.testnow.com**), do this by recruiting a panel of thousands of Internet users. They then pay testers to review Web sites and offer their feedback. Unfortunately, TestNow is only recruiting (and paying) U.S. Internet users, although this may change in the future. Using TestNow's Survey Builder, you create questions about your Web site that you want the panel to answer:

While TestNow is not an inexpensive service (it costs U.S. $995 for 100 testers to review your site), an independent review of your site will help to ensure that your site is meeting its objectives.

Another company to consider is SurveySite (**www.surveysite.com**), a Canadian service that uses "pop-up" survey software to randomly interview visitors to your Web site. Like TestNow, SurveySite allows you to customize the questions that you want to ask your users. Once you have implemented the SurveySite software on your Web site, visitors will be chosen at random, and a pop-up window similar to the following will appear:

Users have the option of declining to participate in the survey if they wish.

The result of this survey process is a comprehensive Web Evaluation Report that you can use to assess your Web site on factors such as content, organization, ease of navigation, uniqueness, visual appeal, visitor experience, sources of frustration, and other features.

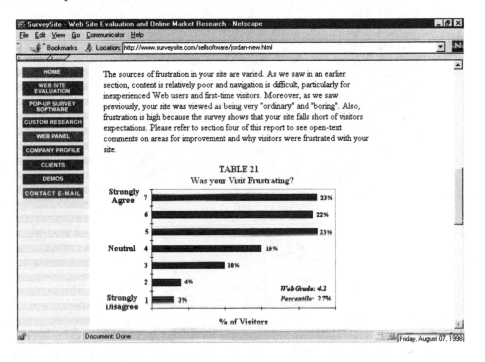

For each factor in the report, SurveySite will assign your site a "WebGrade" that ranges from 1 to 10 (with 10 being the highest score). These rankings show you how your Web site compares to other similar Web sites in the SurveySite database on factors that were evaluated in the survey. For example, your site might receive a WebGrade of 6.5 on "Navigation," which might hypothetically place your site in the sixtieth percentile in your product category. This means that 40% of other Web sites in your product category scored higher than your site did. This information will help you assess how your site stacks up against the competition.

On request, SurveySite will ask visitors to compare your Web site to one belonging to a major competitor. The results are summarized in the final report:

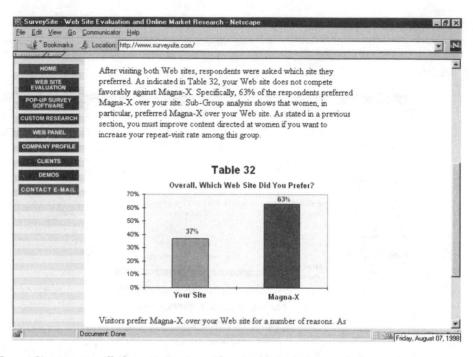

After visiting both Web sites, respondents were asked which site they preferred. As indicated in Table 32, your Web site does not compete favorably against Magna-X. Specifically, 63% of the respondents preferred Magna-X over your site. Sub-Group analysis shows that women, in particular, preferred Magna-X over your Web site. As stated in a previous section, you must improve content directed at women if you want to increase your repeat-visit rate among this group.

Table 32

Overall, Which Web Site Did You Prefer?

Visitors prefer Magna-X over your Web site for a number of reasons. As

The SurveySite report will also give you specific recommendations to help you increase repeat visits to your Web site and overcome the site's major weaknesses.

In addition to randomly interviewing visitors to your Web site, SurveySite has a "Web Panel" of Canadian and U.S. Internet users that are paid to answer surveys about Web sites and/or participate in online focus groups. One advantage of SurveySite's panel is that it includes Canadian Internet users, unlike TestNow's panel, which only includes U.S. users, as we pointed out earlier.

We highly recommend that you consider using a service like SurveySite or TestNow to evaluate your Web site. This type of independent audit will give you new insights and perspectives into your Web site that you may not have noticed before.

12. Are you using intuitive names for the links on your Web pages?

When you design a Web site, the names you give the links to other pages on your site should be clear and unambiguous. In other words, when a user sees a link on your Web site, it should be obvious what type of information the link will lead users to. Many Web site owners come up with creative or "funky" names for various sections of their Web site. Although this may make your Web site more interesting, it's difficult for users to navigate through your site if they have to constantly guess what's behind the links.

For example, here's the Web site for New Balance (**www.newbalance.com**), manufacturer of the popular athletic shoes. The navigation icons along the left-hand side of the screen are supposed to help you navigate the site, but it's not clear what the images represent. For example, one of the icons is a picture of a runner sprinting past a large green dollar sign, but it's not at all obvious what that symbol means:

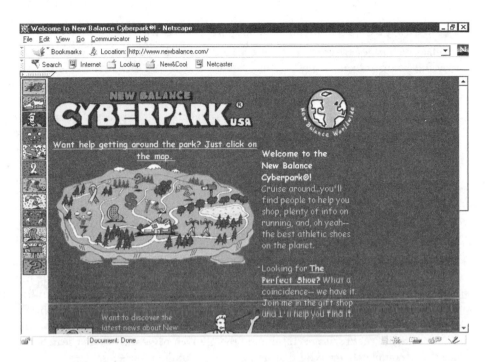

The names assigned to some areas of the site are just as confusing:

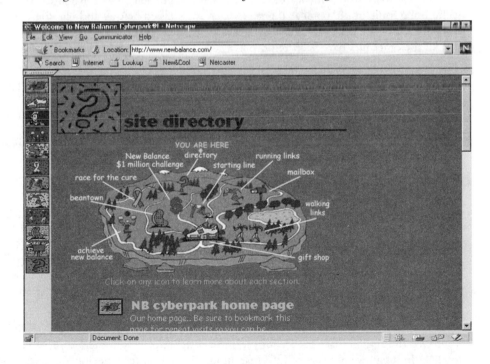

Labels like "starting line" and "beantown" aren't very descriptive.

13. Does your site have any orphan Web pages?

Orphan Web pages are pages that don't have a link back to any other pages of your site. Someone may find a page of your Web site while doing a search on a search engine and will end up accessing your site using that page instead of coming through your Web site's main entry page. If that page isn't linked to the rest of your Web site, the user won't be able to access your other Web pages. To prevent this type of situation from happening, all the pages of your site should include a link back to the homepage and, as we discussed earlier, a navigation bar that indicates where they are within the overall structure of your site.

The three link-checking programs that we reviewed earlier in the chapter (SiteSweeper, Linkbot, and HTML PowerTools) will also let you know if there are any orphan pages on your Web site.

14. Are old Web pages from your site still showing up on search engines?

When you are updating your Web site, you may remove links to Web pages that you no longer want users to access. However, even though these Web pages may not be visible to your Web site visitors, these pages will still show up on search engines unless you delete them from the computer that is hosting your Web site. We have encountered many organizations with this problem. They have updated their Web sites but forgotten to remove the older Web pages from their Web servers. The result? Internet users are still finding the old Web pages on Internet search engines and accessing them, completely unaware that newer versions of the pages exist.

How do you find out if your organization has this problem? Do a search for your organization's name using some of the popular Internet search tools (listed below) and see if any old Web pages show up. Or better yet, do a thorough review of all the files on your Web server, and make sure that all the older files have been removed.

POPULAR INTERNET SEARCH TOOLS

AltaVista	**www.altavista.digital.com**
Canada.com	**www.canada.com**
Excite	**www.excite.com**
HotBot	**www.hotbot.com**
Infoseek	**www.infoseek.com**
Lycos	**www.lycos.com**
WebCrawler	**www.webcrawler.com**
Yahoo!	**www.yahoo.com**

15. Does your Web site have too many layers of information?

Your Web site should make it easy for users to get the information they want. Don't force people to click through several layers of information in order to get to a specific Web page. Provide a menu on the main page of your Web site that gives users direct access to most of the major pages on your Web site. A good example of this technique can be found on the Web site of the Ontario Corn Producers Association (**www.ontariocorn.org**). This organization provides a dropdown menu on its front page so that users can choose the area of the site they want to go to:

How can you create a similar dropdown menu on your Web site? Using a program called LinkLaunch (available from **www.webgenie.com**), you can create a dropdown menu for your site in less than five minutes, and no technical knowledge is required. This program will create your dropdown menu using JavaScript, a popular programming language for the Web that can be understood by most Web browsers.

Here's how it works. Once you have downloaded the program, you create a list of the pages on your Web site and their associated Web addresses:

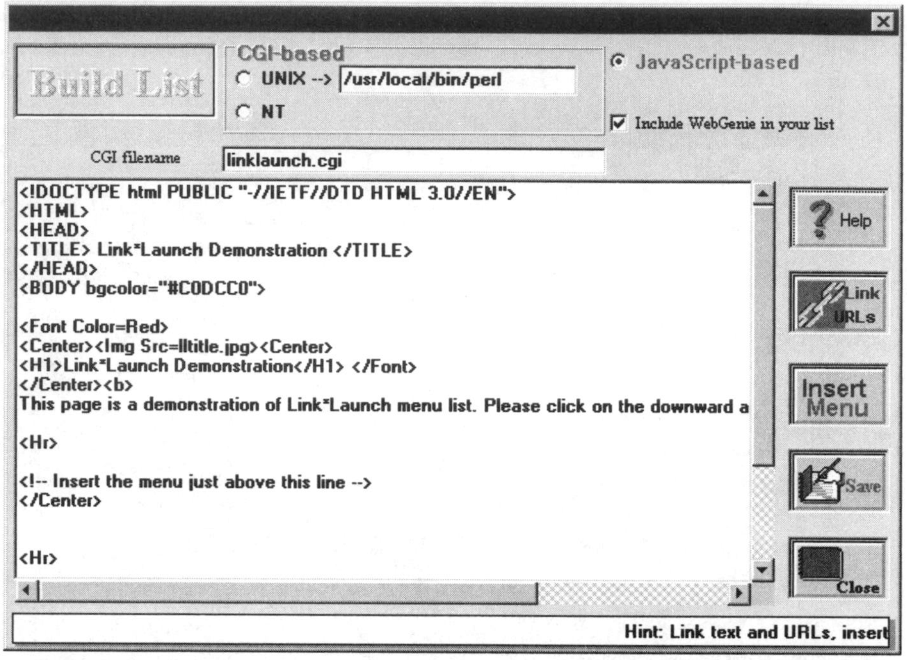
Build List
CGI-based
UNIX --> /usr/local/bin/perl
NT
JavaScript-based
Include WebGenie in your list
CGI filename
linklaunch.cgi
<!DOCTYPE html PUBLIC "-//IETF//DTD HTML 3.0//EN">
<HTML>
<HEAD>
<TITLE> Link*Launch Demonstration </TITLE>
</HEAD>
<BODY bgcolor="#C0DCC0">
<Font Color=Red>
<Center><Img Src=lltitle.jpg><Center>
<H1>Link*Launch Demonstration</H1> </Font>
</Center><b>
This page is a demonstration of Link*Launch menu list. Please click on the downward a
<Hr>
<!-- Insert the menu just above this line -->
</Center>
<Hr>
Help
Link URLs
Insert Menu
Save
Close
Hint: Link text and URLs, insert

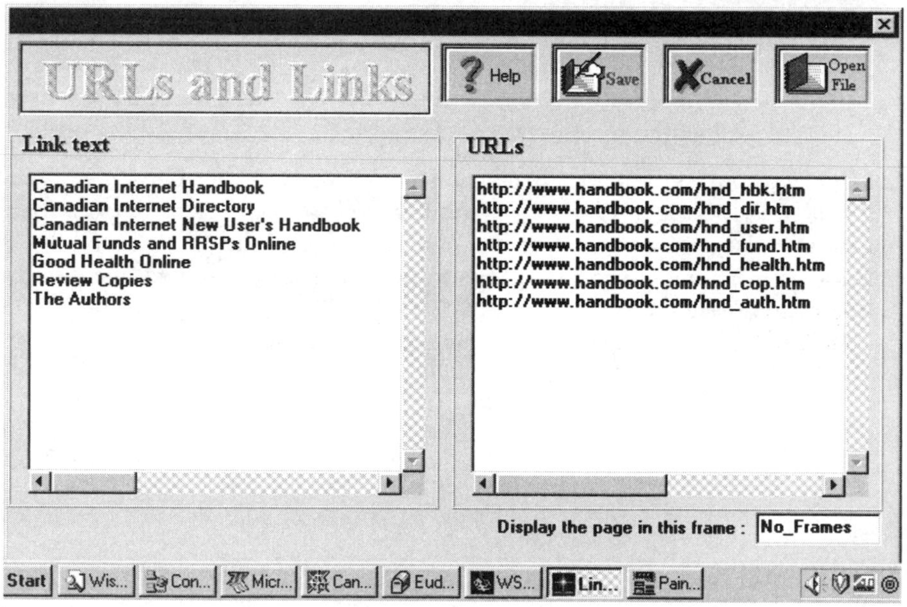
URLs and Links
Help
Save
Cancel
Open File
Link text
Canadian Internet Handbook
Canadian Internet Directory
Canadian Internet New User's Handbook
Mutual Funds and RRSPs Online
Good Health Online
Review Copies
The Authors
URLs
http://www.handbook.com/hnd_hbk.htm
http://www.handbook.com/hnd_dir.htm
http://www.handbook.com/hnd_user.htm
http://www.handbook.com/hnd_fund.htm
http://www.handbook.com/hnd_health.htm
http://www.handbook.com/hnd_cop.htm
http://www.handbook.com/hnd_auth.htm
Display the page in this frame :
No_Frames
Start
Wis...
Con...
Micr...
Can...
Eud...
WS...
Lin...
Pain...

Then you insert your list of links into a page of pre-prepared HTML code that comes with the program:

```
Insert the Link*Launch menu.                                          [X]

   (i)   The URLs have been linked. Now you must insert the code in the HTML file. Please
         position the cursor where the Link*Launch menu should appear and press 'Insert Menu'

                                [  OK  ]
```

```
                                                                           [x]

  ┌─────────────┐   CGI-based                          (•) JavaScript-based
  │             │   ( ) UNIX --> /usr/local/bin/perl
  │  Build List │   ( ) NT                             [ ] Include WebGenie in your list
  └─────────────┘

        CGI filename      linklaunch.cgi

  <FORM>                                                              [?] Help
  <script language="Javascript">
  <!--
  function go36191822(form)                                          [ Link
  {                                                                    URLs ]
    var tU = new Array();
    tU[0]="http://www.handbook.com/hnd_hbk.htm";                     [ Insert
    tU[1]="http://www.handbook.com/hnd_dir.htm";                       Menu ]
    tU[2]="http://www.handbook.com/hnd_user.htm";
    tU[3]="http://www.handbook.com/hnd_fund.htm";
    tU[4]="http://www.handbook.com/hnd_health.htm";
    tU[5]="http://www.handbook.com/hnd_cop.htm";                     [ Save ]
    tU[6]="http://www.handbook.com/hnd_auth.htm";

    location = tU[form.sel_URL.selectedIndex];
  }                                                                  [ Close ]
  //-->
  </script>

                Hint: Link text and URLs, insert the code and 'Save'
```

Then you edit and transfer the completed file to your Web site. In just a few minutes you will have a dropdown menu on your Web site, just like the one below, which you can see on the Web site for our books (**www.handbook.com**):

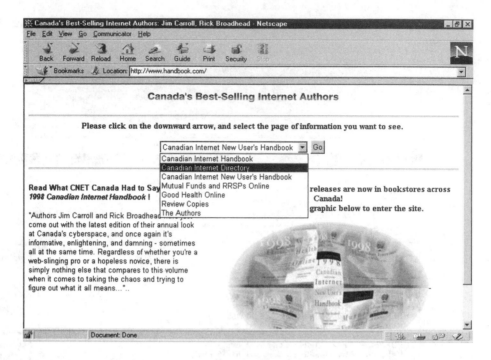

SiteInspector: A Multipurpose Web-Testing Program

A program called SiteInspector (**www.siteinspector.com**) will allow you to test your Web site for many of the problems discussed in this chapter. You can obtain information about "broken links," check the spelling on your Web site, find out whether your Web page will work with different Web browsers, check the overall design of your site, and determine how long your site will take to download with different types of Internet connections.

Simply visit the site, indicate what Web page should be tested, and choose the reports you want to run:

You will then get back a concise report about that page, with each test graded in terms of the number of "smiley faces" awarded. This will help you to determine if you have problems with any pages in your site:

It's simple, it's free, and it's effective, so it's definitely worth a visit.

Other Design Issues

There are many other issues to think about in putting together or updating your Web site, and there are many documents on the Internet that you can refer to.

tip Useful Web Usability Resources

One of the best collections of Web usability resources we have seen is at Usable Web's Guide to Web Usability Resources (**www.usableweb.com**). This site provides links to hundreds of documents about Web site design issues. Another excellent resource is the Web site of User Interface Engineering (**world.std.com/~uieweb**), a Massachusetts-based consulting firm that specializes in product usability issues. The company's Web site includes many useful articles on Web design and usability.

A good place to start is by using the major search engines. Use search phrases such as "Web design," "Web page design," and "Web design tips." For example, when we did a search in AltaVista for "web page design," we found many pages with useful tips and guidelines on what to think about in designing a Web site.

Also check Yahoo! under the "Computers & Internet" section. Once you have selected the "Computers and Internet" category from the main page of Yahoo!, follow this path to get to the Web design section: "Information and Documentation"; "World Wide Web@"; "Page Design & Layout@." Here is an example of some of the links to the useful sites that we found:

```
Yahoo! Arts:Design Arts:Graphic Design:Web Page Design and Layout - Microsoft Intern...   _ 8 x
File    Edit   View   Go   Favorites   Help                                                  e
Address  http://www.yahoo.com/Arts/Design_Arts/Graphic_Design/Web_Page_Design_and_Layout/  Links
```

- Common Problems in Web Design - ...and how to avoid them.
- Crafting a Nifty Personal Web Site - just one big, fat opinion.
- Design-O-Rama! - use this reference material for all of your HyperText Markup Language needs and your site might just look as good as Glassdog.
- Dzine - an online guide to good design.
- Eightfold Path to Enlightened Websight, The - distillation of Web design principles from teknozen @ction websites.
- Graphic Design Resources - categories include fonts, cgi, web design guidelines, image collections, image viewers, sound libraries, validation, and web tools.
- Interfacing - An interview with Steve Berlin, editor of The Useless Pages, on how NOT to make a good page.
- ilvNet - a digital drawing board: short essays written on concepts of web design, plus design bulletin boards.
- Kanagawa Design Forum Web Design Contest - entry open to all, deadline January 20, 1998; designer of the winning Web site will receive 1,000,000 Yen, approximately US $8,300. Entries are viewable online.
- Muskoka19 - web design tips and tricks.
- Netscape/Photoshop Demo Page - demonstrates and explains new features in Netscape and advanced Photoshop techniques. Also contains links, HTML, help and more.

```
                                                    Internet zone
Start  Yaho...  Micro...  Conne...  Paint S...  Some ...              9:10 PM
```

Summary

Most Internet users don't do a good job of keeping their Web sites operating smoothly. In many ways, a Web site is like a car. It's a major investment, and you need to get it tuned up regularly. While most people now recognize the importance of keeping their Web sites up-to-date, usability and accessibility issues are often ignored. We admit that even we have been guilty of many of the problems we have identified. We have no doubt that if you follow the advice outlined in this chapter, you will dramatically increase the satisfaction of visitors to your Web site.

chapter two

How to Improve Your Web Site's Visibility on the Internet

According to CommerceNet, the number one concern for online merchants is how shoppers will find their Web sites.

"New Services Aim to Boost Efficiency of Search Engines," Electronic Advertising and Marketplace Report, July 14, 1998

Highlights

1. Is your Web site listed in all the major search engines and directories? A service called the did-it detective can help you with this task.

2. Include your Web site in specialized search engines and directories that are related to your target market.

3. Use meta-tags and title tags to influence how search engines rank your Web site. Exercise caution when using automated submission programs and search engine optimization services.

4. Tools like WebPosition, PositionAgent, RankThis!, and ScoreCheck can help you monitor and improve your Web site's position on popular search engines.

5. More and more search engines are using a Web site's popularity as a major factor in their ranking criteria. Web site owners should take this into account when planning their online marketing strategy.

About six months ago we noticed that one of our long-time clients had finally established a Web site, so we went and had a look. It was a great site, containing many of the elements that make for a successful Internet presence.

Then we decided to see if the company had taken the next logical step of ensuring that the site was listed in various search engines and directories. We were surprised by what we found, or rather, by what we didn't find.

The site wasn't listed in Yahoo!, Infoseek, or any of the other popular Web directories. They didn't appear in any search engines when we did a search for a phrase that applied to their line of business. They weren't even in any of the indexes that related specifically to their line of business.

They simply didn't show up.

But what fascinated us was that their Web site was designed by a professional Web developer. Intrigued, we examined the Web site in greater depth; we discovered that the designer had not taken advantage of the methods available for Web sites to improve their likelihood of showing up in a search engine or directory. Nor had the designer bothered to help them get listed in the major search engines and Web directories.

In effect, they had built an effective Web site but didn't do anything to help people find them on the Internet.

We began to realize as we looked into the situation further, by examining many other Web sites, that a lot of Canadian Web site owners suffer from the same problem. Far too many individuals and organizations are missing out on some of the fundamental things that must be done to make a Web site easy to find.

In this section we will show you how to fix this problem. We will go through the steps we took when searching for our client, but for our purposes we call this client V.I. Rhodes Insurance Services, an organization specializing in, say, aviation insurance.

Is Your Web Site Listed in the Major Search Engines and Web Directories?

It seems like such a simple and basic thing to do, but we remain stunned by the number of Canadians who don't take the time to ensure that their Web sites are listed in the major search engines and Web directories. Why go to all the time, effort, and expense of creating a Web site, if you don't do what is considered to be the absolute minimum in terms of making people aware of the site?

There are two main places where you should ensure you are listed: search engines and Web directories. Search engines are just that; you use them to do a search of the Web pages they have indexed. Search engines have programs that go out and index every word on every Web page that they can find. The search is then put into a database, which can be searched for a particular word, phrase, or a combination of words and phrases. Web directories, on the other hand, are like a set of Yellow Pages. People working for Web directories select Web sites for the directory and then place those Web sites in the appropriate categories. Although you can do a search for a word or phrase on a Web directory just as you can on a search engine, a directory doesn't index the contents of all the Web pages on the Internet. Web directories only contain listings of selected Internet resources, with a short one- or two-sentence description of each resource. Therefore, when you do a search on a Web directory, you are only searching the titles and descriptions of Web sites that have been included in the directory; you are not searching the entire World Wide Web.

Yahoo! (**www.yahoo.com**), one of the largest Web directories, is considered the definitive directory on the Internet; its Canadian counterpart is Yahoo! Canada (**www.yahoo.ca**). When we started looking for our client, we started at Yahoo! Canada:

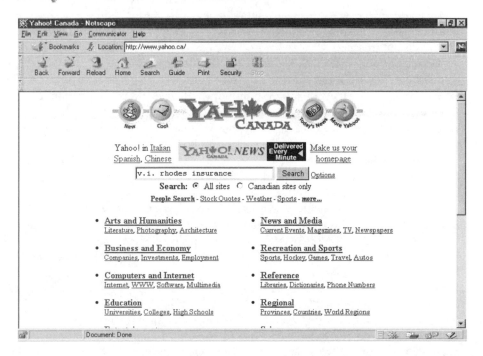

They didn't show up. So if they weren't in Yahoo! Canada, they weren't in Yahoo! since adding yourself to Yahoo! Canada automatically adds you to the main Yahoo! site.

Be sure to list your site on Yahoo! Another directory to get listed on is Snap! (**www.snap.com**), which is partly owned by NBC. While not as popular as Yahoo!, Snap! is rapidly gaining a loyal following on the Internet.

How do you get your Web site listed in a directory? For Yahoo! Canada visit the site and navigate through the list of categories until you find the specific subcategory under which your organization should be listed. At the very top of most subcategory pages is a button labelled "Add URL." Click on it, and follow the instructions that appear. We should point out that Yahoo! Canada is very selective about which Web sites get to appear in its database. One of the reasons why Yahoo! has such a loyal following is that its database is controlled by real people who handpick sites for inclusion in the database, as opposed to a search engine, which indexes everything it can find using automated computer programs called "spiders." As a result of Yahoo!'s screening process, you may have difficulty getting your Web site accepted. So to improve your chances, carefully follow the rules that appear on the Yahoo! Canada site. The rules are in a document called "How to Suggest a Site." There is a link to this page at the bottom of the main page of Yahoo! Canada.

Next, we tried looking for V.I. Rhodes Insurance on some of the major search engine sites. We have listed what we consider to be the most important search engines below. Getting your Web site listed in these search engines is an absolute must. We didn't have much luck finding our client's Web site in any of the sites below; evidently, when the company established its Web site, no one told them that they should take the time to get listed in all the major search engines.

What's involved in getting your Web site listed on a major search engine? All you need to do is visit the search engine's Web site and look for a button or link called "submit URL," "add your site," "submit your site," or something similar. Click on the link or button and fill out the form that appears. Within a few days or weeks (depending on the search engine), your Web site should be added to the search engine's database. However, as mentioned above, search engines use programs that regularly scour the Web looking for new and updated Web sites; the sites are then added to their index. This means that your Web site will likely be found and indexed by the search engines without you having to visit each search engine and manually adding your Web site to their databases. Nevertheless, we recommend that you don't wait for this to happen, or assume that it will happen. Take the time to visit each search engine and submit your site to their database. This way, you'll know that your Web site will be included in their index.

To maximize your Web site's visibility on the Internet, you should register your Web site with all the major search engines listed below (except AltaVista Canada; we explain why below). Many organizations only register their Web site in one or two search engines, figuring that will be enough. But if you ask several Internet users which search engine they use, you will get several different answers. To cover all the bases, make sure you register your Web site in every major search engine. If you don't, there's a good chance that people won't be able to find you, because they're using a search engine that you didn't register with.

We've listed AltaVista Canada below because it is one of the major search tools that Canadians use. However, unlike the other search engines, AltaVista Canada does not allow you to submit your Web site to its database. AltaVista Canada is designed to automatically find and index every Web site that exists within the borders of Canada. If you already have a Web site, it may already be in the index. If you've just created a site, be patient. Eventually, AltaVista Canada will find your site and include it in its index.

MAJOR SEARCH ENGINES

AltaVista	www.altavista.digital.com
AltaVista Canada	www.altavistacanada.com
Canada.com	www.canada.com
Excite	www.excite.com
HotBot	www.hotbot.com
Infoseek	www.infoseek.com
Lycos	www.lycos.com
WebCrawler	www.webcrawler.com

Our experience searching for V.I. Rhodes Insurance Services on the Web is not unusual. Many times we have tried to find a certain company or individual who we definitely know has a Web site, only to come up empty on the major search engines.

Is your Web site listed in all the major search engines?

Are you sure? We strongly recommend that you visit each of the major search engines, as well as Yahoo! and Snap!, and make sure that your site shows up when someone searches for your company name or the primary topic related to your Web site. Some search engines, like Lycos, have a tool on their Web site that allows you to determine if your Web site is in their index. Better yet, try out a free service called the did-it detective (**www.did-it.com**):

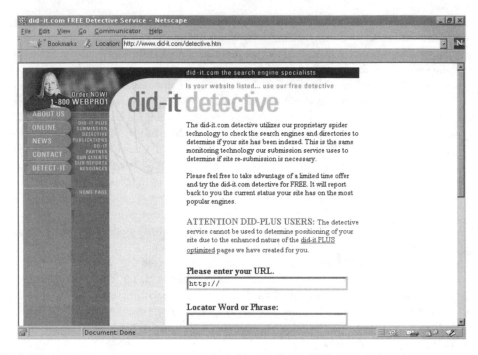

At the did-it detective site you can type in the address of your Web site, and at this point, type in your company name in the "Locator Word or Phrase" box. You provide your e-mail address, and in a little while, you will receive an e-mail message back advising you whether you are listed in the major search engines and directories of the Internet:

Have You Chosen the Right Categories?

It isn't enough to ensure that you are listed in major directories like Yahoo! You must be in the appropriate categories within such a site. So don't simply make sure that you are listed; make sure that you are listed in the specific categories where people will likely look for you. And since new categories are sometimes added to directories like Yahoo!, constantly monitor these sites for new categories that your Web site should be listed under.

You should expect to find V.I. Rhodes Insurance listed in Yahoo! within a variety of categories, such as:

Business and Economy:Companies:Insurance;

Business and Economy:Companies:Aviation.

After all, these are the categories that a pilot or someone in the aviation industry might look into when looking for aviation insurance. We should point out that Yahoo! reserves the right to change your category selections if they don't agree with your choices. Don't pick categories that are unrelated to your business just so that you can increase the number of places where you appear on Yahoo! Once you have submitted a site to Yahoo!, they will visit your Web site to ensure that the category or categories you have chosen match the content on your Web site. But don't be afraid to register your site under more than one category. Put yourself in the shoes of potential customers. What categories would they be searching on Yahoo! in order to find an organization like yours?

tip Online Marketing Resources

For an excellent index to resources that will help you market your Web site, visit SearchZ at **www.searchz.com**.

Is Your Web Site Listed in Major Industry and Topic Directories and Specialized Search Engines?

While many people may find you in the major search engines and directories discussed above, others may come across you when searching within Web sites that contain specialized industry or topic directories.

Spend some time looking around, and you will probably discover that for any particular industry or topic, there are a number of specialized online directories and search engines. For various reasons individuals and organizations are taking the time to establish comprehensive lists of Web sites related to a particular industry or topic and work hard at notifying people interested of the existence of such directories.

This means that a pilot looking for insurance might not necessarily search Yahoo! or Excite to find aviation insurance specialists, but might look at a specialized aviation directory for such information. That is why you should ensure that you are listed in the various specialized directories that are appropriate for your Web site.

You might be surprised at the extensive number of specialized directories that are available for any particular topic or industry. We checked the Aviation category in Yahoo! and found that there were quite a few directories specific to the Aviation topic:

We then visited one of the first ones we saw, entitled "Aviation Internet Resources." It turned out to be an extensive list of thousands of Web sites related to aviation and was likely a place where people within the industry look for information, including, perhaps, insurance services:

We had a look and found that the directory did include a specific category related to aviation insurance, but V.I. Rhodes Insurance was not listed:

This, perhaps, might be a missed opportunity. The point is, if you don't take the time to list yourself in some of the key topic and industry directories, then you could be missing out on a valuable opportunity for people to find you.

But now a word of caution. Some would-be entrepreneurs have established such directories but charge a fee to be listed. Unless you have compelling evidence that the directory is used widely throughout the industry or topic area, be careful. There are a lot of initiatives, but our experience is that few of them really succeed.

What do we suggest? Undertake an extensive search of the Internet for directories related to the topic or industry that is related to your Web site. Be broad; don't be too restrictive in the way you categorize where you might fit. Take time to visit all the directories that you discover, and determine if you can add yourself to the directory. If you must contact someone to get yourself listed, do so, and be prepared to justify why your particular Web site should appear.

In many cases it is easy to get listed. Many of the directories include a "submission" section in which you can "submit" your Web site for inclusion in the directory. For example, the Aviation Internet Resources site that we mentioned above includes a page to do just that. This site asks for general company information as well as contact information and company description/history. It also allows you to specify the category in which your Web site best fits:

Where do you begin to find topic or industry directories? We suggest several places:

- Definitely start out at Yahoo! Find your industry or topic, and see if there is a "Directories" or an "Indices" category. For our example there are quite a few, making this the best starting point.

- Then do a search in various search engines such as AltaVista for particular phrases. In our case, we looked for the phrases "aviation directories," "aviation listings," and "aviation sites." We found quite a bit of useful content; for example, this page of related Web sites:

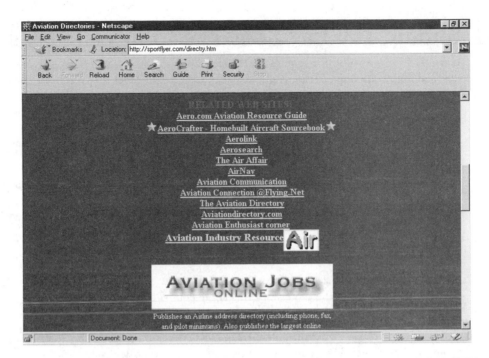

One of our best search phrases was "aviation links," which provided an extensive list of Web sites related to the aviation industry:

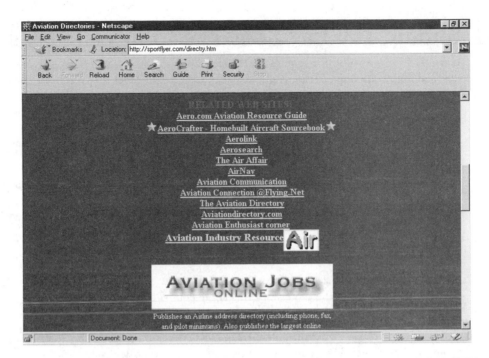

tip Should You Pay Someone to Register Your Site?

If you have an e-mailbox, it is quite likely that at some point you will have received an e-mail message from someone offering to register your Web site in "over 200 search engines." The message was likely a piece of junk mail. Or perhaps you have found links to companies or software programs that promise to take the time to register you on all kinds of sites when you are surfing the Web.

Should you use either type of service? Be cautious here. We don't encourage anyone to do business with someone who contacted you through a junk e-mail message, since many of the companies behind such efforts are clearly fraudulent in their intent. Signing up with a service to register you might help you get listed in various sites, but perhaps not the specific search indexes and directories that we talked about in this section.

In addition, many of these services and software programs use unethical techniques to try to increase your site's visibility on the major search engines.

As a result, we suggest that you approach such offers and programs with an extreme degree of caution and carefully assess the professionalism of the company involved.

Perhaps the most important comment we can make is the following. Most Internet users, when looking for a Web site, will visit one of the popular search engines or directories that we discussed earlier in the chapter. They don't go to the hundreds of other Web sites that these submission services promise to list you in. Therefore, you won't get a lot of additional exposure by using these services. As for the main search engines and directories, you can easily register with these services yourself, as we discussed above.

If you are still intent on checking out some of the major site promotion services and programs, here are some of the more popular ones:

TrafficBuilder	**www.cyberindustrial.net**
Dynamic Submission 2000	**www.apex-pi.com**
SubmitWolf Pro	**www.msw.com.au/swolf**
Submit It!	**www.submit-it.com**

Does Your Web Site Show Up When Someone Is Searching for Keywords or Phrases Related to Your Business?

Once you have followed our guidance for getting your Web site listed on the Internet, your next task is to ensure that your site is getting the best possible placement on Internet search engines and directories. Now it is time to determine if people will find you if they happen to type in the words and phrases that you think they might use when looking for sites like yours. You have to work hard to ensure that when people are doing a search, your Web site appears in the first few pages of the search results.

What you need to do is write down all the words and phrases that you think people could use if they are trying to find your site. You're going to use this material to see how well positioned your site is in various search engines and directories.

Assessing Your Site

We suggest that you visit did-it detective again, a site we mentioned earlier. This time, type in your Web address, one of the search words or phrases that you think someone could use, and then type your e-mail address. Within a couple of hours, you will get a detailed e-mail report advising you not only if you are listed in all the major search engines, but where your site ranks for the particular words or phrases that were used:

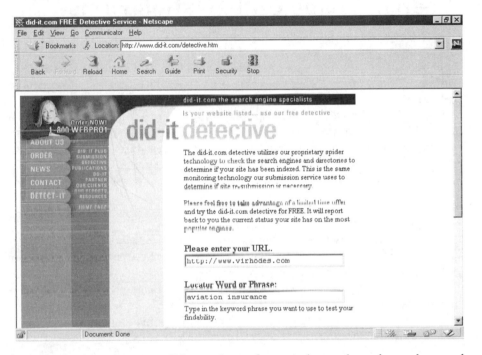

In other words, the did-it detective will let you know, for particular words or phrases that people might be searching for, whether your site shows up in the top 10, top 100, or whether it shows up at all.

Keep in mind that studies have shown that if you don't appear on the first few pages of a search result, people won't find you at all, since they rarely go past these first few pages before starting a new search.

So how do you go about getting your Web site closer to the top of search engines' results lists? You have to code your Web pages better, in particular, by taking advantage of meta-tags and page titles (or title tags). Don't let these words scare you. "Meta-tags" and "title tags" are two of the best ways to ensure that your Web site shows up when someone searches for the products or services you offer.

Many searches on the Internet generate thousands or tens of thousands of hits. Most users will only examine the first two or three pages of results before reformulating their search and trying again. So it's important to design your Web page to optimize your position on search engines and directories. You want to do everything you can to make sure that when someone searches a topic related to your Web site, your own site appears near the top of the list. Otherwise you will rarely get noticed.

There are certain techniques to use to influence your ranking on search engines and directories. Two of the most popular are using meta-tags and title tags.

Meta-tags are pieces of code that you bury in your Web site source code to influence the description that search engines and directories give your Web site (this is called a "description meta-tag") and to influence the words the engines associate with your site (this is called a "keyword meta-tag"). A page title, or "title tag," is the specific title that is generated by Web browsers when anyone visits a Web site. It's the heading that shows up in the upper left-hand corner of the browser.

tip Search Engine Optimization Firms

There are services on the Internet that promise to send traffic to your Web site without using meta-tags and without modifying any of the content on your Web site. How do they do it? They build one or more Web pages for you that include keywords related to your business. These pages are called "bridge pages." They are coded in such a way that they will show up on a search engine when an Internet user does a search for a particular word or phrase. When users click on a bridge page, they are redirected to the company's actual homepage. An example of a company that provides this type of service is Web-Ignite Corporation (**www.clientdirect.com**). Bear in mind that because bridge pages aren't naturally occurring Web pages, there is disagreement within the Internet community over whether the use of bridge pages is an ethical practice. As a result, we recommend that you use search engine optimization firms at your own discretion.

Meta-Tags

Let's show you how we used "meta-tags" for our Web site about our books (**www.handbook.com**). You can look at our meta-tags by viewing the "source code" we used to create our Web site. The source code for our Web site is shown in the screen below. When using Netscape, you can look at a Web site's source code by choosing "View" from the list of options at the top of your browser, then select either "Page Source" (for Netscape 4 users) or "Document Source" (for Netscape 3 users). Users of Microsoft's Internet Explorer should select "View" from the menu bar, then "Source":

```
Netscape - [Source of: http://www.handbook.com/]                          _ 8 X

<HTML>

<HEAD>

<META HTTP-EQUIV="Content-Type" CONTENT="text/html; charset=iso-8859-1">
<META HTTP-EQUIV="Bulletin-Text" CONTENT="Canada's Best-Selling Internet Authors: Jim Carroll, R
<META NAME="Author" CONTENT="Web Designs by Wright">
<META NAME="Description" CONTENT="Canada's Best-Selling Internet Authors: Jim Carroll, Rick Broa
<META NAME="keywords" CONTENT="canadian internet handbook, canadian internet, jim carroll, rick
<META NAME="GENERATOR" CONTENT="Mozilla/4.02 [en]C-DIAL  (Win95; U) [Netscape]">
<TITLE>Canada's Best-Selling Internet Authors: Jim Carroll, Rick Broadhead
</TITLE>

</HEAD>

<BODY TEXT="#000000" BGCOLOR="#FFFFFF" LINK="#000000" VLINK="#000000" ALINK="#000000" TOPMARGIN=
<CENTER>
<IMG SRC="http://www.handbook.com/h_bannertop.gif" BORDER=0  ALIGN=CENTER>
</CENTER>
<BR>
<CENTER>
<TABLE BORDER=0 CELLSPACING=0 CELLPADDING=0 WIDTH="100%" >
<TR>
<TD ALIGN= LEFT VALIGN=LEFT WIDTH="40%" >
<FONT FACE="arial" COLOR="#000000" SIZE=-1>
<B>
Read What CNET Canada Had to Say About the
<I>1998 Canadian Internet Handbook
</I>!
</B>
</FONT>
<P>
```

Look at the sixth line in our source code; this is our "description meta-tag":

    <META NAME="Description"
    CONTENT="Canada's Best-selling Internet Authors: Jim Carroll, Rick Broadhead">

The information in a description meta-tag is used to create a summary of your Web site. When someone uses a search engine or a directory, the Web site summary is the one- or two-line description that appears under the title of each document named in the search results. For example, here's the page AltaVista produced when we searched for Web pages containing the phrase "montreal expos." The brief description you see under each document name is called the site summary:

```
AltaVista: Simple Query "montreal expos" - Netscape
File  Edit  View  Go  Communicator  Help

Back  Forward  Reload  Home  Search  Guide  Print  Security  Stop        N

Bookmarks   Location: http://altavista.digital.com/cgi-bin/query?pg=q&what=web&kl=XX&q=%22montreal+expos%22

1. Montreal Expos Bulova Wall Clock
   Montreal Expos Bulova Wall Clock. Item Number: #BU-SB515. Price: $19.95. Supplier:Bulova. Select. to begin the
   ordering process. Official Logos and Colors.
   http://www.onlinesports.com/pages/I,BU-SB515.html - size 2K - 28-Mar-97 - English - Translate

2. Features - Won Over by the Montreal Expos
   Monday August 18, 1997 Edition. Sports. Won Over by the Montreal Expos. Tom Regan, Special to The Christian
   Science Monitor. BOSTON -- In related news:...
   http://www.csmonitor.com/durable/1997/08/18/feat/sports.2.html - size 11K - 27-Jan-98 - English - Translate

3. CNN/SI - Baseball - Box Score: Montreal Expos at Atlanta Braves - September 20
   Sports News from Cable News Network(CNN) and Sports Illustrated Magazine.
   http://cgi.cnnsi.com/baseball/mlb/nl/scoreboards/1997/09/20/finalbox.atlanta.montreal.0327.html - size 17K -
   27-Jan-98 - English - Translate

4. THE BASEBALL CONNECTION- Montreal Expos
   Multiple links to baseball sites covering the Montreal Expos
   http://www.thebaseballconnection.com/baseball/expos1.stm - size 33K - 27-Jan-98 - English - Translate

5. THE MONTREAL EXPOS PAGE
   Montreal Expos Mailing List: expos@janus.sdsu.edu Send Subscription Requests To: expos-reuqest@janus.sdsu.edu
   Ticket Information: (514) 8GO-EXPOS. *...
   http://www.cif.rochester.edu/users/flashy/baseball/expos.html - size 1K - 19-Apr-95 - English - Translate

Document: Done
```

Many Internet users (including the authors of this book) use these Web site summaries to help them decide which sites to visit. It's therefore important to create a description for your site that accurately and concisely reflects its purpose. What happens if you don't include a description meta-tag on your site? The search engine or directory will create its own summary for any Web page site using the information it finds on that page. Often this description won't accurately convey what your Web site is about, so it's advisable to create your own summary using the description meta-tag. This will automatically override the abstract created by the search engine or directory, but only if the search engine or directory obeys meta-tags; some don't (more on this later).

Let's go back to the source code for our book Web site. Look at the seventh line down; this is where we have included the following line:

```
<META NAME="keywords" CONTENT="canadian internet handbook, canadian internet, jim carroll, rick broadhead,
    Canadian Internet, Canadian Internet Handbook, Jim Carroll, Rick Broadhead">
```

This is what a "keywords meta-tag" looks like. Notice that we have separated each word or phrase in our keywords list using a comma.

A keywords meta-tag increases the chance that your Web site will appear high on the results list whenever someone does a search using any of the words or phrases that appear in your tag.

For our Web site notice that we have listed the following words and phrases in our keywords meta-tag:

- canadian internet handbook
- canadian internet
- jim carroll
- rick broadhead
- Canadian Internet

- Canadian Internet Handbook

- Jim Carroll

- Rick Broadhead

One thing we don't do is use the word "internet" as a meta-tag; it is far too popular on the Web. The more unique the tags you use, the better.

You may be wondering why all the entries appear twice, first in lowercase, and then with the first letter of each word capitalized. Most search engines (like AltaVista) do not require initial capitals on words, which speeds the typing of words you're searching for. However, some search engines and directories are case-sensitive (meaning they distinguish between uppercase and lowercase words). We want to ensure that if someone types in "Canadian Internet Handbook" in a search (rather than "canadian internet handbook"), our Web site will still show up near the top of the list.

When creating your keywords meta-tag, it is important to choose words and phrases you think potential customers will use when searching for Web sites like yours. On our Web site we have used our names (Jim Carroll and Rick Broadhead), the name of one of our books (Canadian Internet Handbook), and the phrase "canadian internet." Also, where possible, make your meta-tags as descriptive and distinctive as possible. For example, placing the word "canada" in our meta-tag will do little to increase our site's chances of being found on the Web, because it's such a popular word.

When creating your description meta-tag, we recommend that you don't repeat the same keyword more than once as a way to increase your Web site's ranking. Some search engines and directories will lower your Web's site's position in their index or remove your Web site altogether if they discover you repeating the same keyword many times. You should also be aware of the limitations on the length of meta-tags. On AltaVista, the limit for both description and keyword meta-tags is 1,024 characters of text (for the entire list of keywords), while on Infoseek, the limit is 1,000 characters for keyword meta-tags (for the entire list) and 200 characters for description meta-tags. Therefore, to accommodate all the search engines, you should keep your description meta-tag under 200 characters of text and your keyword meta-tags under 1,000 characters in length.

A good example of meta-tag usage is on the Web site belonging to Zesto Holdings, a British Columbia-based citrus-spice company:

Check out their site, and you'll see that they have the following meta-tags in their source code: Zesto's "description meta tag":

    <meta name="Description"

    content="Zesto - A novelty product for baking and cooking - No More Grated Knuckles">

Zesto's "keywords meta tag":

    <meta name="keywords"

    content="Zesto, lemon, orange, peel, citrus, rind, zest, cooking, baking">

Their keywords meta-tag will improve the likelihood that people searching for information about cooking with citrus or lemon will come across this site. For example, typing the following words into AltaVista Canada:

    baking with citrus or lemon

produced the following results screen, with Zesto's Web site on the first page of results:

Similarly, when we searched AltaVista Canada for the words "lemon" and "baking," the Zesto Web site showed up in the top 10 matches. While it's unlikely that the meta-tags alone were responsible for the site's high ranking within AltaVista, they certainly helped. However, meta-tags are only one of many criteria that search engines and directories use in determining a Web site's ranking in their index. For example, where the keywords actually appear in your text, and how often can also make a big difference. On Zesto's Web site you'll notice the words "citrus" and "lemon" appearing more than once on Zesto's main Web page. It's the combined effect of several techniques that will help your Web site to get a good ranking on search engines and directories.

To get a feel for how Internet users search for information on the Web, visit the WebCrawler Search Voyeur (**www.webcrawler.com**). It is a scrolling ticker that shows you the search phrases people are using on the Web—right now. When you click on one, you are whisked off to the same search results someone just found:

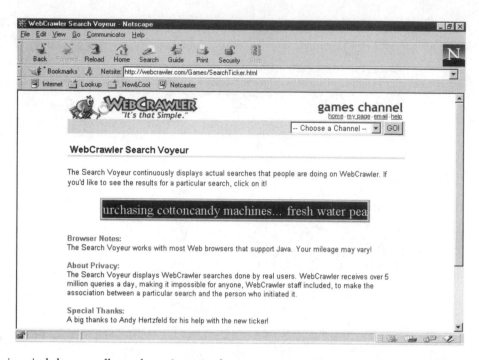

Keep in mind that not all search engines are alert to meta-tags. AltaVista, HotBot, and Infoseek are, but Lycos and Excite seem to ignore them. Furthermore, for search engines and directories that do pay attention to meta-tags, they are only one of several factors used to rank your Web site for users' searches. Therefore, meta-tags are no panacea for getting your site to the top of search engine lists; they are just one of many things you need to do to improve your site's chances of being found on the Web. Most search engines and directories include help files describing techniques to improve your site's ranking in their database. For example, Lycos (**www.lycos.com**) has a page called "Your Site in Lycos," which provides several tips and pointers to help you optimize your Web site's ranking in their index:

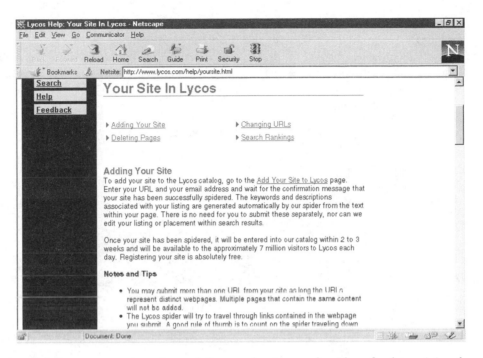

Keep in mind that every search engine and directory has its own algorithms for determining the ranking of Web pages in its index. Meta-tags are only one factor. For this reason, review the advice each search engine and each directory gives on its Web site and try to accommodate as many of the suggestions as possible in order to optimize your position on all the Internet search engines and directories.

tip Help With Meta-Tags

A great tool to help you create meta tags for your Web site is TagGen (**www.hisoftware.com**). This program doesn't require any technical knowledge to use, and it can automatically update your Web pages with the meta-tags you have created.

Title Tags

Now let's look at page titles, or "title tags." Looking back at the source code of the Web site for our books, you will see the title tag beneath our keywords meta-tag:

<TITLE>Canada's Best-Selling Internet Authors: Jim Carroll, Rick Broadhead</TITLE>

Most search engines and directories pay special attention to the words in your Web site's title when they index your site. In other words, you increase the likelihood of appearing higher up on a directory or search engine's results list if the words in your title closely match what an Internet user is looking for. This means that you should create a title for your Web site that is as descriptive as possible. The title tag is also important for another reason. When you create your title tag, you are determining the title that an Internet user will see for your site in a directory or search engine's list of results. It's important to remember that when people search the Web, they often get thousands of results for a single query. Creating a good, descriptive title for your site is one way to make it stand out from the rest. Internet users are most likely to click on Web sites that have clear, descriptive titles.

Let's look at an example of a title tag. Consider the Web site of the Pacific Coast Feather Company, shown below. Notice the title the company is using for its Web site: "Welcome to Pacific Coast." (Remember that the title is whatever appears in the upper left-hand corner of the Web browser when you visit a Web site; it is not what appears on the first page of an organization's Web site. It's just coincidence that Pacific Coast's title is also the same as the banner that appears in big block letters on the first page of its Web site.)

"Welcome to Pacific Coast" isn't a very effective title. A better title would be

> "Pacific Coast Feather Company – down pillows, down comforters, and featherbeds."

Why is our suggestion better than the title the company is currently using? By referring to the company's down products in the title of its Web site, the company can improve its chances of showing up on a search engine or directory when someone does a search for phrases such as "down pillows" or "featherbeds." The company's current Web site title doesn't mention the company's product line and, hence, is a less effective choice for a title.

Entering Meta-Tags and Title Tags on Your Web Site

What's involved in adding meta-tags and title tags to your Web site? Is it complicated?

Not really. If you use a software program to create your Web pages, it usually has a place where you can enter the meta-tags and title tags that you want to use.

Let's take a look at how this works using Netscape Communicator, a program for creating and maintaining your Web site. When you create a page, you can define the "page properties." This gives a screen where you can assign a title (the title tag), description (the description meta-tag), and keywords (the keywords meta-tag) to a Web page. Netscape Communicator then inserts the appropriate meta-tags and title tag information into the Web page:

Page Properties ☒

General | Colors and Background | META Tags |

Location: file:///Untitled

Title: Canada's Bestselling Internet Authors: Jim Carroll & Rick Broadhead

Author: Web Designs by Wright

Description: Canada's Bestselling Internet Authors: Jim Carroll & Rick Broadhead

Other attributes

Use commas to separate multiple words or phrases.

Keywords: canadian internet handbook, canadian internet, jim carroll, ri

Classification:

[OK]   [Cancel]   [Apply]   [Help]

Let's recap some important points:

- For both the meta-tags and title tag, use words that you think people might use when trying to find Web sites like yours. Keep in mind that the information you place in the title tag is what appears at the top of a searcher's Web browser. The title tag also determines the title that appears for your Web site in a directory or search engine's results list.

- Try to make your title as descriptive and relevant as possible. The title tag should accurately describe the nature of your business.

  For example, suppose you run a forensic accounting firm under the name "Smith, Jones, and Brown." Rather than just using the name of your firm as the title of your Web site, go one step further. Use a title like this instead:

  `<TITLE>Smith, Jones and Brown - Forensic Accounting Specialists</TITLE>`

  By including the words "forensic accounting" in the title, you stand a better chance of showing up on a search engine when a user does a search for those words.

- Not all directories and search engines pay attention to meta-tags, but some do. More importantly, every directory and search engine uses a different algorithm for ranking Web pages. Make sure you read the online help files provided by most search engines. This will help you understand what you need to do to get a good ranking for your Web site on the respective search engines.

  Finally, be aware that there is some debate over whether the time and effort spent "tweaking" your meta-tags actually results in some improvement in your placement on various directories and search engines. Some individuals and organizations have gone too far in the way that they manipulate their meta-tags, using too many instances of the same word, for example, with the result that search engines are beginning to crack down. There is a law of diminishing returns in terms of your effort. While intelligent use of meta-tags may help to move you up a few pages with just a little bit of effort, getting on to page 1 or 2 might prove to be an impossible task, regardless of how much time you dedicate.

To keep up-to-date with the evolving world of meta-tags, visit Web Marketing Today (**www.netb2b.com**), an online site that contains links to many articles related to Internet marketing and business activities. Look under the Knowledge Database section. Doing several searches for meta-tags and search engines, we were able to find several wonderful articles that helped to put meta-tags into perspective. A sample is seen below:

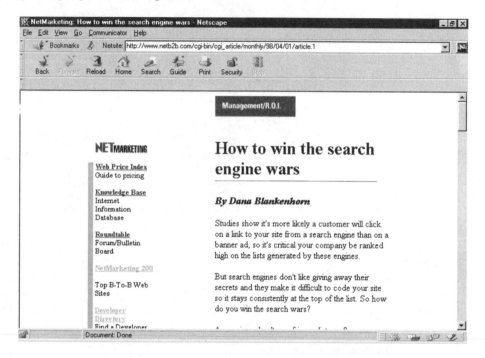

University Training in Web Positioning

Proving just how important the topic of search engine positioning has become to the business community, a U.S. university has accredited the first university level course for Web positioning in North America. Missouri-based Kennesaw State University is now offering a continuing education program on Web positioning strategies. Graduates will earn a certificate from the university and receive a Continuing Education Credit in Web Positioning Tactics. Participants also receive an official logo to place on their own Web site confirming successful completion of the course. The course takes place on the Internet. For more information visit **www.jergroup.com/web**.

WebPosition

If you really want to get into managing your meta-tags to try to improve your ranking on various search engines, then check out WebPosition, a software program available from Missouri-based First Place Software (**www.webposition.com**).

WebPosition is a wonderful tool for Windows 95 that will do a detailed check of the position of your Web site, or specific pages within your Web site, on various search engines and directories. It does so by testing a variety of search words and phrases that you provide to these engines. It does the type of thing that the did-it detective does, but in a far more detailed manner.

Not only that, but the program will run on a scheduled basis and advise you if your particular position on a search engine has improved or worsened over time, thus giving you an opportunity to further tweak your meta-tags to improve the situation, if necessary.

You can learn how to use WebPosition within minutes, but you will discover that it can take days and weeks to really learn how to take advantage of its features, given the information that it provides regarding how you are ranked on various search engines.

You first provide details about the Web site that you want to check:

Then you are given the opportunity to specify the words or phrases that people might use to find your site on the Web:

Assessing the Effectiveness
of Your Web Site

Protecting Yourself Online

Improving Your Productivity
on the Internet

Enhancing Your Web Site

You can also specify which search engines and directories should be queried:

Once you have done this, WebPosition queries each search engine. You can set up a schedule so that this occurs while you are not using your computer, since it can take a little while. Once it has finished, it builds a variety of reports:

V.I. Rhodes Insurance

Last Results on July 24, 1998 03:26 PM

Concise Summary Report **	Excellent overview of your search positions by keyword and Search Engine. It even shows your last reported positions.
Summary Report	Summary showing what ALL your listings look like on each Engine. Make sure they look good to get the best response.
Detail Report	Shows exactly what is positioned above and below you. Analyze these pages to see what you could do to better your competition.
Alert! Report	Alerts you to places where you've declined in rank or have been dropped entirely! Once your rankings are good, make sure they stay that way.
Trend Report	Shows a summary of your rank statistics over time by Engine and keyword. This guide will help you meet your long-term goals for each Engine and keyword.
Log Report	Records the last Mission statistics and includes the complete *unmodified* results from the search engines.

The main report you will use is the one detailing your ranking on each search engine for each particular search phrase. In this case, we are advised that for our company, we are not even in the top 30 listings and, hence, don't appear in the first three pages (we can specify these limits):

WebPosition Concise Summary Report

V.I. Rhodes Insurance

Report created July 24, 1998 at 03:35 PM by WebPosition version 1.20.4

Registered To: Reviewer Eval..

[Back To Menu]

Jump to Keywords for: [AltaVista] [Excite/AOL NetFind] [InfoSeek] [HotBot] [LinkStar] [Lycos] [WebCrawler] [Yahoo] [YellowPages] [Magellan]

AltaVista

Keyword	Position	Page	Last Position	Change	URL
aviation insurance	>30	>3	NA	NA	No pages found.

If you examine the detailed report, you can find out who is listed above and below you on various search engines for certain search words and phrases. This can be useful for monitoring your competitors and for determining what others are doing differently to get themselves positioned higher on a search engine:

You can try out a 30-day evaluation version of WebPosition. The cost of the program is U.S. $99 (at time of writing). Given what you can accomplish in such a short period of time with this program, we believe it to be money well spent.

PositionAgent

Although much less powerful than WebPosition, you should also look at PositionAgent (**www.positionagent.com**). This program will monitor your Web site's position on the major search engines and directories and provide weekly status reports by e-mail. This is a commercial service and ranges in price from U.S. $60 to U.S. $1,400 for a 6-month licence, depending on how many Web pages and keywords you want to track. You can try out PositionAgent by using the free trial available on their Web site:

Name	Status	Position			Page	
Alta-Vista	done	1			1	
Magellan	done	—	—	—	—	—
Yahoo	done	—	—	—	—	—
Excite	done	3			1	
HotBot	done	—	—	—	—	—
WebCrawler	done	—	—	—	—	—
InfoSeek	done	—	—	—	—	—
Lycos	done	1			1	
LinkStar	done	—	—	—	—	—
Galaxy	done	—	—	—	—	—
YellowPages	done	—	—	—	—	—

RankThis!

We also like RankThis! (**www.rankthis.com**), a free tool that helps you determine your Web site ranking based on different keyword sets in 10 of the major search engines. This site will tell you if your site ranks within the top 200 for the keywords you have chosen to search on; it also lists the sites that are in the top 10 for that keyword(s) search, thus providing some "competitive research." While you, of course, can find out this same information by visiting the search engines directly, RankThis! makes it easy to query any of the major search sites from one page. Unfortunately, a major limitation of RankThis! is that you can only query one search site at a time:

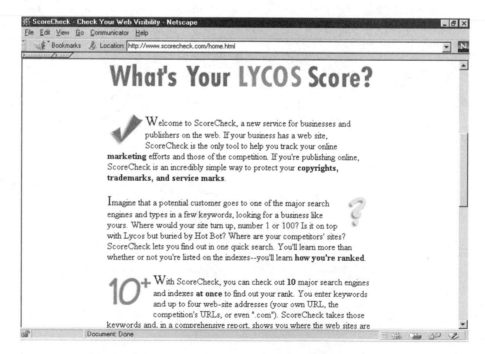

ScoreCheck

ScoreCheck (**www.scorecheck.com**) is a similar service that will "score" your Web site and send you a report by e-mail:

You can obtain a free "ScoreCard" for your Web site by visiting the ScoreCheck Web site. You can also sign up for ScoreCard's commercial service, which allows you to check more search engines, schedule your ScoreCards, and have your reports archived on the Web. The cost is U.S. $20 for three ScoreChecks.

tip How "Popular" Is Your Web Site?

In order to determine which pages show up at the top of a results list, search engines rely on a number of factors, some of which we have discussed in this chapter. However, search engines are increasingly using a site's popularity as an important factor when ranking the results of a search. In other words, when a user does a search on a search engine, more popular Web sites show up higher in the results list. How can a search engine measure how popular a Web site is? One method is to examine how many other Web sites link to it. Alternatively, a search engine can track which Web sites in its index are getting the most visits and use this information to organize the results of a user's search. To see an example of a search engine that uses popularity to rank its search results, visit Google at **google.stanford.edu**. Other major search engines are using a technology called Direct Hit to help them rank Web sites for users. For more information, visit **www.directhit.com**.

How does this affect you? Web site owners who want to get their Web sites listed prominently on search engines need to think about ways to increase the popularity of their sites. One way to do this is to encourage other Web sites to link to you. The more Web sites that link to you, the more popular your Web site will be in the eyes of the search engines.

Summary

Your success on the Internet will be due in large part to how well you market and promote your Web site. Successful online marketing includes designing your site in such a way that you optimize its ranking on popular search engines and directories.

As a result, we suggest that you invest the time to carefully examine the position of your Web site on the various search engines and directories and assess how you can take advantage of some of the methods outlined in this chapter to improve the visibility of your site on the Web. Remember, your Web site isn't serving you well if no one can find it.

chapter three

Tips From Canadian Webmasters

People are demanding more than ever from the Web as a communication medium. It must be informative, easy to navigate, fast to load, entertaining, current, accessible, and the operative "I" word—interactive. These demands have prompted a reactive rather than proactive process of building and communicating information on the Web.

Jenny Winterbottom, Web site developer, Vancouver Aquarium

Highlights

1. This chapter contains valuable insights from leading Canadian Webmasters regarding what makes a successful and winning Web site.

2. In addition, they provide valuable comments on the most common problems that exist with Web sites and the tools they use to manage and build some of the largest and most comprehensive Web sites in Canada.

In assessing the design, reliability, and effectiveness of your Web site, the best advice that we can give you is to learn from the experience of others. To help you in this regard, we sent a message containing three questions to the Webmasters of a variety of Canadian organizations with Web sites. Based on the flood of responses we received, we realized that many of those involved in the Internet across Canada are eager to share their experiences and what they have learned. So here are the questions we asked, the panel of Webmasters, and their replies:

1. If you could offer four (nontechnical) tips to Canadian Web site owners to help make their sites more effective, what would they be? We are thinking about issues related to design, layout, marketing strategy, promotion, etc. We are not interested in technical issues, such as servers used, etc.

2. What is the most common mistake that you see Web site designers/owners making?

3. What Internet utilities (shareware or commercial) do you recommend to our readers to help with effective design or management of a Web site?

Our panel covers a wide range of organizations, in terms of the type of organization as well as the size. Their answers to our first two questions provided the greatest amount of detail. Therefore, we have organized their responses to these questions in a way that emphasizes common concepts and issues.

Our Panel

Ellen Agger
Webmaster, Alzheimer Society of Canada
www.alzheimer.ca

Virginia Brailey
Manager, Communications, Noranda Inc.
www.noranda.com

Jean Pierre Burdett
Internet Content Designer, Dell Canada
www.dell.ca

Wayne Carrigan
Webmaster, tsn.ca
www.tsn.ca

Addy Ching
Internet/Intranet Marketing Coordinator, Hong Kong Bank of Canada
www.hkbc.com

Simon Cohen
Webmaster, AOL Canada
www.aol.ca

Tom Dawson
Webmaster/Partner, ICanGarden.com
www.icangarden.com

Thomas Hader
Webmaster, Clearnet
www.clearnet.com

Mike Hyttinen
Web Site Designer, Sony Music Canada
www.sonymusic.ca

Theresa Jobateh
Internet Administrator, Canadian Egg Marketing Agency
www.canadaegg.ca

John Pullam
National Manager, Electronic Commerce
Sears Canada Inc.
www.sears.ca

Paul Schwartz
Webmaster, Reader's Digest Canada
www.readersdigest.ca

Hart Steinfeld
Webmaster, Canadian Airlines
www.cdnair.ca

Sandy Wills
Webmaster, Molson Breweries
www.molson.com

Jenny Winterbottom
Web Site Developer, Vancouver Aquarium
www.vanaqua.org
www.clamshell.org

General Motors of Canada Internet Marketing Organization
(replies from a panel)
www.gmcanada.com

Webmaster, Alliance Video Store
(name withheld by request)
www.alliancevideo.com

Question 1:

If you could offer four (nontechnical) tips to Canadian Web site owners to help make their sites more effective, what would they be? We are thinking about issues related to design, layout, marketing strategy, promotion, etc. We are not interested in technical issues, such as servers used, etc.

1. Understand Your Target Market

Ellen Agger, Webmaster, Alzheimer Society of Canada:

"Be clear on why you are creating a site, and know what you want it to do for you. Know who your audiences are—what they want from your organization and from your site. Is it information, entertainment, the latest news, or sports reports? The clearer you are when planning your site, the better you can choose the design features, the navigation scheme, and the elements that will make it work for your visitors. A good site works for both your organization and your visitors."

General Motors of Canada Internet Marketing Organization:

"Let the design, content, and functionality of your Web site be driven by your users' needs; think about what they want, not what you want to tell them."

Jenny Winterbottom, Web Site Developer, Vancouver Aquarium:

"The Web is a visual medium that depends on good design for good communication. It is also perhaps the most difficult medium in which to achieve successful design. The most challenging role a Web designer has is to make sense out of information and convey it to users under a wide variety of conditions. Differences in modem speeds, computer platforms, browsers, and monitors can create a design nightmare if a site is not developed and tested to accommodate these differences.

"Know your audience, then design with them in mind. For example, the Aquarium's Web-based game was developed for use in schools. Therefore, it was essential that we created a site that ran efficiently on lower quality computers with slower connection speeds."

Simon Cohen, Webmaster, AOL Canada:

"Begin with the end in mind. Understand why people are coming to your site, and make sure that your site delivers. Nothing disappoints visitors more than to find the information they were searching for wasn't there or worse, wasn't available to them for a technical reason."

Tom Dawson, Webmaster/Partner, ICanGarden.com:

"It has been my experience that people use the Web to find information. If we deliver that information, they will visit often, and we have an opportunity to present our message or product. Instead of "pumping" a product, the visitors increasingly rely on the site as a trusted source of information. As in every business, the more you know your visitor, their needs and desires, the more attractive your site will be and a place they want to visit. Unless you are a brand new business, you probably already know a lot about your target audience. All you have to do is adapt your knowledge to building a Web site. Start with looking at your company's product and service. Examine them to see what kind of information that you could adapt to something that you can update on a regular basis that will keep visitors coming back on a regular basis. If you don't think you know what would interest your clients or visitors, start with something that is of interest to you or your business. Make the content relevant to your audience. Information became the hot commodity of the 90's and, in my opinion, will become even more important in the new millennium."

2. Keep It Simple

Simon Cohen, Webmaster, AOL Canada:

"Avoid 'bells and whistles.' Flashy is fun, and if that's your business, then great. However, most folks don't have the bandwidth to support it, and unless it makes their lives easier, chances are good they won't appreciate it. Stick to the basics—if it can be done with fewer tricks and less technology, do it."

Paul Schwartz, Webmaster, Reader's Digest Canada:

"A FAQ and a few photos about your product/service/hobby will be far more popular and appreciated than a big, expensive and difficult to modify and maintain multimedia extravaganza! Web sites are real give-and-take affairs. If you want something (orders, fame, whatever), then you're going to have to give of yourself and your knowledge and experience. There are no short-cuts."

Hart Steinfeld, Webmaster, Canadian Airlines:

"If you are just starting out, or even if you are an expert, one of the best pieces of advice I can give is the KIS rule. keep it simple. Some of the best Web sites out there are the ones that don't use a lot of graphics and fancy toys.

"Avoid huge scrolling pages full of text. It just simply won't be read. Studies have shown that if you can't say what you want to say in a few paragraphs, forget it!"

Theresa Jobateh, Internet Administrator, Canadian Egg Marketing Agency:

"Be careful with using the latest bells and whistles (i.e., multimedia, Java), since some visitors may not be "up-to speed" with their browsers, modems, and sound and video capabilities."

3. Use Clear Navigational Aids

Sandy Wills, Webmaster, Molson Breweries:

"The key to a successful Web site is proper navigation. The navigation of your site should always be foremost in your mind when developing content and design. You should be able to guide the user to specific content through simplistic navigation. It is essential to build your navigation for all levels of interaction. If a person coming to your site has limited Web experience, you run the risk of overwhelming that user with extravagant navigational choices. If a person coming to your site has extensive Web experience, you can offer him or her clear navigation with optional abilities. It is mandatory to have navigation present on every page of the site. Keep in mind that most users come to your Web site with a preconceived expectation of content and will not spend time searching for it."

Tom Dawson, Webmaster/Partner, ICanGarden.com:

"When you create your site, think about the layout of your site. Make it understandable, easy to follow, with a natural flow from one area to another. Don't fall into the trap of having the standard links like every other site. Allow the visitor to explore the site and be pleasantly surprised when they 'discover' something new."

4. Define Your Objectives

Jenny Winterbottom, Web Site Developer, Vancouver Aquarium:

"One of the most important, but frequently overlooked, aspects of creating a Web site is strategic planning. Without a well-defined process for developing and implementing a Web site, no amount of information or great design will ensure success. Questions you should be asking are: Why do you need a Web site? How can the Web assist your business needs? Define concrete objectives for your site and how they fit into the overall goals of your business. Develop a mission statement to remind yourself of the goals you are trying to achieve. Know where you are going and the outcomes you want to accomplish; develop a budget and project timeline; finally, target milestones to achieve, then monitor your progress as the site develops. By defining goals before you start, you will be able to make more informed decisions about how technical functionality and design will play a role in the development process. For example, if one goal of your site is to generate revenue, then you may want to include secure online credit card transactions. Seek input from colleagues to ensure your Web site meets the needs of the organization as well as your audience. Establish working groups and select the appropriate team players to help achieve your goals. Remember, simply because your IS department has the technical skills doesn't mean they will create an effective Web site. The Vancouver Aquarium's Web site, for instance, was developed within the Education Department because the mission of our site is to provide educational content."

Virginia Brailey, Manager, Communications, Noranda Inc.:
"A Web site is a communications tool that requires a defined strategy and must be evaluated relative to the company's business strategy and desired image."

5. Promote Your Web Site Address

John Pullam, National Manager, Electronic Commerce, Sears Canada Inc.:
"Put your URL on everything. Every business card, every sign, every piece you mail."

Hart Steinfeld, Webmaster, Canadian Airlines:
"Try to get your Web address out there as much as possible. If you want to drive people to your site, you need to make people aware that you have a site. Once your site is live, make sure that every piece of collateral you send out, every business card you hand out, and anything with your name on it has those three W's on it!"

6. Make It Easy For Visitors to Contact You

Simon Cohen, Webmaster, AOL Canada:
"Make sure there is a "real person" behind the virtual presence. There should always be a way for the visitor to contact you. If it's e-mail, answer it within 24 hours. Phone numbers are even better; it's surprising how many people still want that 'personal touch,' even in the age of the Internet."

General Motors of Canada Internet Marketing Organization:
"Ensure that a user is never more than a click or two away from being able to send you an e-mail no matter where they are in the site. Use this opportunity to respond promptly and thoroughly; it will be greatly appreciated."

7. Develop Useful Content For Your Web Site

Paul Schwartz, Webmaster, Reader's Digest Canada:
"Don't go crazy with JavaScript, Java, animated GIFs and other "fun stuff." It's hard (and often expensive) to make these work properly and look good, and the appeal wears off really quickly. Take the time and money you would have spent on this sort of thing and put it towards your content. Your site visitors will appreciate it more, and it will get you more traffic and repeat visits."

John Pullam, National Manager, Electronic Commerce, Sears Canada Inc.:
"Make sure your site gives the customer really useful content...don't waste your space or time writing corporate histories."

8. Focus on Content Before Design

Jenny Winterbottom, Web Site Developer, Vancouver Aquarium:
"Content drives design, not the other way around. Deciding what content to include on your site and how people will access the content will determine the structure of a site. An effective Web site should add value and supplement existing content, not merely re-purpose it in another format. For example, the Aquarium's Web site supplements on-site exhibits by building online exhibits that create a community for guests to return to after visiting, or for those who are unable to visit in person. Ask questions such as, What can a Web medium do for this content that no other medium could? How will users employ and interact with the content? You can then select the most appropriate technologies to make your site functional and effective. Should you use HTML, animation, FlashTM, or complex databases to incorporate and display content effectively? Consider adding sound, video, or animation to present content in innovative ways."

Paul Schwartz, Webmaster, Reader's Digest Canada:
"Let the design grow out of the content. Don't design a site and then fit in your content. The most effective design for your particular site will become apparent as you attempt to build the pages, so don't worry about the design too much when you first begin. I always finish the text first, then add the graphics."

9. Use Innovative Marketing Techniques When Promoting Your Web Site

Mike Hyttinen, Web Site Designer, Sony Music Canada:
"In addition to an online banner ad campaign, advertise using traditional means such as print, TV, and radio. Tie the mediums together into one consistent campaign that focuses on the Web site. Use giveaways, online coupons, and other incentives to drive traffic. Advertising innovative tools and content on your site also can work well (calculators, real-time data, exclusive content). Try partnering with other companies and organizations that will complement your overall online strategy. Try sponsoring pages on other sites, or have others sponsor pages on your site. Develop campaigns that are content-rich and provide information in addition to giving the sell. (Have you seen those interactive banner ads from Met Life that take you straight to content-rich information on their Web site?)"

10. Get a Friend or Colleague to Critique Your Site

Simon Cohen, Webmaster, AOL Canada:
"As often as possible, get someone to visit your site who can give you constructive criticism. This will not only find weaknesses in the site's design and functionality; it may turn up some questions you had never thought of. (They may also find that broken link that your developer missed.)"

11. Find the Right Balance of Information

Jenny Winterbottom, Web Site Developer, Vancouver Aquarium:
"Prioritize and be selective with text. In the age of information overload, too much information will overwhelm a user, while too little information frustrates. Putting an entire journal online is not effective, while taking excerpts from one journal article may pique a user's interest to seek out more. Determine hierarchies of information to help users navigate through layers of content. One good piece of information presented effectively is 1,000 times more powerful and persuasive than many bits of poorly presented information. Take advantage of the Web's strength as an evolving, flexible medium. Update content regularly, and adopt changes in technology as they are introduced online to keep content fresh."

12. Give Your Visitors an Escape Route

Mike Hyttinen, Web Site Designer, Sony Music Canada:

"Providing escape routes helps a user navigate through your site. A way to get back to the home-page from anywhere is essential. Remember, never assume that users will always come to your Web site through the first page. They may have arrived at your site through a bookmark sent by a colleague or through a search engine."

13. Solicit Feedback

Wayne Carrigan, Webmaster, tsn.ca:

"Ask users for feedback about your site and take action on it."

Addy Ching, Internet/Intranet Marketing Coordinator, Hong Kong Bank of Canada:

"Use your site as a communication channel and learn from your visitors."

Paul Schwartz, Webmaster, Reader's Digest Canada:

"If you don't have log files, ask your visitors for feedback, and be prepared to respond promptly when they e-mail you (even just to thank them for their feedback)."

14. Keep Your Expectations in Check

Webmaster, Alliance Video Store:

"Until Internet purchasing takes a greater hold in consumer behaviour, expect up to 70% of the ultimate purchase of your product to occur at retail. The Internet is still considered an 'information gathering' tool for a majority of consumers."

15. Keep Your Web Site Up-to-Date

Sandy Wills, Webmaster, Molson Breweries:

"Current and informative content is essential for a Web site to be successful. Successful Web sites are revisited by a user. If a person comes back to your site and the content is stale, he will not return. If the user comes to your site after hearing your new product spot and it is not reviewed on your site, she will not return. Try to treat your site as a constantly evolving company brochure. You would not hand a five-month-old newsletter to a prospective client, would you?"

Tom Dawson, Webmaster/Partner, ICanGarden.com:

"The more frequently you update, the more likely you will develop a faithful following to the site. Developing a consistent time of updating the Web site builds an expectation into the visitors, and like a favourite magazine, they will look forward to its arrival. When we started our site a little over two years ago, we made a commitment to update our site every Sunday. We missed two Sunday updates when we went to Mexico and couldn't get our Internet connection to work. Even that early in our Web site development we heard about it from our visitors."

16. Don't Forget That the Web Is Only One of Many Media You Need to Use

Ellen Agger, Webmaster, Alzheimer Society of Canada:

"A Web site is a fantastic communication tool. But it needs to be part of a larger mix of ways that an organization communicates with people, complementing, for example, newsletters, brochures, and ads. The Alzheimer Society of Canada's Web site has allowed us to reach people at any time of day, anywhere in the country (and the world), and to provide opportunities for caregivers to interact with each other as well as with our offices across the country. But we know that not all the people we want to reach have access to the Internet. It's important to keep that in perspective unless your audiences are all hard-core computer users who are already online."

17. Start Off Small

Paul Schwartz, Webmaster, Reader's Digest Canada:
"Start off small. It's much easier to add to a small site than to modify and maintain a monster. Besides, you'll never really know what people want and what works until you try it, so start off with a few items and see what people click on."

18. Develop Online Promotions in Concert With Your Internet Service Provider

Webmaster, Alliance Video Store:
"Evaluate the 'equity' your product holds to Internet service providers and trade that equity for banner page promotions and online consumer promotions. Internet service providers are always looking for points of difference to market against the competition; allow them to utilize the brand recognition of your product to 'brand' their promotion in exchange for the design/execution of the promotion.

"If you do not share a demographic with a service provider, act as a prize provider in their promotions. Establish contact and express interest to several providers; your relationship should only be exclusive within the promotional period. Participate as often as you can."

19. Give Credit When Using Ideas From Other Web Sites

Paul Schwartz, Webmaster, Reader's Digest Canada:
"Don't be afraid to borrow ideas from other sites, but ask first, and give credit where credit is due. Common courtesy applies to the Internet too!"

20. Experiment With Different Typefaces

Thomas Hader, Webmaster, Clearnet:
"From a design perspective, using lots of tiny type in order to get a lot of text on a page is a strain on the eyes, and it requires the visitor to hunch over and get closer to the monitor. I think it's a good idea to vary type sizes and experiment with typefaces to enhance the look of the page and make it easier to read."

21. Design Your Site With Accessibility Issues in Mind

Ellen Agger, Webmaster, Alzheimer Society of Canada:
"Our site, for example, uses plain language, rather than medical jargon, to make the information—the heart of our site—as accessible as possible. We chose a plain background, rather than a busy image, to make the type easier to read, especially for older eyes. And we've kept the 'bells and whistles' off our site, so people who are looking for information can get it quickly and easily, without needing the latest browser or special software. For an informational site like ours, these design/development decisions have meant greater access to information for our visitors. The feedback we receive supports this."

Jean Pierre Burdett, Internet Content Designer, Dell Canada:
"Make the site accessible to different browser types and modem speeds. Don't forget people with disabilities; they represent your market too."

Theresa Jobateh, Internet Administrator, Canadian Egg Marketing Agency:
"Don't assume everyone uses 800×600 resolution for Pete's sake! If you design your site for 800×600, let your visitors know. It's a real pain using the scroll/slide bar when visiting a site."

22. Look For Cost Efficiencies

General Motors of Canada Internet Marketing Organization:

"Look for opportunities to deliver those services that benefit both you and your user. Things like online support and ordering, product specs, schedules, and account status are all of tremendous value and can be delivered more cost effectively in many cases than by traditional means."

23. Make Popular Content Easily Accessible

Wayne Carrigan, Webmaster, tsn.ca:

"Review traffic patterns and bring the content that is more popular forward. Keep your layout simple; try and keep all content within three clicks of the homepage."

24. Remain Consistent

Mike Hyttinen, Web Site Designer, Sony Music Canada:

"One of the more important user interface rules is to ensure your site remains consistent in every way possible. Physical location of navigation/utilities should always be predictable, and use of consistent verbiage and nomenclature throughout is a must (is it a "site map," sitemap," "site-map," "site index," etc.).

"It's OK if your pages look different (in fact, it may aid in the navigation between sections). Think of how a magazine is laid out. You can have a different look throughout each section of the mag, but there are common elements that keep the overall feel of the magazine together."

Sandy Wills, Webmaster, Molson Breweries:

"It seems to me that the design element of a Web site today is either hugely misplaced or overexposed. It is very important to have a consistent look and feel to your site. If your design layout is sectional, users will feel like they have left your site even though they are just viewing a subsection of your site."

25. Encourage User Interaction

Sandy Wills, Webmaster, Molson Breweries:

"Incorporating a community within your site is extremely important. Initializing user input and regulating the feedback is a valuable asset to your Web site. Empowering the user with capabilities such as message boards, chat, e-mail, etc., directly involves him or her into your community site. The instant feedback function of these capabilities will enable you to monitor the site's evolution."

26. Put Yourself in the Shoes of a Typical Web User

Ellen Agger, Webmaster, Alzheimer Society of Canada:

"Think about what works for you as a Web user and what doesn't. I like a site to deliver what it promises on the homepage, give me a full picture of what's available, make it easy and logical to get there (a good navigation scheme), give me information once I do get there (too many sites are skimpy in this department), and be pleasant to look at. What makes me crazy? Unclear navigation (where can I go next? how can I get back to a page I visited several pages ago? what's available on this site?); unnecessary blinking visual images that blink too frequently and jump out and hit me over the head; complex graphics that take too long to download; and bad, long-winded writing."

Wayne Carrigan, Webmaster, tsn.ca:

"Design matters. Have you ever pulled on a door when you were meant to push? A lot of people do, and they feel inadequate about themselves, especially since the door has a push sign on it. Well, the main reason for this phenomenon is that often the wrong handle is on the door. Many doors have pull handles on them where you are meant to push. It is actually a design fault. My point is that design not only effects people but affects them too. You have a responsibility as a Web designer to think about how your users will feel about using your Web site. A little more time spent on planning can make your users' experience better."

27. Refresh the Design/Appearance of Your Web Site

Wayne Carrigan, Webmaster, tsn.ca:
"Periodically make visual design changes to give users a fresh experience."

28. Make a Long-Term Commitment

Thomas Hader, Webmaster, Clearnet:
"Be bold. Break some rules. Hog some bandwidth. Never be afraid to try new things on your site. Treat your site as a living, growing, and changing thing that is never quite finished. Web sites are projects that continue long after you get the first version up on the server and indexed with the search engines. Be ready to devote plenty of time and energy to make it a popular Web destination. Anybody who remarks casually that 'anybody can build a Web site' is right, but he or she probably hasn't done it yet."

29. Use a Professional For Graphics

Sandy Wills, Webmaster, Molson Breweries:
"Graphics should only be done by a creative and experienced individual. The user's initial reaction to your Web site is activated by the design; therefore, file size, creative layout, and colour placement are all very important aspects of the site."

30. Provide Fast and Easy Access to Product Information

Webmaster, Alliance Video Store:
"Your pages should showcase your product first and foremost and be fast and easy to click through. There should be a clear path for consumers to gain the information they seek and commit to purchase painlessly. Offer choices along this path to gain information about your other products as well, but make sure a straight path to purchase can be navigated by a committed buyer."

31. Periodically Revisit Your Site's Objectives

Jenny Winterbottom, Web Site Developer, Vancouver Aquarium:
"Evolution means evaluation. Revisiting the goals of your site frequently will ensure it is achieving what it was originally intended to do. Once a site has been up for a period of time and it takes on new roles, you may find your goals need to be altered."

32. Create a Good Impression

Jean Pierre Burdett, Internet Content Designer, Dell Canada:
"Anyone interested in doing business over the Net should take the time and care to make their site look, feel, and work as good or better than their other communications. The company must look reputable if people are to feel comfortable handing over their credit card."

33. Make the Web Site "Personal"

Tom Dawson, Webmaster/Partner, ICanGarden.com:
"Make the site personal. Let the readers feel there really is someone behind it. You always hear that the Internet is the greatest leveller ever, since every business has the same chance to present its products whether they are large or small. You don't need massive budgets for advertising or storefronts; all you need are imagination and commitment. The look and feel of your Web site need to be as unique as you. This levelling effect can also be a curse, since the Internet can be very impersonal and leave people

wondering if there is actually a human behind the site. You're a person, unique. Your business is an extension of your values and beliefs. Make your Web site echo that sentiment. Allow your visitors to get to know you; they will be enriched, and you will have a chance to make a 'world' of new friends."

34. Learn Programming Fundamentals

Sandy Wills, Webmaster, Molson Breweries:
"The fact that almost everyone who gets involved with the Internet strikes immediately into composition of a Web site clearly indicates the ease of Web site development. However, it is my opinion that there are far too many people developing business Web sites without learning the programming fundamentals. I truly believe one must learn the raw coding and programming and not depend on an editor to compose a site. One must be able to decipher the clutter that the editors place in the source to continually update and evolve the site."

35. Measure the Success of Your Site in Different Ways

Jenny Winterbottom, Web Site Developer, Vancouver Aquarium:
"The Aquarium monitors its Web site success by tracking hit statistics through server logs, offering coupons online, which can then be tracked when redeemed on-site, providing online contests and counting entries, and through visitor feedback forms. Another way to monitor success is not only in terms of number of visitors, but also in terms of the site itself. How has the site grown? Is it accomplishing what it was supposed to do? Is content maintained and current?"

36. Have Fun

Paul Schwartz, Webmaster, Reader's Digest Canada:
"Keep it fun and manageable. A Web site can be much more informal than traditional corporate communication. Avoid comedy, but don't get too stuffy in your language or presentation unless that's what you're actually trying to convey. A good site should be fun for the Webmaster too. If it's a burden, then there's probably something wrong, and it probably isn't fulfilling your or your visitors' needs."

Question 2:

What is the most common mistake that you see Web site designers/owners making?

1. Assuming That Visitors to Your Web Site Are Technically Inclined

Mike Hyttinen, Web Site Designer, Sony Music Canada:
"Face it. Most users are casual surfers with little or no technical ability or Net savvy. Even I don't understand some of the options presented to me at some Web sites, and I'm in the industry! Assuming that everyone has the most current browser or is Net savvy enough to figure out how to download and install plug-ins is a big no-no.

"Sites should be designed with the (relatively) lowest common denominator in mind. This is not to say you shouldn't use emerging technologies like Flash; just use them in a way that the user doesn't have to think about technical options. (Design your site so that features like Flash are transparent to the user. If the user already has the plug-in, then send him or her to the plug-in-enhanced page. Don't ask users if they want to use it; the answer should be pretty obvious if they already have the plug-in.)"

John Pullam, National Manager, Electronic Commerce, Sears Canada Inc.:
Don't use overly complex technology jargon that cuts out a significant portion of your users (most people do not run the latest, greatest browsers and add-ins). You can easily alienate or disappoint customers if you aren't sensitive to this."

2. Having a Web Site When You Don't Need One

Hart Steinfeld, Webmaster, Canadian Airlines:
"It's starting to slow down a bit now, but for a while there anybody and everybody had a Web site (most of them very poor sites). Before you sit down and have someone write a bunch of code for you, ask yourself who is going to be using the site and why they would come. Make sure a Web site is right for your company. For example, not every company advertises on the television. You have to decide what medium is right for you."

3. Not Checking Spelling

Theresa Jobateh, Internet Administrator, Canadian Egg Marketing Agency:
"I think designers are preoccupied with the design and layout but forget how to spell or to check for spelling errors!"

4. Crowding a Web Site

Ellen Agger, Webmaster, Alzheimer Society of Canada:
"Too much information on the homepage with too many typefaces, flashing banner ads, poor writing, loud backgrounds. This translates into visual overload for the visitor."

Jenny Winterbottom, Web Site Developer, Vancouver Aquarium:
"Complex graphics, oversized pages, and confusing navigation will quickly lose the two-second average time you have to grab a user's attention. Less is more in Web design. Keep pages simple and easy to navigate with a consistent look and feel for your site. Image is everything, which doesn't mean that a beautifully designed site will make a successful site, but rather, a professional and well-executed site will portray a professional and successful business. Pay careful attention to details such as spelling, grammar, and accurate content. Ensure links are correct, images are not broken, and minimize server downtime. A broken Web site is a forgotten Web site."

5. Not Including Enough Useful Content

Ellen Agger, Webmaster, Alzheimer Society of Canada.
"Not providing enough useful information, making people feel like their time has been wasted looking for what's not there."

6. Trying to Do Too Much Too Quickly

Paul Schwartz, Webmaster, Reader's Digest Canada:
"Pick just one thing and do it well. One really good page is all it takes to make a good Web site. Once you have a solid, basic site, it's easy to build on your successes and learn from your mistakes."

7. Not Including Contact Information

Thomas Hader, Webmaster, Clearnet:
"I still run into sites where I cannot contact anybody. No e-mail links, no phone numbers, nothing."

8. Approaching the Internet Haphazardly

Tom Dawson, Webmaster/Partner, ICanGarden.com:
"I am continually amazed that Web site designers and business owners don't seem to take the Internet seriously. I don't know any business that would ever consider not answering their phone yet getting an answer to an e-mail can sometimes be almost impossible. Similarly, they would never consider creating a brochure or advertisement without putting in their best effort, nor would they use tired, trite graphics. When it comes to the Web site, however, so many sites look like they were

'slapped' together with little or no thought—a short description of their business, a couple of pictures of their products, and 'borrowed' images. Webmasters would be well advised to diligently note what they like (or dislike) in sites they visit so they can use this information in developing their own sites. Nor would any serious business owner develop a business without promoting it. Yet they never consider expending the same energy promoting their Web site. How tragic when all it requires is commitment and willingness to take the impact of the Internet seriously."

9. Not Planning Your Internet Strategy

Wayne Carrigan, Webmaster, tsn.ca:

"Try and understand why you want to have a Web site (your competitor has one isn't a valid reason), who you want to cater to, and how you are going to keep your Web site up-to-date."

Sandy Wills, Webmaster, Molson Breweries:

"The primary mistake Web site owners are making is improper planning in the site's development. It is crucial to create a site essence that encompasses all objectives of your business. The majority of time spent developing the site should be invested in the content architecture and design structure before a single page has been placed online. If the site's focus is created, maintained, and regulated by a team all armed with the same critical path, the site will succeed."

Jenny Winterbottom, Web Site Developer, Vancouver Aquarium:

"The most frequent mistakes that Web site owners make are not only a lack of planning before creating a Web site, but also a lack of planning after the site has been created. Keeping your site alive and generating repeat visitors require effort. Set up a maintenance schedule for updating content, then let visitors know about new changes. The Aquarium's SurfScene e-mail newsletter informs visitors of new features on our Web site each month. The Web is a communication medium, so use it to communicate about your site. Register your site on search engines, solicit other sites to exchange links, and generate excitement by sending out press releases to newsgroups, newspapers, and other media."

10. Designing Your Site So That It Can Be Easily Read By Web Log Analysis Tools

Thomas Hader, Webmaster, Clearnet:

"I would also advise to keep your method of statistical reporting in mind when you design the site. Extensive use of frames and JavaScript to populate your frameset is decidedly unfriendly to any reporting tool that crunches your log files. As good as the tool might be, if you aren't careful in planning your navigation architecture, you are still going to wind up spending considerable time 'creatively interpreting' what your stat report spits back. I know this from experience."

11. Lack of Commitment

Addy Ching, Internet/Intranet Marketing Coordinator, Hong Kong Bank of Canada:

"Building a Web site is not a one-time campaign, but an ongoing process. Make sure you are committed before you start building a Web site."

Thomas Hader, Webmaster, Clearnet:

"I would say the single biggest mistake is launching a site and then thinking that it's 'over.' Owners go through the trials of intense initial builds, get the site out there, and then relax. You're not finished; you just got started. Now it's time to begin thinking about, and planning, functionality enhancements and content updates."

General Motors of Canada Internet Marketing Organization:

"The tendency of companies to stand back and let a first- or second-generation Web site exist is an ongoing testament to their inability or reluctance to fully exploit this medium. Lacking the commitment to dedicate the necessary resources, combined with an inability to develop a useful strategy and support it with meaningful content, will cause many companies to develop a poor reputation with their wired customers."

12. Not Optimizing the Web Site For Users With Dial-Up Modems

Simon Cohen, Webmaster, AOL Canada:

"Far too many designers and owners never experience their own site using a conventional dial-up connection. The truth is, any site is going to perform tremendously when viewed over the company LAN or on the designer's workstation. The rest of the world still works at 28.8 (if you're lucky). Remember, if you're running out of patience waiting for your site to load, the average visitor has probably given up already."

Question 3:

What Internet utilities (shareware or commercial) do you recommend to our readers to help with effective design or management of a Web site?

Ellen Agger, Webmaster, Alzheimer Society of Canada:
Microsoft's FrontPage98 [Web site creation and management software]
www.microsoft.com/frontpage.

Mike Hyttinen, Web Site Designer, Sony Music Canada:
Macromedia's Dreamweaver [Web site design software] **www.macromedia.com**

Theresa Jobateh, Internet Administrator, Canadian Egg Marketing Agency:
NetIntellect [Web log analysis software] **www.netintellect.com**

John Pullam, National Manager, Electronic Commerce, Sears Canada Inc.:
HotMetal Pro [HTML editor] **www.softquad.com**
Coast Webmaster [Web site management software] **www.coast.com**
Paint Shop Pro [Image editor] **www.jasc.com**

Hart Steinfeld, Webmaster, Canadian Airlines:
HomeSite [HTML editor] **www.allaire.com**
Microsoft's FrontPage98 [Web site creation and management software]
www.microsoft.com/frontpage

Wayne Carrigan, Webmaster, tsn.ca:
Homesite [HTML editor for PCs] **www.allaire.com**
BBEdit [HTML editor for Macintosh computers] **www.barebones.com**
Adobe Photoshop [Image editor] **www.adobe.com**
CuteFTP [FTP program for PCs] **www.cuteftp.com**
Fetch [FTP program for Macintosh computers]
www.dartmouth.edu/pages/softdev/fetch.html

Paul Schwartz, Webmaster, Reader's Digest Canada:
BBEdit [HTML editor for Macintosh computers] **www.barebones.com**

Sandy Wills, Webmaster, Molson Breweries:
Inspiration [Web site mapping software] **www.inspiration.com**

Simon Cohen, Webmaster, AOL Canada:
HTMLed [HTML editor] **www.ist.ca**
Dreamweaver by Macromedia [Web site design software] **www.macromedia.com**
WS_FTP [FTP software] **www.ipswitch.com**

Tom Dawson, Webmaster/Partner, ICanGarden.com
TextPad [text editor] **www.textpad.com**
DerekWare HTML Author [HTML editor] **www.geocities.com/~gilpo/dwhtml.html**
Image Composer [image editor] **www.microsoft.com/imagecomposer**

General Motors of Canada Internet Marketing Organization:
Screen Ruler [virtual ruler for measuring objects on your screen] **www.kagi.com/microfox**
Small Screen [helps you simulate small monitor sizes without having to change your current screen resolution; for Macintosh computers]
ftp://ftp.pht.com/pub/mac/info-mac/dev/small-screen-13.hqx
Color Picker Pro [colour translator for designing Web pages; for Macintosh computers]
www.rootworks.com
The Web Site Garage [tune-up program for your Web site] **www.websitegarage.com**

Jenny Winterbottom, Web Site Developer, Vancouver Aquarium:
Photoshop [image editor] **www.adobe.com**
Homesite [HTML editor] **www.allaire.com**
GIF Construction Set [GIF animation kit] **www.mindworkshop.com/alchemy/alchemy.html**

Thomas Hader, Webmaster, Clearnet:
Linkbot [link checker for your Web site] **www.tetranetsoftware.com**
Opera [Web browser] **www.operasoftware.com**
NetIntellect [log analysis software] **www.netintellect.com**
WebTrends [log analysis software] **www.webtrends.com**

Summary

Clearly, the above tips from the Canadian Webmasters are a lot to absorb. What should you do? Sit back, and take a good, hard look at your Web site. Read each and every comment that the Webmasters have provided, and examine your own site in the context of these comments.

We believe that this will prove to be one of the most effective means of sprucing up your Web site.

Protecting Yourself Online

Security is probably one of the most significant concerns for Canadians who use the Internet. That is why we have devoted one of our themes to this topic this year.

First is Chapter 4, "Dealing With Viruses and Vandals on the Internet." During the last year, we have been hit by more viruses than ever before and put the blame squarely on the connectivity offered by the Internet. Quite simply, because of the Internet it is now easier than ever before to distribute viruses. And now viruses can also take advantage of special Internet capabilities, such as Java and ActiveX. We take a look at the many methods of dealing with these pesky critters in this chapter.

There is another risky issue: we think many Canadians are not backing up their Web sites. We are seeing an increasing number of small Internet service providers disappear; when they disappear, so do all the Web sites they hosted. If those Web sites are not backed up, they're gone forever and will have to be reconstructed. We provide guidance on what to do in Chapter 5, "Backing Up Your Web Site."

Privacy remains a major concern online. In Chapter 6, "Protecting Your Privacy Online," we take a look at the many ways available to shield or hide your identity online. Contrary to public opinion, shielding your identity isn't only for lawbreakers; it's for average, everyday Canadians who use the Net. In the absence of any privacy legislation in Canada, it is important to understand how your privacy is at risk and what you need to do to protect it.

Next to privacy, security is probably your biggest worry. In Chapter 7, "Securing Your Connection to the Internet," we take a good look at the unique hacking culture found on the Internet. We also point you to some of the major sites where security exploits are shared. No doubt you will get the sense that even as a dial-up user, you are increasingly at risk when you use the Internet. Specifically, we look at PC firewall software, which you can use to protect yourself, and the concept of "ethical hacking." Ethical hacking is an arranged break-in: you get someone to break in to your computer. This will help you identify how to plug any "holes" that were discovered.

chapter four

Dealing With Viruses and Vandals on the Internet

It's every computer owner's worst nightmare. Besides a direct hit from a lightning bolt, a virus is about the most destructive thing that can happen to a home computer.

John Breeden, "Infectious Enthusiasm: Viruses on Your PC," *The Washington Post*, May 29, 1998

There's good news and bad news about some new computer viruses. The bad news: These viruses, which can afflict Java or ActiveX programs, can damage more data than any other viruses in history.

"Java, ActiveX Files Can Be Virus Victims," *Investor's Business Daily*, October 10, 1997

Highlights

1. The number of new viruses is growing at a substantial rate. By some accounts, the threat of virus infection is 20 times more likely today than it was two years ago.

2. As a result of the Internet, viruses can spread faster than ever before, primarily through e-mail messages and downloadable software. The interactive nature of the Internet means that new types of malicious viruses are emerging which cause embarrassment to their victims.

3. In addition to viruses, Internet users also need to worry about Internet "vandals," harmful computer programs that can damage your computer.

4. As computer programs and computer operating systems become tightly integrated with the Internet, your computer is more susceptible to viruses and Internet vandals.

5. Many of the virus warnings being circulated on the Internet are hoaxes. Carefully investigate any virus reports you receive before alarming others.

6. To protect yourself from viruses and Internet vandals, use antivirus and antivandal software. For maximum protection make sure that you update your virus software regularly.

We admit that, until recently, we have been somewhat skeptical of the whole virus paranoia thing. But our experiences in the last year have caused us to change our perception of just how risky and prevalent viruses can be.

Perhaps we had become jaded; both of us have been using personal computer technology for a combined total of over 25 years, and we have had but a few instances of viruses in the past. This has, no doubt, contributed somewhat to our skepticism of the frenzy and media hysteria that sometimes surround the concept of the computer virus.

But there have been a few recent instances where a virus has caused actual damage to one of our computers or resulted in a lot of wasted time. In all of these cases, we received the virus through the Internet, either by means of a file that we had downloaded or within an attachment that we received with an electronic mail message.

In a few of those instances the virus came from the most unlikely of sources: staff at our publisher and even our editors have sent us at least three e-mail messages containing various chapters of our books that have contained a virus. Their word processing software had become contaminated with a virus from a document they had received from someone else, and the nature of this particular virus is that it attaches itself to every document they worked on.

Viruses are real and are becoming more of a problem. According to statistics on the site of Dr. Solomon's (**www.drsolomon.com**), a well-known developer of virus software, as of mid-1998 the number of identified viruses was growing at an alarming rate:

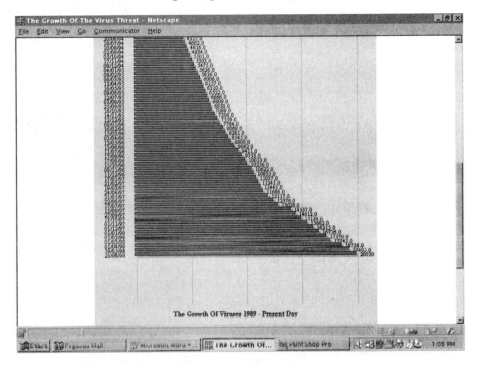

Other sources confirm this trend. Some "virus research centres" have discovered and identified at least 20,000 known computer viruses and are reporting that they are discovering hundreds of new viruses each and every month. Other studies indicate that at least 98% of all corporations experience virus problems every year and spend a significant amount of time and money dealing with the problem.

According to some in the computer industry, infection of your computer with a virus is 20 times more likely today than it was two years ago. The blame for this state of affairs rests, to a large extent, with the rapid growth and adoption of the Internet, as we will describe below.

What Exactly Is a Computer Virus?

There are many definitions about, but to keep it simple, we will simply say that a computer virus is any computer program or computer code that causes damage to the files or programs on your computer, crashes your computer, accesses and misuses personal information, prevents you from adequately using your computer, or is a prank or hoax that wastes a lot of your time.

Computer viruses do not just happen; they are created by someone. How do they get onto your computer? They attach themselves to other files, such as word processing documents or software that you receive over the Internet, on a CD-ROM, or on a computer diskette. Once you bring these files onto your computer, the viruses in turn can attach themselves to other files on your computer, which you could unwittingly send on to someone else.

The best places to get detailed and up-to-date information on viruses are the Web sites of antivirus software manufacturers, for example, this Web site maintained by Dr. Solomon's (**www.drsolomon.com**):

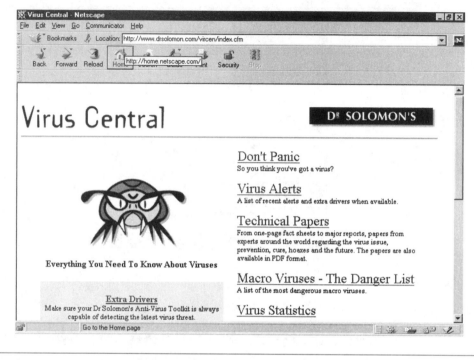

MAJOR ANTIVIRUS VENDOR SITES

Dr. Solomon's	**www.drsolomon.com**
McAfee	**www.mcafee.com**
Network Associates	**www.nai.com**
Network Associates Virus Information Centre	**www.nai.com/vinfo**
Norton AntiVirus Research Center	**www.symantec.com/avcenter/index.html**
Symantec Corporation	**www.symantec.ca**

Most of these sites provide general and detailed background about viruses, including in-depth information on thousands of different computer viruses that now exist.

The Internet's Impact on Viruses

The Internet is linking together individuals and computers around the planet in an unprecedented fashion. But with its positive impact comes the reality that it is largely responsible for the rapid growth in the number of viruses in existence and the number of people being affected by them. The Internet is causing several problems:

- **Viruses are more easily distributed**. Quite simply, with the emergence of the Internet and e-mail systems linked to the Net, there has been a massive increase in the exchange of file attachments between people and organizations. A few years ago the Internet was still relatively new, and e-mail addresses didn't often appear on business cards. Today, however, Internet e-mail is ubiquitous throughout the corporate world, and some statistics state that one of five Canadians is using the Internet from home.

  The result is that more and more people are using the Internet to exchange word processing documents, spreadsheets, and other information within computer files. This increases the opportunity for the rapid distribution of computer viruses within these files.

  One of the fastest-growing categories of computer virus is the "macro" virus, which is most often found in Microsoft Word documents. Some estimates are that 80% of the viruses found on the Internet are macro viruses; not surprising, given that they are distributed quite easily when you send an infected document to someone else in an e-mail message. We have been hit with these viruses several times over the last year.

- **The acceptance of the concept of downloadable software.** The Internet has been of great benefit to the concept of "demoware," "shareware," "freeware," and other forms of software that you can try out for free. Software developers can quickly make a new program or version of a program available to existing and potential customers for very little cost by making it available on the Internet. Software repositories have been created throughout the Internet that make it easy to access new programs and update existing programs.

  It isn't just demoware/freeware/shareware that is having an impact. Software and hardware companies make updated versions of their programs or drivers available for downloading on the Internet, given that this can result in a significant decrease in the cost of support.

  As these trends have evolved, it has meant that a lot of people have become familiar with the concept of using the Internet to obtain new software and drivers. They think nothing of using the Internet to go off and find the latest version of a program, obtain an updated driver, or try out a new program that they have read about. And sometimes what they obtain is an infected computer file.

  We will say this: the vast majority of software repositories on the Internet are safe. Visit a site like TUCOWS (**www.tucows.com**), which we refer to throughout this book, and chances are that the stringent virus testing that the organization does will ensure that you get a file that is not infected. Download the latest driver for your networking card from Intel, and there is a strong likelihood that it is virus-free. While there are sometimes problems with reputable software sites, the vast majority of such software is OK.

  But start to download trial programs from other places around the Internet, and you might be playing with fire. Try out a new shareware program without running it through a virus checker, and you are putting yourself at risk.

  It is with the unknown that the greatest potential for damage can occur.

- **New types of computer viruses.** The Internet is leading to the emergence of a new type of virus. In the past, a virus may have been restricted to doing damage to your computer. Now, since your computer is linked to many others through the Internet, virus developers have new opportunities to undertake their malicious activities, and the viruses themselves have become more malicious.

  For example, at the time we were writing this chapter, a new virus had been discovered that posts your word processing documents to discussion groups on the Internet. This takes virus programs beyond causing damage through the loss of important computer files. Now there is potential embarrassment and even significant legal risk by posting confidential information in a public forum.

- **A renegade culture.** There is no doubt that there is a culture on the Internet that encourages the development and distribution of viruses.

  There are renegade sites where information about new methods to develop viruses is eagerly shared. Discoveries of problems and weaknesses within new programs or operating systems which might allow a new type of virus are eagerly traded online like baseball cards. A culture of irresponsibility flows like an electric current through some areas of the Internet.

  The concept of virus programming can seem tantalizingly romantic to some, with images of a dashing young super-cyber-hacker. Also fuelling the growth in viruses is the anti-Microsoft rant, which can be found throughout the Internet. Quite simply, there are a lot of people developing viruses for the Windows environment, simply because they like to do anything they can to strike a blow against Microsoft, perceived by many within this culture as the evil empire of the 1990s. This is an issue that we examine in a later chapter, when we take a look at security issues impacting the Internet.

All of these factors have contributed to the current situation: computer viruses are far more prevalent than they were even a few years ago.

The Bulgarian Virus Factory

During the late 1980s and early 1990s, most viruses came from one country in particular, Bulgaria. In 1990, Bulgaria was the origin of more viruses than any other country in the world. Why was Bulgaria such a hotbed for viruses? Experts say that during this period, Bulgaria had an abundance of skilled but unemployed programmers who had a lot of time on their hands. Lacking any legitimate outlets for their talents, they turned to virus production as a means of rebelling against society.

The New Kid on the Block: Internet Vandals

Viruses aren't the only problem you need to worry about. When surfing the Web, your computer can be infected by malicious Java "applets" and ActiveX "controls" that are based on the Java and ActiveX programming languages.

Both Java and ActiveX allow Web developers to create tiny computer programs that download to your computer when you visit a Web page; these are called "applets" (in the case of Java) and "controls" (in the case of ActiveX). They significantly enhance the capability of Web sites, and in many cases, lead to some absolutely wonderful new capabilities online. For example, check out the crossword site at Canada.com (**www.canada.com**), one of the best Java-based applications we have seen on the Internet in terms of design and reliability (not to mention fun):

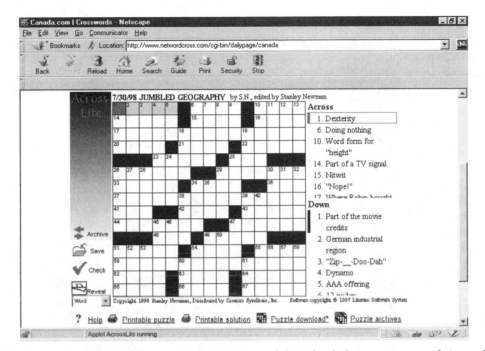

But the very emergence of these new programming capabilities has led to a new type of virus called an "Internet vandal." An Internet vandal is a malicious computer program that is invisibly down loaded onto your computer through an ActiveX control or Java applet. An Internet vandal can destroy data on your hard disk, upload private information from your hard disk to the Internet, or sabotage your computer in other ways. There are many such programs emerging; visit the Hostile Java Applets page (**www.rstcorp.com/hostile-applets/index.html**) to get an idea of the risks that exist:

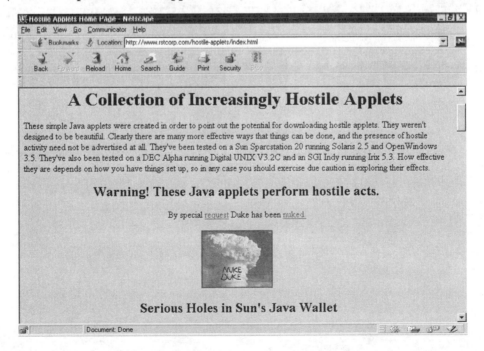

For an example of a malicious ActiveX control, visit **www.axent.com/swat/1attacks/win95/Showfile/showfile.htm**. This Web page will read a Microsoft Word document off your hard drive and e-mail it to someone else's e-mail address:

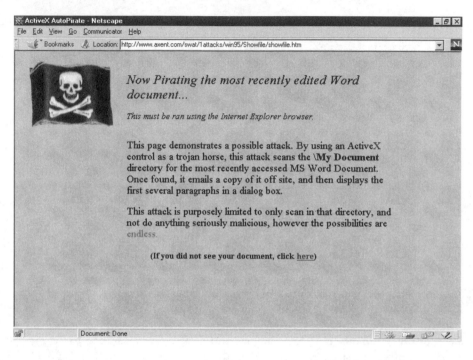

tip Test Your System—For Free

SurfinTest is a free program that shows you how much Java and ActiveX activity is occurring on your computer when you access the Internet. The program will also alert you if any security violations occur. You can download the software at **www.finjan.com**.

Java and ActiveX not only increase your chances of being infected with a virus, but they pose increased security risks as well. If you are technically inclined and you really want to understand the risks with Java, visit the Java Security Hotlist at **www.rstcorp.com/javasecurity/links.html**.

Is the talk of potential problems with Java and ActiveX far-fetched? Not at all. It is such an issue that an entire book has been written on the topic, *Java Security: Hostile Applets, Holes & Antidotes*. In addition, other books cover the topic in-depth. There is a great deal of concern about the risk within the Internet programmer community:

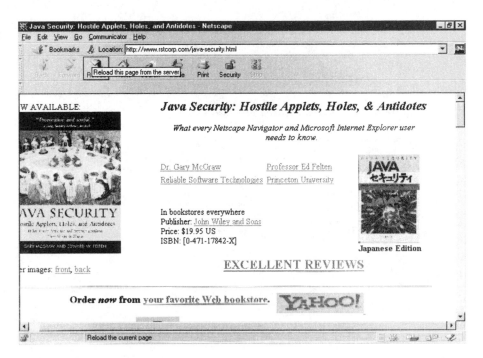

Access to encrypted passwords stored on your hard drive is perhaps the biggest potential problem with hostile Java and ActiveX applications. An encrypted password is a password that has been "scrambled" so that it appears as gibberish to someone who tries to read it. If you use the Internet to access your bank account, for example, your bank password will be stored in an encrypted form on your computer's hard drive so that it can't be read by an intruder.

The Hostile Java Apps homepage (**www.rstcorp.com/hostile-applets/index.html**) is a fascinating place to visit to learn about the nature of the risk posed by Java. There we found a program that can easily unscramble an encrypted password just like that:

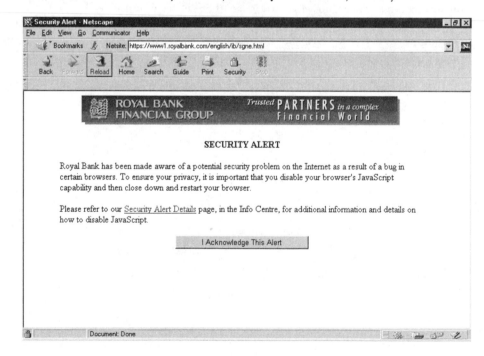

Related to the risk posed with Java and ActiveX are risks with JavaScript, a language used on many Web sites. JavaScript doesn't share much in common with Java other than the name. JavaScript itself presents a number of potential security threats, one of which we learned about when we went to access our bank accounts at the Royal Bank (**www.royalbank.com**) one day:

As pointed out by Netscape on its site, anyone who knows how to take advantage of this particular security weakness in JavaScript would be able to figure out the user ID and password that we use to sign in to our bank account. In addition, the individual would be able to figure out all the other Web sites that we had visited during this particular browsing session.

The point is this: technologies such as ActiveX, JavaScript, and Java are leading to some very real security exposures that all Internet users should be aware of. There is a fine line between what might be considered a virus or Internet vandal and what might be considered a security risk, but the fact is that Java and ActiveX present all kinds of opportunities for problems.

Looking Into the Future

The risk of a virus or Internet vandal doing damage to your computer will increase with the continued growth of the Internet. Consider the following two trends:

- **The integration of programs to the Internet is leading to potential new problems that have yet to surface.** With the emergence of the Internet there are wonderful opportunities to add new capabilities to computer programs by linking them to the Internet. Your word processor program will soon be able to automatically grab documents from anywhere on the Internet or run a special spell checker that is obtained from a Web site. Your spreadsheet will have the ability to obtain automatic financial updates from a corporate Web server. Your calendar program will be able to grab a list of free time slots to automatically determine if it is possible to line up a meeting with someone else. Far-fetched? These capabilities are already emerging in many programs, as computer software is married to the capabilities of the Internet.

No doubt, by linking computers around the world, the Internet is leading to a whole new era of computerization. We will see fascinating software developments through the next decade.

But the fact is that this tight integration of computer programs to the Internet is also leading us down a path that is fraught with risk and is presenting individuals with dishonourable intent marvellous new opportunities to do damage.

Consider this scenario. You download an innocent-looking program from the Internet that promises to allow you to search the Web more effectively. You install it, try it out, and it does what it purports to do, so you keep on using it. What a great tool, you think.

Unbeknownst to you, the program has another purpose that is entirely hidden from you. In the background, unseen and unknown to you, it grabs various files from your computer and uploads them to the software developer. Password files. Electronic banking files. A listing of Web sites that you visit.

Far-fetched? Not at all. We have often found ourselves using a computer program that is linked to the Internet and have wondered whether the program could be doing anything behind our backs. This type of problem is already occurring. On the Dr. Solomon's Web site you can read about the T-Online virus, which steals the user IDs and passwords of a certain German Internet service provider while they are online. Users never know that it is happening, unless they use a virus application.

We think that this type of "virus" will become far more prevalent in the not-so-distant future. What is challenging is that it would be very difficult for you to determine whether any of the programs you use on your computer are actually doing anything wrong.

- **Computer operating systems are being integrated to the Internet.** Finally, the future of computing is found in a closer integration of the operating system to the Internet, a fact which in itself presents all kinds of potential problems in terms of viruses and security.

  This is the direction being taken by both Microsoft and Apple. Consider the benefits: tightly link the massive bits of information found on the Internet to your desktop, and it will become far easier for you to search for information. Integrate the Web browser directly into the operating system, and information on your computer and on the Internet become one. This is a good concept; it's no wonder Microsoft fought so hard to integrate the Web browser into the operating system in Windows 98.

  But this integration also leads to the potential for significant problems. We will see an increase in nefarious computer viruses that take advantage of the close link between a computer and the Internet. The warning signs were found with an early version of Internet Explorer, which featured a close link from the Web browser to the operating system. This link allowed anyone with a bit of technical knowledge to put a link on his or her Web site that would run a program on a visitor's hard disk. Someone with a little knowledge could easily create a Web site which, when visited, would cause the visitor's hard disk to be erased.

  Microsoft quickly issued a patch to fix that problem, but others have popped up. The anti-Microsoft rant prevalent in some areas of the Internet means that there are many people working hard trying to discover every little security hole, problem, and risk within Microsoft operating systems, each of which can be used for a nefarious purpose or could lead to some new form of virus.

  Many also believe that Microsoft, in its rush to claim the Internet as its own by tightly integrating the Internet to Windows, is making very sloppy mistakes that have a terrible security impact. There seems to be an entire culture online intent on finding and exploiting every single Microsoft program weakness that exists. Expect the number of problems in the Windows environment to grow as a result. This is a topic that we will examine later in a separate chapter on Internet security issues.

  These two trends will increase the risk to your data, your computer, and your personal information. We don't want to sound alarmist, since there is certainly enough sensationalism about computer viruses in the mainstream media. But we do believe that anyone using computers and the Internet has to be cognizant of the increased risks of this new era and that we must do what we can to protect ourselves.

Virus Hoaxes

One thing to keep in mind is that if you receive an e-mail warning that you are not to open a message that contains a certain phrase, it is probably a hoax. In fact, there are so many virus hoaxes being circulated on the Internet that some organizations say they are spending more time debunking virus hoaxes than dealing with real virus threats.

We have been inundated through the last year with messages warning us about some new type of virus that is transmitted by e-mail and cautioning us not to open certain e-mail messages that contain a subject line with a certain phrase. We usually check one of the virus hoax pages below and confirm our suspicions that the virus is a hoax.

Virus hoaxes are very real and extremely common. Perhaps the best known is the "Good Times" virus: you are warned not to open an e-mail message from an America Online user.

Viruses cannot be transmitted and attack your computer simply by reading an e-mail message, which is what these hoaxes often warn you about. However, they are frequently transmitted through an e-mail attachment; hence it is with the e-mail attachment that you need to take the most care.

If you receive an e-mail message alerting you about a virus, check one of the Web sites below to see if it's a hoax before sending the warning message to all your friends.

PAGES THAT PROVIDE DESCRIPTIONS OF VIRUSES KNOWN TO BE HOAXES	
The U.S. Department of Energy	ciac.llnl.gov/ciac/CIACHoaxes.html
Symantec's List of Virus Hoaxes	www.symantec.com/avcenter/hoax.html
Computer Virus Myths	kumite.com/myths

How Can You Protect Yourself From Viruses and Internet Vandals?

The best protection, of course, is to isolate your PC from the world, but that's not practical in the era of the Internet.

As a result, the more time you spend on the Internet, the more important it is that you use an antivirus program that is "Internet-aware." These programs differ from regular antivirus programs in that they do special things to account for the increased risk that can come from being linked to the Internet, such as scanning e-mail messages, either automatically or on demand, for viruses found in e-mail attachments, or scanning files that you download from the Internet for problems. But as discussed in this chapter, viruses aren't the only problem you have to worry about. You also need to be concerned about Internet vandals, such as hostile Java applets and ActiveX controls. Hence, in addition to getting an "Internet-aware" antivirus program, we recommend that you obtain an anti-vandal program, software that will protect your computer from Internet vandals. Fortunately, it is now possible to obtain both antivirus and antivandal protection in a single program. Examples are WebScanX and eSafe Protect, both of which we describe below. Both antivirus and antivandal programs can usually be obtained from computer retail stores or purchased from the vendor's site on the Internet. Most vendors will allow you to download a trial version of their antivirus and/or antivandal software for free. Some of the most popular antivirus and antivandal programs are listed below, along with the Web addresses where you can obtain further information.

POPULAR ANTIVIRUS AND ANTIVANDAL SOFTWARE

WebScanX from McAfee	**www.mcafee.com**
eSafe Protect from eSafe Protect Technologies	**www.esafe.com**
VirusScan by McAfee (antivirus only)	**www.mcafee.com**
Norton AntiVirus by Symantec (antivirus only)	**www.symantec.ca**
SurfinShield Xtra from Finjan Software (antivandal only)	**www.finjan.com**

WebScanX

McAfee (**www.mcafee.com**), acquired in 1997 by Network Associates (**www.nai.com**), is one of the most popular antivirus software program developers in the computer industry today. McAfee's WebScanX provides both antivirus and antivandal protection. You can instruct WebScanX to automatically scan any files that you download through the Internet for a virus:

In addition, you can have it check Java and ActiveX programs for any unauthorized activity:

If you visit a site that contains a hostile Java applet or ActiveX control, you will get a warning:

In most cases, you will want to deny the applet from doing what it wants to do.

WebScanX will also examine the files that are attached to e-mail messages (for certain e-mail programs) that you receive, further helping you to guard against damage. And like most virus programs, you can obtain updates automatically over the Internet that provide details on new viruses and hostile Java/ActiveX programs.

eSafe Protect

Another good example of a program that provides both antivirus and antivandal protection is eSafe Protect, from eSafe Technologies (**www.esafe.com**). We tried it out on a site that had a few hostile Java applications, and the program immediately advised us that something was wrong:

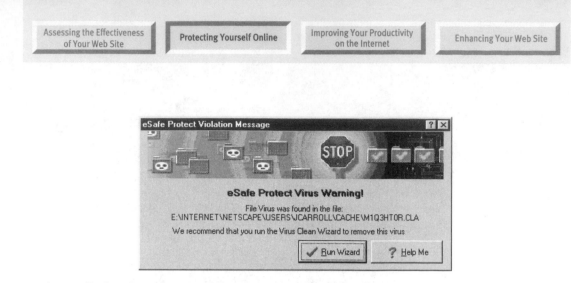

It then walked us through a process to eliminate this particular Java application and also discovered a few others on our hard drive that we weren't aware we had acquired. Fortunately, the viruses had not yet done any damage:

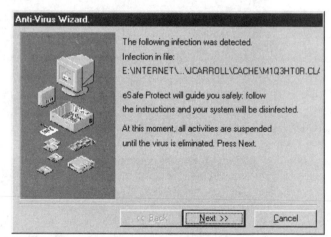

eSafe Protect will also protect you from viruses in the files that you download as well as examine certain e-mail messages for the same.

The Importance of Updating Your Virus Program

We want to underscore the importance of regularly updating your Internet-aware virus program once you obtain one. Because new viruses are being discovered all the time, it's really important that your virus program be aware of all the latest viruses. Most antivirus software vendors provide their users with regular updates that can be downloaded from the Web. The point is this: if you don't update your virus program regularly, you increase your risk of being infected with a virus. *Your virus program is only as good as its most recent update.*

No Virus Program Is 100% Effective

You should also be aware that while a virus program will substantially reduce your chances of being infected with a virus, no virus program is 100% effective. Why? Since new viruses are emerging every day, it's impossible for a virus program to know about every possible virus. As a result, while virus programs will reduce your risk of getting a virus, they will never eliminate that risk completely.

Our Recommendations

We suggest that, at the minimum, you do several things to protect yourself from the risks described in this chapter:

- Install both an antivirus program and an antivandal program on your computer or use a program that provides both types of protection, such as WebScanX or eSafe Protect. As suggested above, make sure that you update your virus program on a regular basis.

- Regularly visit the Web pages of antivirus and antivandal vendors to keep yourself informed of any new viruses, Internet vandals, and other virus or security threats. For example, the Network Associates Web site (**www.nai.com**) keeps users apprised of new Internet security threats:

- Check with your Internet service provider to find out if they are using any products that scan the e-mail messages entering their network for viruses. These programs provide an extra layer of protection, since they try to detect viruses within e-mail messages before they have a chance to reach your personal computer. If you have not yet chosen an Internet service provider or are thinking of switching, this may be a factor to take into consideration.

- Recognize that security holes are found on an ongoing basis with both Netscape and Microsoft Web browsers. As a result, you should always try to use the most recent versions. The latest version of Netscape can always be found at **www.netscape.com**, and the latest version of Internet Explorer is available at **www.microsoft.com/ie**.

- Always run a virus program before doing any backups of your computer files; it doesn't make sense to back up your viruses to disk. If you have to restore some files after they have been destroyed, you would simply be bringing the virus back again.

- If you do get a virus, follow the instructions that come with the antivirus program you use. Most are very good at describing the steps you need to follow. And if you have suffered some damage, then take a look at the Web sites of the leading antivirus software developers mentioned above, since they usually provide some straightforward guidance on the alternatives available to you.

chapter five

Backing Up Your Web Site

It's not whether your computer will go down, it's when.

Stephen H. Wildstrom, "Don't Be a Crash Dummy," *Business Week*, **April 13, 1998**

Everyone knows you're supposed to brush your teeth, wear a seat belt and back up your hard drive. But a recent survey of 1,000 users around the world shows less than 20 percent do regular backups.

Bob Rankin, "Backup Basics," *Newsday*, **February 4, 1998**

Highlights

1. It is important to back up your Web site in case the company hosting your Web site goes out of business or experiences a massive computer failure. It can happen to you.

2. One option for backing up your Web site is to use a product like Flypage Web Backup, which will make a full copy of your Web site for use in an emergency. Alternatively, you can use an FTP program or an offline browser like WebSnake.

3. In addition to backing up your Web site, you should back up your critical Internet files. They include your bookmarks, cookie files, e-mail files, and passwords.

4. Internet backup services like Connected Online, Atrieva, and @Backup allow you to securely back up all your computer files to an off-site computer located somewhere on the Internet. If any of your files are ever lost or damaged, you can retrieve them over the Internet, even when you are travelling.

Do You Have a Backup of Your Web Site?

Ask yourself this question: if the company that hosts your Web site had a hard disk crash, do you know for sure that they have an adequate backup of all the important files, including a complete and recent copy of your Web site?

Imagine discovering that they don't. To your horror, you are suddenly in a situation where you have to spend a huge amount of time and resources to recreate your Web site, since you haven't kept a master copy of it on your own computer.

We wouldn't be surprised if a lot of Canadian corporate and individual Web site owners found themselves in this situation. Consider what happened to one of Canada's most popular Web sites in 1998: the computers that store the user data for Molson's I Am Online Web site crashed, and Molson lost the user profiles for the hundreds of people who use the site. Immediately following the incident, Internet users who visited the Molson site were greeted with a message asking them to resubmit vital data to the site to help Molson recreate their personas:

Assessing the Effectiveness
of Your Web Site

Protecting Yourself Online

Improving Your Productivity
on the Internet

Enhancing Your Web Site

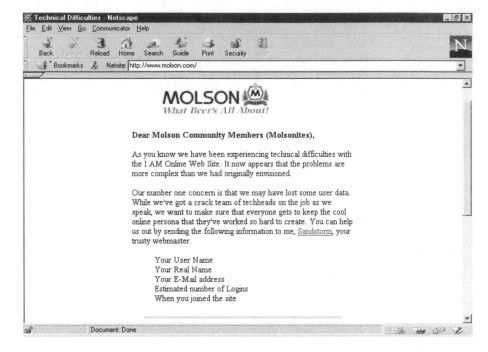

The point is that computer failures do happen, and, inevitably, valuable data get lost as a result.

We suspect that the vast majority of Canadian organizations that host Web sites have regular and reliable backup procedures, but one can never be too sure. Not only that, but some Internet service providers and Web-hosting companies have suddenly gone out of business. Their servers simply disappeared from the Internet, as soon as certain telecommunication lines were cut for lack of payment. Consequently, the owners of Web sites on those services had no way of accessing their sites and, hence, were unable to recreate them elsewhere.

tip Protect Yourself Against Theft

In addition to the risks we have already described, there is also the possibility that the computers hosting your Web site could be stolen from your Internet service provider or directly out of your offices if you're running your own Web servers. This happened at the headquarters of Merriam Webster (**www.m-w.com**), one of the world's most popular dictionaries. Burglars broke into the firm's office and, believe it or not, walked off with the company's entire Web site. Fortunately, Merriam Webster had their Web site backed up, and it was online again within a few days.

This is why it is important that you put in place procedures to automatically make backup copies of your entire Web site on a periodic basis, so that you can recreate your Web site in a hurry if necessary. The first thing you should do, however, is understand whether the Web-editing program that you use keeps a complete local copy of your Web site on your own hard disk. Some do automatically; be sure to check out the specifications of the Web-editor program that you use to understand if backups are made, and if so, test the backup to ensure that you could recreate your Web site if necessary. Even that might not be good enough; consider your other options as well.

There are a few alternatives available that allow you to automatically back up your Web site on a periodic basis. In this chapter we review the following three options:

- Web site backup software;
- Web site download software;
- FTP software.

Web Site Backup Software

A new category of software is emerging which is dedicated to the task of providing a full copy of your Web site for use in an emergency. The first program out of the gate in this category is the Flypage Web Backup program (**www.flypage.com**).

You set up the program by providing details of where your Web site is located and information on how you connect to the Internet. This will be used by the program to dial in to the Internet when it needs to do a backup. If you are not permanently connected to the Internet, the Flypage program will dial in automatically at the time you specified when you configure the program.

Since the program notifies you by e-mail when it has made a backup copy of your Web site, you must also provide some information regarding your e-mail configuration:

Assessing the Effectiveness
of Your Web Site

Protecting Yourself Online

Improving Your Productivity
on the Internet

Enhancing Your Web Site

You then specify how frequently you would like your Web site to be backed up:

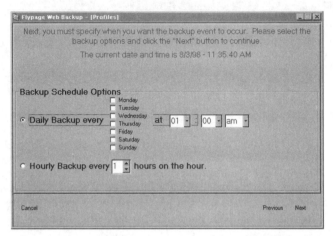

After doing that, Flypage dials in to your Internet connection and accesses your Web site files using FTP, to ensure that everything is set up and configured correctly. (FTP is a special method of accessing files over the Internet.) You then indicate which files you want to back up:

And that's it. From this point on you will get a regular transfer of the files from your Web site to your hard disk, which you can then use if your Web site goes down. In addition to the e-mail notification you receive when a backup copy has been made, you can also access a log within the program at any time to ensure that the backup is working properly:

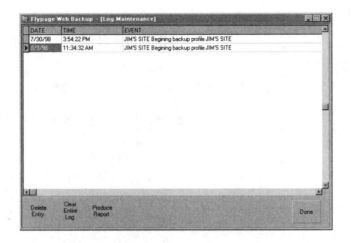

Web Site Download Software

In addition to using a program like Flypage, you can also use any one of the many "offline browsing programs" that have become available. You usually use such programs to download a Web site so that you can view it later while you aren't connected to the Internet. Take a look at the "Offline Browsers" category in TUCOWS (**www.tucows.com**), where you can find a number of these very useful programs:

Fortunately, a few of these programs will, in downloading a site, let you make a backup copy of most of the elements that make up your Web site. One of our favourites is Anawave WebSnake (**www.anawave.com/websnake**), a small, compact program that includes a number of useful features.

In WebSnake you can indicate that when you download a site, you want to "snake a mirrored copy of a Web site including directory structure." If you choose this option, you will get a download of your entire Web site in a format that will be almost completely suitable for the purpose of recreating your Web site online:

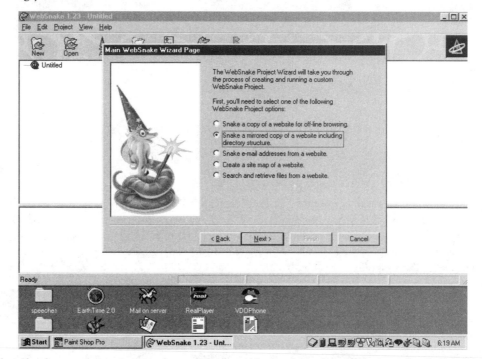

To download your entire site, simply provide the address of the site you want to "snake" and indicate how many levels within your site you want to retrieve:

WebSnake Mirroring Wizard, Page 1

A WebSnake Mirroring Project can copy a remote website including the directory structure to your local hard drive.

In order to create a WebSnake Mirroring Project, you'll need to select a starting address/URL (such as http://www.websnake.com or www.websnake.com).

Starting Address/URL: http://www.handbook.com

Next, you'll need to provide a name for this project.

What would you like to name this project?

Project Name: Handbook

< Back | Next > | Finish | Cancel

WebSnake Mirroring Wizard, Page 3

Warning!

Many websites are very large, and a Mirroring Project can fill your hard drive with tons of files. You can configure this project to Snake limited levels of HTML documents, and you can also set a limit to the remaining hard drive space used before a WebSnake Project stops.

☑ Limit the number of levels snaked to: 8

Stop project if space left on local drive is less than: 10 MB

< Back | Next > | Finish | Cancel

WebSnake reads your site, downloads every page and image, and stores a copy on your local computer. All the Web addresses are adjusted to include the directory structure of your site, which allows you to use the downloaded pages to recreate your site:

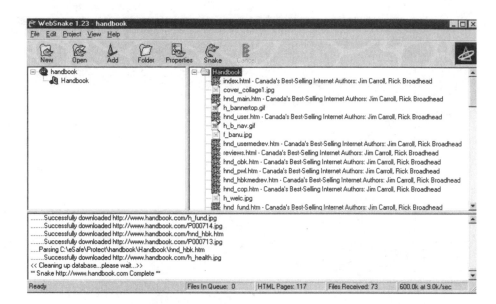

This means that you can take these files, upload them to your Web server, and have a fairly good immediate working copy of your Web site. The program isn't perfect; there may be some links that you have to fix, and it won't download any special scripts, files, or programs that process forms or perform other special activities on your site. But it will give you enough to recreate your site with very little effort.

Finally, since the program includes a scheduling feature, you can set it up to automatically download your entire Web site on a regular basis.

FTP Software

If you don't use either of the alternatives above, then make sure that you at least use your FTP program on a regular basis to download a complete copy of your Web site to your own computer. Many such programs now include scheduling capabilities, so with a little effort you can set things up so that you can automatically download your site on an ongoing basis. You can find a lot of good FTP programs at the TUCOWS site (**www.tucows.com**).

Test Your Backup!

No backup is worthwhile if you don't test it to make sure that it works. The computer industry is full of horror stories of people who thought they had a backup of their files, only to discover, upon restoring them, that some small configuration problem had rendered the entire backup invalid. The only way to be sure that you have a good, working backup of your Web site files is to try to restore them.

To do this, we suggest the following:

- Check the backup policies of the company that hosts your Web site, and, if necessary, insist that they allow you to perform a full recovery and restore operation to ensure that you can actually recreate your Web site from their backup files.

- Regularly back up your Web site files using one of the methods described in this chapter, then test restoring these files to your Web server to make sure that it works.

- Redundancy is important. Don't rely on one backup; do several. The authors of this book actually have copies of their Web sites stored on several computers, different backup tapes, and on other computers on the Internet.

Causes of Data Loss

Power failure/surge:	45.3%
Storm damage:	9.4%
Fire or explosion:	8.2%
Hardware/software error:	8.2%
Flood and water damage:	6.7%
Earthquake:	5.5%
Network outage:	4.5%
Human error/sabotage:	3.2%
Heating, ventilating, air-conditioning failure:	2.3%
Other	6.7%

Source: *Contingency Planning* (via **www.apcc.com**).

Have You Backed Up Your Critical Internet Files?

Even if you decide not to use an online backup service, you should at the very least make frequent backups of your important Internet files. Some of the files that may be most important to you are:

- **Your bookmark file(s).** We don't know how many times we've lost this important file due to our own carelessness. And it hurts when we do it. After all, our bookmark file contains many sites that we want to go back to and visit later. Once we've done something to lose our bookmark file, either by reinstalling a Web browser and overwriting our existing one or through some other action, we end up wasting a lot of time looking for those important and useful Web sites.

- **Your cookie file(s).** Many Web sites make use of "cookies," special files on your computer where information about your preferences for certain Web sites is stored. For example, if you have joined a Web site that requires a user ID and password to visit, some sites will give you the option of saving your user ID and password in your browser so that you don't have to type them in every time you visit the site. The Wall Street Journal (**interactive.wsj.com**) is an example of a site that gives users this option:

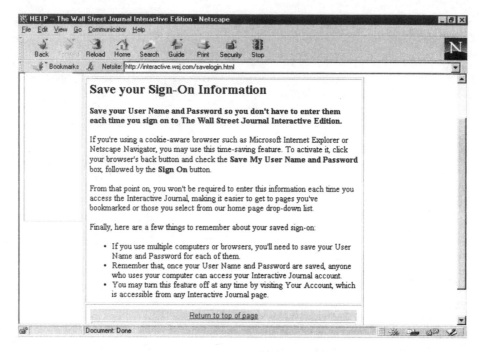

When a Web site provides you with this option, the information is stored in your cookie file. If you lose that file on your hard disk, then you will have to retype in your user ID and password for that site and all the other sites that store your user IDs and passwords in your cookie files. We're willing to bet that you won't remember a lot of that information! Cookie files are also used by services like My Yahoo! (**my.yahoo.com**), which allows you to set up a personalized page of stocks and news headlines that you are interested in. If you lose your cookie file, you will lose all of these settings, and you will have to reconfigure your settings from scratch.

tip How to Find Your Bookmark or Cookie File

If you are using a Netscape browser, use the "Find" command in your Windows or Macintosh system to find the bookmark.htm, bookmark.html, or cookies.txt file. The "Find" command can be accessed from the "Start" button in your Windows task bar:

If you are using Microsoft's Internet Explorer, your bookmarks are called "Favourites." You will find your "Favourites" and "Cookie" folders in the Windows directory of your computer:

- **Your e-mail messages and e-mail addresses.** As you use the Internet more and more, you will come to truly appreciate the importance of e-mail to your business and personal activities. Lose your inbox one day, and you'll recoil in horror. Lose your entire e-mail program, and you will regret having lost all the e-mail addresses you accumulated. This is why it is important to ensure that you at least undertake a regular and complete backup of your e-mail system and all of your e-mail messages. If you use an address book in your e-mail program (an address book is a program that allows you to store the names and e-mail addresses of people you correspond with regularly), make sure you back that up as well. One of the authors has gone so far as to archive most of the e-mail messages he has sent and received since 1984, a topic we address later in this book.

- **Your passwords.** If you keep any Web site passwords or usernames in files or programs on your computer, make sure you back these up as well. In addition, if you use an FTP program, remember that passwords for the various sites you access are usually stored in the program. If you were to ever lose or accidentally delete your FTP program, you would lose all the information stored in the program, which includes all your user IDs and passwords. For this reason, it's important to back up your entire FTP program.

Internet Backup Services

Finally, if you aren't doing regular backups of your computer, you might begin to question your sanity. You may find yourself in a pretty miserable situation if your computer hard drive crashes or if your computer is stolen.

Many people avoid doing a regular backup simply because it tends to be a hassle: you have to be there to put the backup tapes in the machine, and you have to check to make sure that it is working correctly. Depending on the backup device that you have, you may find yourself switching backup tapes on a regular basis. It can be a real hassle.

But one trend that is occurring with the Internet, which we believe will be significant, is the emergence of Internet backup services that are aimed at consumers and small businesses.

POPULAR INTERNET BACKUP SERVICES

REX	**www.infosure.com**
Connected Online Backup	**www.connected.com**
Atrieva	**www.atrieva.com**
@Backup	**www.atbackup.com**

These services allow your data to be backed up to a computer somewhere on the Internet, usually for a monthly fee. You can immediately restore any lost or damaged files by retrieving them through the Internet. If you have a disaster, many of the companies will send you a CD-ROM or series of CD-ROMs containing an exact copy of all the files on your computer as of the last backup. These services can also be used to create backup copies of any Web sites that you operate.

Consider some of the benefits of using an online backup service:

- **Your data are stored at an off-site location.** When you do a backup to tape or some other device, you should ensure that you store a copy off-site. After all, suppose you had an office fire that destroyed both your office computers and your backup tapes. When you use an Internet-based backup service, a copy of your data is stored off-site, removing the risk of destruction of your backup with whatever might have caused destruction of your computers in the first place.

- **You can get your data from anywhere in the world there is an Internet-connected computer.** Many of the Internet-based backup services allow you to restore your files directly through the Internet, while others only send a CD-ROM of your complete backup the next day. For those that let you restore online, this means that you could use the service to obtain an important file if you are travelling away from the home or office.

- **You have access to unlimited capacity.** Although most online backup services provide a basic amount of storage, most are willing to let you back up any amount of data that you want for an additional fee.

- **You don't have to purchase any special hardware.** Many people who have bought tape backups and attempted to configure them for their system, particularly internal tape backups, have found that the entire process of installing and configuring such a system can be a real challenge, particularly when their computers fill up with other conflicting hardware and software. Online backup services don't suffer from these challenges.

Your Privacy Is Protected

Most Internet backup services encrypt (i.e., scramble) your files so that no one can read them. This means that not even the owners and technical support staff employed by the online backup service can get access to your data.

Connected Online Backup

A good example of an Internet backup program is Connected Online Backup (**www.connected.com**). Recognizing that the market is likely to become busy with a number of different options available to the consumer, this company announced a flat rate pricing model for unlimited backup for a fee of U.S. $19.95 per month.

When you install Connected Online, you first go through a process to create an account on the Connected Online service. This occurs automatically through the Internet:

Registration Complete

Congratulations! Registration is complete. Your new account number is:

10126-46213

In case your computer or hard drive is lost or damaged, you'll need information about your account in order to recover your data.

We recommend that you print out your account information and store it in a safe place away from your computer.

[Print Account Information]

If you need help, press the Help button on any screen for information on how to contact our Technical Support department.

Welcome!

| < Back | Next > | Cancel | Help |

Then you identify how frequently you would like to see the backups occur:

Schedule

Please indicate when you would like to run backups. We strongly recommend that backups be done daily to minimize the risk of losing any important data.

○ Backup on manual command only

● Backup automatically on specified days at scheduled time

Schedule Settings

☑ Sun ☑ Mon ☑ Tue ☑ Wed ☑ Thu ☑ Fri ☑ Sat

Start the backup at a random time between the specified hours:

From: 9:00 PM   To: 5:00 AM

☑ Prompt for Backup each time Windows exits

< Back   Next >   Cancel   Help

You also provide a special word that will be used to encrypt your data when stored on the Connected Online computers, so that it cannot be accessed by the staff of Connected Online. You also specify whether you should back up all of your files right away, so there is a master copy at Connected Online, or whether you should only back up files that you have created recently:

Including Old Files

You can choose to back up only new or recent data files, or you can back up all your data files regardless of age.

If you choose to back up files regardless of age, the first backup may be very large. After your first backup, however, subsequent backups will be much smaller because they will store only data that's newly created or changed since the previous backup.

Please choose:

○ Back up only newly-created data.

I'm trying out this backup service. Until I'm sure, I don't want to backup my old data.

● My oldest data is already backed up elsewhere or isn't important.

Back up data files created or changed since: (dd/mm/yy)

○ My old data files are important. Back up my data files regardless of age.

I understand that my first backup may be large if I have lots of old data.

< Back   Next >   Cancel   Help

This is an important issue to understand, since it will help you realize that when you do a backup, you are not necessarily always uploading each and every file on your computer. Here is how these programs work:

- They scan your entire computer. Any program files common to you and Connected Online, such as those related to Microsoft Windows, or specific computer program files, such as those for Netscape, are not backed up. Instead, a record is kept that these files were on your computer. If they ever need to be restored, Connected Online will do so from a master copy of these programs that it keeps. This significantly reduces the length of time that it takes to back up your computer.

- All of your unique data files and computer program files that are unknown to Connected Online are uploaded the first time you use the service.

- Then each time you do an automatic backup, only the newest or modified files are sent to Connected Online.

  This means that the first time you do a backup, it could take quite a long time, since there are a lot of files to upload. But once that is done, each subsequent backup should only take a little while, since only the newest data files are uploaded as well as any new program files that you installed and are not known to Connected Online.

When you first install the Connected Online program, it scans all the files on your computer and determines which ones need to be uploaded. You will also see an X listed beside any files that will not be backed up because they already exist at the master Connected Online site, that is, they are program or Windows files known to Connected Online:

You can also take a look at which computer programs are known to Connected Online:

Once you have done this, Connected Online will do your first backup and will then undertake a scheduled backup on a regular basis.

To restore files, you simply choose the "Restore" option. Your computer connects to Connected Online through the Internet and provides you with a complete listing of your files. You then simply choose which ones you wish to restore.

Should you have suffered a complete crash of your system, or if you want additional protection, you can request a copy of your files on a CD-ROM.

tip Your Virtual Briefcase

In addition to the Internet backup services we have already listed, we also recommend you check out a service called Visto Briefcase (**www.visto.com**). Visto Briefcase continuously backs up your favourite computer files, calendar, address book, and bookmarks to a secure Web site called a "briefcase." You can access your private "briefcase" from any computer in the world that has access to the Internet, making this service useful to business travellers who frequently forget important computer files on their office PCs. A unique aspect of the Visto Briefcase service is that it will keep both your home and office PCs in sync with each other. In other words, if you make a change to your Internet bookmarks on your office PC, Visto Briefcase will automatically update your home computer's bookmark file with the same change. In order for this synchronization to work, however, both computers need to be continuously connected to the Internet. The service costs U.S. $9.95 per month for 20 MB of storage.

Issues to Think About

There are a few other things to think about when it comes to backing up your Web site and using Internet backup services.

First, it is probably a good idea to back up your files using several methods and ensure they are stored in several places, particularly if you are using an online service. After all, you can never be absolutely sure of the stability of the company offering the backup service. Before you choose an Internet backup service, find out what the firm's own backup procedures are. What happens if the firm you are using has a massive computer crash? Do they make backup copies of the data you are sending to them?

Second, be sure to check your system for viruses before backing up; otherwise, you will simply be creating problems if you ever need to restore your files after a virus gets you.

But these may be relatively minor issues. The key thing is to make sure that you take the time to back up not only all the files on your computer, but your Web site as well.

chapter six

Protecting Your Privacy Online

Some of the largest commercial sites on the World Wide Web have agreed to feed information about their customers' reading, shopping and entertainment habits into a system developed by a Massachusetts company that is already tracking the moves of more than 30 million Internet users.

"Big Web Sites to Track Steps of Their Users," *The New York Times*, August 16, 1998

Although many Internet service providers have policies protecting the privacy of their subscribers, they have frequently turned over records, including subscribers' real names, to law enforcement authorities.

Amy Harmon, **"Canadian Ruling Unmasks a Company's Internet Critics,"** *The New York Times*, July 14, 1998

Highlights

1. When you visit a Web site, you leave behind an electronic trail of information that can sometimes be used to reveal your name and/or e-mail address. Anonymous remailers and services like the Anonymizer can help you conceal your identity when sending e-mail and using the Web.

2. Before disclosing any information to a Web site, see if there is a privacy policy. And even if a privacy policy does exist, be aware that the company may be misleading users about how it intends to use the information it collects from you.

3. Many Web sites use "cookies" to track the activities of their users. While the information contained in cookie files is usually anonymous, the potential for abuse exists. Programs like Cookie Pal and Anonymous Cookie can help you monitor and control cookie activity on your computer.

4. Information that you publish on the Internet may be archived without your knowledge. Services such as DejaNews and Reference.COM archive messages that people have posted to thousands of Internet discussion groups and bulletin boards. And a project called The Internet Archive is creating a permanent record of the Web by copying Web pages and preserving them in a digital archive. Your Web site could be in this archive.

Personal privacy has become one of the hottest issues related to the Internet. And it's no wonder. There is a distinct clash occurring between the desire by many companies to obtain as much information as possible about visitors to their Web sites and the desire by many users to ensure that their activities online remain anonymous or undetected.

In this chapter we take a look at five important privacy issues and offer some practical tips on what you can do to protect yourself online.

1. Do You Know How to Remain Anonymous on the Internet?

If you are concerned about companies or the government tracking what you do on the Internet, you can take steps to ensure that your online activities remain anonymous. Not only can you remain anonymous when sending e-mail and USENET messages; you can be anonymous when browsing the Web as well.

Why would you want to do this? Your first thought might be that anyone trying to remain anonymous on the Internet must be breaking the law, but that isn't the case. There are many reasons why people wish to remain anonymous: there are lots of people who participate in electronic mail or USENET discussion groups on sensitive support topics (e.g., alcoholism) who don't want their identity to be known. You could be researching or using Web sites that have a similar degree of sensitivity and don't want any information linked back to yourself. Perhaps you simply don't like the current aura that surrounds the Internet, where many organizations seem to be almost giddy to learn details about who is visiting them online. Or maybe you disagree with certain government policies, such as those proposed by Elections Canada, which propose making anonymous free speech illegal on the Internet. There are probably many other reasons as well.

tip Hide Your Tracks!

Cover Your Tracks (**www.ffsoftware.com**) is a privacy tool for Internet users who use the Netscape Web browser. This program will delete specific references to information on your computer: which Web sites you recently visited and your cookie, cache, and history files. Other programs that erase evidence of your Internet surfing are CyberClean (**www.thelimitsoft.com**) and WebSweep (**www.luckman.com**). Both CyberClean and WebSweep work with Netscape and Internet Explorer.

What Is the Nature of the Problem?

Most people are well aware that e-mail sent through the Internet which has not been encrypted is not secure. Anyone at your ISP or one of the companies involved in transmitting the message can easily read the contents.

And when you visit a Web site, your computer provides certain basic information to the site. Much of this information is stored in Web log files that track what you do on the site and includes details such as your IP address (i.e., the number assigned to you when you connect to the Internet) and details about your Web browser.

What can Web site owners learn when you visit their Web site? They can figure out the IP, or Internet address, you are coming from. They might be able to use this later to determine who you are (more about that later, in the "cookie" technology section). In addition, depending on the Web browser you might be using, they might be able to figure out your e-mail address.

To get an understanding of the type of information that can be discovered, visit Consumer.net (**www.consumer.net**), a site dedicated to consumer privacy and protection. Once you have connected to the site, click on the menu option "Analyze the privacy of your Internet connection" (found near the bottom of the homepage); you will have to wait a few minutes while it analyzes what it can learn from you. The results are fascinating:

Privacy Analysis of your Internet Connection

Some Information that is collected about you when visiting a web site

☆ ☆

Internet privacy software for Netscape (NSClean)   Order Now ✓
www.software.net

(For Internet Explorer use IEClean)
☆ ☆

(Please wait for analysis to complete, it may take 2 or 3 minutes)

Related pages: How this analysis works   Internet Privacy

Traceroute Page - The network tools used here. Run a trace on any computer on the Internet.

Your IP address: 24.112.72.92

Your computer name (if it has one): cr943611-a.wlfdle1.on.wave.home.com

Consumer.net shows you how easy it is for another Web site to figure out your IP address and whether your Web browser is revealing your e-mail address to Web sites that ask for it (older versions of Web browsers did this):

Does your browser give out your e-mail address?

Your browser does not supply your e-mail address by asking for the HTTP_FROM value.

Your browser provides the following information when making an FTP request:

FTP username is: anonymous

FTP password is: WinGate@

Who registered your domain? (if computer name has a 'fully qualified' Internet name ending in .com, .net, .org, .uk, ... see list. For other domains look it up here):

Registrant:
Home Network HOME-DOM
  425 Broadway
  Redwood City, CA 94063
  US

Domain Name: HOME.COM

You can do a similar privacy test at the Anonymizer site (**www.anonymizer.com**), which we discuss below. This site provides a particularly good summary of the type of information that can be determined when you visit a Web site and provides an equally good summary of how this information can be misused:

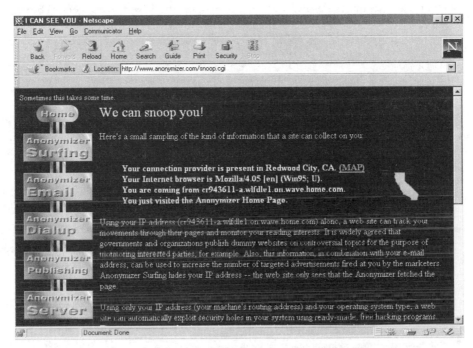

What is the real risk here? Web sites can identify who you are. As we mentioned above, each Web site you visit can learn your IP address. As users of a Yahoo! chat group discovered in 1998, their IP addresses were used under a court order to identify them in a proceeding in which a Hamilton, Ontario, company, Philip Environmental, felt it was being abused online. Hence Web logs that contain your IP address can be linked to ISP access logs to identify who you are.

tip Will Your Internet Provider Protect Your Privacy?

The Philip Environmental situation caused many Internet users in Canada to question the privacy of their Internet activities. Philip Environmental was able to obtain the identities of several Canadian Internet users by serving their Internet service providers with court orders. Several ISPs complied with these orders, raising the ire of many of their customers. What would your ISP do in a similar circumstance? We encourage you to find out. Check with your ISP to see if they have a policy regarding customer privacy.

And if you have a dedicated connection to the Internet through a cable modem and have a Web site accessible through that cable modem, then any Web site that you visit could determine precisely who you are, simply by looking at your IP address and then travelling to your Web site.

Should you be worried at all if you aren't doing anything of an illegal nature online? Should you care if you can be identified? To answer that question, stay on the Consumer.net site and read the article "Can your E-mail address be traced when visiting a Web Site?" (**consumer.net/trace.asp**). The article describes how, with a little bit of detective work, Web site owners can identify the e-mail addresses of people who have visited their Web sites:

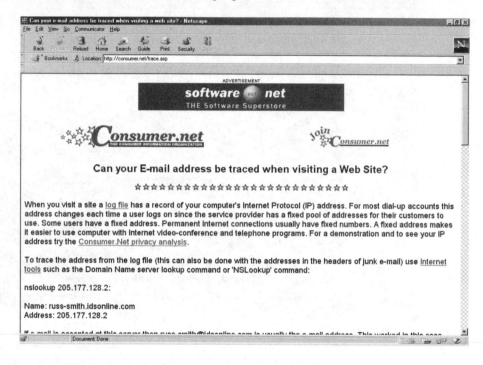

If privacy is important to you, then surfing anonymously might be too. Let's look at how you can do things anonymously on the Internet.

Sending Anonymous E-mail

There are a number of free and commercial services online that you can use to send and receive anonymous e-mail.

To find the free e-mail services, check the sites of various groups on the Internet dedicated to protecting freedom of speech. Organizations that provide Internet services to dissident communities in countries where freedom of speech is not a constitutional right (e.g., China and Burma) are also places to check. A good example is the Global Internet Liberty Campaign's Web site (**www.gilc.org/speech/anonymous/remailer.html**):

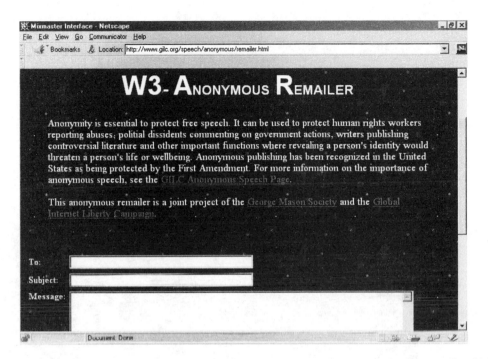

Should you need the ability to send and receive anonymous e-mail on a regular basis with a high degree of reliability, there are services that you can pay for. Examples are Nymserver (**www.nymserver.com**) and MailAnon (**www.mailanon.com**):

Surfing the Web Anonymously

As we pointed out earlier, your identity isn't protected when you visit a Web site. It is possible for the Web site owner to discover your e-mail address and therefore identify you. One of the main services that allows you to remain anonymous while browsing the Web is the Anonymizer (**www.anonymizer.com**).

The service is free. Simply type in the address of a Web site that you would like to visit, and your identity will be concealed when you visit that site:

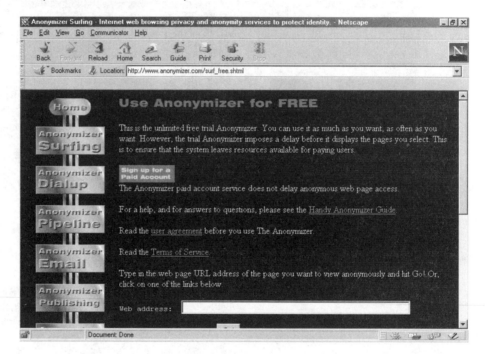

When you use the Anonymizer, you will experience a short delay before you can connect to the Web page that you want to visit. This is deliberate. They want to encourage you to sign up for the Anonymizer's commercial service, available for U.S. $30 per month, which will allow you to connect to Web sites anonymously without experiencing any delays.

You can also check out the Lucent Personalized Web Assistant (**lpwa.com:8000**). Unlike the Anonymizer, the Lucent Personalized Web Assistant doesn't force you to visit its Web page every time you want to visit another Web site anonymously. Instead, this service works by allowing you to set it up as the default "proxy" for your Web browser. What this does is configure things such that each and every time you travel to a Web page, the request goes through the Lucent service automatically, with the effect that all of your browsing is completely anonymous, automatically. The Lucent site provides straightforward instructions on how to set up your Web browser so that it goes through the Lucent proxy; it is a fairly easy change. After this, the Lucent proxy will show up as the address in any Web site logs rather than your own.

The service also includes several innovative features and capabilities, for example, the ability to automatically make anonymous the e-mail address you may be asked to provide to various Web sites. This allows you to have several anonymous e-mail addresses that you provide to various Web sites that require them, such as when you register with a new Internet service.

The Lucent service is a good example of how sophisticated anonymous services are becoming on the Internet and, hence, is well worth a visit simply to find out where we are headed:

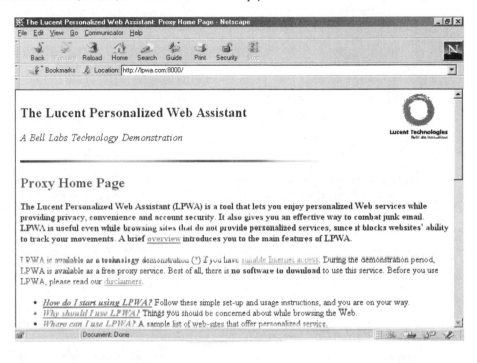

tip Keeping Your E-mail Private

If you're worried about sending a private document to a friend, co-worker, or colleague by e-mail, consider using a product called DataSafe SE. This program secures your data using a 16-character combination that you supply. The great thing about DataSafe is that the recipient of the secure document doesn't need to have the program. To unlock your file, the recipient only needs to provide the combination that you created. You can download a free demonstration of DataSafe SE at **www.novastor.com**. For highly sensitive business communications that require secure delivery over the Internet, check out the UPS Document Exchange from United Parcel Service (**exchange.ups.com**).

2. Do You Check Web Sites For Privacy Policies?

We remain amazed at the number of Internet users who willingly hand over to Web sites all kinds of private information, without wondering whether that information will be kept private. A Web site that collects information about you may sell your data to marketers without your knowledge. How rampant is this problem on the Web? Even some of the largest Web sites on the Internet seem to be guilty of this practice. Have you heard of Geocities (**www.geocities.com**), the popular service that allows Internet users to create their own free Web pages? To the dismay of thousands of their users, Geocities was investigated by the U.S. government for misleading customers and secretly selling personal information about them to marketers. The investigation prompted the company to change its privacy practices by putting in place new safeguards to protect the privacy of its users.

In the *1998 Canadian Internet Handbook* we dedicated an entire chapter to this issue. At the time we wrote:

> *perhaps the biggest security and privacy risk online is barely covered in the press at all: many Canadians willingly part with all kinds of private information, without stopping to think about the information they are giving away and without wondering about what might happen to that information. And we find that the businesses requesting this private information online do little to provide assurances to people that such information will not be misused.*

We don't think that things have changed much in the last year:

- The fact remains that few Canadian organizations seem to have bothered establishing a privacy policy on their Web site. This echoes an experience in the United States: the government issued a warning to Web site owners to implement online privacy policies. But a year later only 14% of the 1,400 largest Web sites had complied.

- Many people still willingly hand over private information to Web sites, without realizing that in the absence of any Canadian laws with respect to the use of private information by the private sector, Web site owners can do whatever they like with that information.

It isn't surprising that many Canadian companies have not adopted privacy policies for their Web sites; there's no legislation in Canada with respect to the privacy of information accumulated by companies in the corporate sector. Anything goes!

As a result, when it comes to Web sites that ask for private information, we suggest that you first look for a privacy policy. If one does not exist, then perhaps you should think twice before going any further.

What are your options? Provide the information, or leave the site and not take advantage of any information or services offered there. Or adopt an alias. In one survey two-thirds of the survey participants said that when asked for private information when not entering an economic transaction, they provided an alias so that they could not be identified.

A privacy policy is simply that: it is a statement by a company, provided on their Web site, advising what you can expect that company to do with any information you provide. An excellent example of a privacy policy is found on the IBM Canada Web site (**www.ibm.com/Privacy/**). The IBM privacy page provides details on what protection you will get after providing any information to them; it also includes links to additional pages and sites that expand on some of the points that are raised:

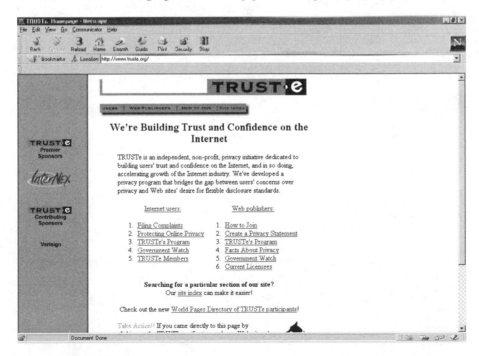

IBM notes on its page that it is a member of TRUSTe (**www.truste.org**), "an independent, non-profit, privacy initiative dedicated to building users' trust and confidence on the Internet." TRUSTe is one of several initiatives emerging online to help protect the privacy of Internet users:

A similar initiative, which seeks to provide assurances not only of privacy but of the safety of economic transactions and other activities through a Web site, is WebTrust (**www.cica.ca/WebTrust**), a service provided by the American Institute of Certified Public Accountants and the Canadian Institute of Chartered Accountants. A site that displays the WebTrust seal has met a number of criteria, for example: "the entity maintains effective controls to ensure that private customer information is protected from uses not related to the entity's business." Hence you can be reasonably assured that a company displaying the WebTrust seal has a privacy policy. You can learn more about WebTrust at the CICA Web site:

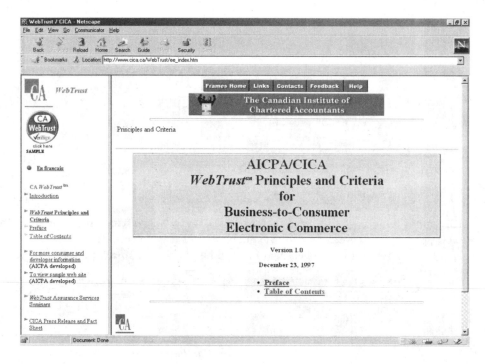

Look for the WebTrust and TRUSTe seals on Web sites you visit. Any Web sites displaying these seals have taken steps to protect your privacy.

3. Are You Protecting Yourself From Inappropriate Use of "Cookie" Technology?

You are probably aware that when you visit a Web site, the site might place a file called a "cookie" on your computer's hard drive. (If you are using one of the services that provide anonymity, you will still get a cookie, but at least you will have guaranteed your anonymity when it comes to that cookie.) The cookie contains a unique piece of computer code that can be used to identify you. The cookie file doesn't necessarily identify you personally, but it can be used by Web site owners to track what sections of the Web site you looked at, what online advertisement you saw, and what products you ordered. This allows Web site owners to track the habits of their visitors. This information can then be used to customize the information that customers see the next time they visit the Web site.

For example, suppose you visited the Web site of a major airline and looked up the cost of a flight to Hong Kong. If the airline is using cookie technology on its site, it could then add information to your cookie file indicating that you are interested in a trip to Hong Kong. The next time you return to the Web site, your cookie file would alert the airline that you are interested in Hong Kong, and any specials on flights to that destination would automatically be displayed on the screen for you.

Cookies are also used by some Web sites to store an Internet user's password and user ID so that you can automatically connect to Web sites that you subscribe to without having to type in your user ID and password each time you visit.

Some firms, like Engage (**www.engage.com**), use cookie files to create enormous databases that contain profiles of Internet users. They then use this information to target online advertisements to the users most likely to buy specific products and services. Engage's database contains profiles of more than 30 million Internet users. Shocking, isn't it?

There has been a lot of hysteria about the privacy risks associated with cookies. Although a cookie file is usually anonymous (your e-mail address and name are not normally contained in a cookie file), it is possible for a Web site to manipulate the cookie information in such a way that your privacy is invaded. For example, a Web site owner may be able to link the information in your cookie file to a registration form you filled out when you first visited the site. Because the registration form likely asked for your full name, the Web site owner may be able to associate this information with your cookie file and therefore identify you. Despite these privacy risks, cookie files don't pose any security risks to you or your computer. They cannot be used to plant a virus on your computer, nor can they pluck personal information off your hard drive.

tip Wash Away Your Cookies

Cache and Cookie Washer (**www.webroot.com**) is a useful program that will delete your cookie files from your hard drive. You can select which cookie files you want to delete and which you want to keep, allowing you to retain the ones that contain preferences or log-in information for sites that you visit regularly.

How can you protect yourself from cookie files? Fortunately, there are a number of different programs that can help you to manage your cookies. A good example is Cookie Pal (**www.kburra.com**). When a cookie is sent to you, Cookie Pal displays a box asking you if you want to accept it:

We should point out that some Web sites depend on cookies to operate. This means that if you reject a cookie from a Web site, you may not be able to access the site at all, or certain sections of the site may be unavailable to you.

You can also use Cookie Pal to see a list of all the cookies that have been placed on your hard drive:

X-RAY VISION software (**www.intracept.com**) will monitor your Internet connection and scan all data before it enters your Web browser or leaves your PC through the Internet. Using this program, you can prevent cookies from being deposited on your hard drive and customize your privacy settings for Web sites that you frequently visit. @Guard (**www.atguard.com**) is another useful program that allows you to selectively accept or deny cookies for specific Web sites.

Note that cookies are not all bad; in fact, when they are used to store passwords and user IDs for sites that you use frequently, they are very convenient. And as many Internet users have already discovered, it can be a big hassle trying to prevent cookie files from accumulating on your hard drive. The steady stream of warning boxes appearing on your screen can become extremely annoying and will eventually slow down your use of the Internet. Nevertheless, some Internet users feel better using a cookie detection program like Cookie Pal, because then they at least have some control over the information that is being collected about them.

POPULAR COOKIE MANAGEMENT SOFTWARE

Cookie Pal	**www.kburra.com**
Cookie Crusher	**www.thelimitsoft.com**
Anonymous Cookie	**www.luckman.com**
NSClean and IEClean	**www.privsoft.com**
Cookie Terminator	**www.4developers.com**

4. Are You Aware That Information on the Internet Can Live on, Forever?

As you work with the Internet, keep in mind that the information you place online, whether on your Web site or on a Web-based bulletin board, USENET discussion group, or mailing list, might be archived and kept forever. What you say today might come back and haunt you tomorrow.

Imagine, for example, that you have joined an online discussion group in USENET related to some personal problem that you have. You post a few items, try to get some questions answered, and generally discover the collaborative power of the Internet.

But your postings have been archived in DejaNews (**www.dejanews.com**) or Reference.COM (**www.reference.com**), services that archive messages that people have posted to thousands of Internet discussion groups. Years later, when you apply for a job, the prospective employer does a search for you online, finds what you posted in DejaNews or Reference.COM, and rejects you because she doesn't like what she saw. Far-fetched? We don't think so. In fact, our advice is to keep this in mind when posting any personal information on an Internet discussion group.

5. Is Your Web Site Being Archived Without Your Knowledge?

Finally, not only can your conversations in Internet discussion groups be archived forever, but the information that you have on your Web site may become part of a permanent Internet archive as well. A project called The Internet Archive (**www.archive.org**) is making a copy of the Internet every 30 to 60 days. The purpose of this initiative is to make a permanent record of the Web that can be used by historians, scholars, the government, and business researchers. This means that even if you delete a Web page from the Internet, it may have already found its way into The Internet Archive. The privacy implications are chilling. Consider this scenario: a student currently going to college creates his own Web site and then removes it from the Internet when he graduates. Years later, he runs for the leadership of a major Canadian political party. The Internet Archive would make it possible for his adversaries to recover his Web site from his college days and perhaps use the information against him. How do you stop this from happening to you? Visit **www.archive.org:80/webmasters.html**, where you can find instructions on how to prevent your site from being included in the archive.

Are You Privacy Conscious?

Privacy on the Internet is an ongoing issue and to deal with it properly, you should work hard to keep up-to-date with new areas of concern, new technologies, and new risks.

To do this, visit the following Web sites: the Online Privacy Alliance (**www.privacyalliance.org**), the Electronic Frontier Foundation (**www.eff.org**), the Center for Democracy and Technology (**www.cdt.org**), and the Electronic Privacy Information Center (**www.epic.org**). Any one of these sites is an excellent starting point to learn about privacy issues, what you can do to protect yourself, and other related topics.

And for a unique Canadian spin, be sure to check the sites of the Privacy Commissioner of Canada (**infoweb.magi.com/~privcan/**) and Electronic Frontier Canada (**www.efc.ca**), both of which contain useful privacy resources.

chapter seven

Securing Your Connection to the Internet

A 22-year-old Canadian man suspected of breaking into a NASA Web site and causing tens of thousands of dollars in damage has been arrested by Canadian Mounties....More than $70,000 worth of damage was caused at the NASA Web site and officials were forced to rebuild the site and change security.

"Suspected NASA Hacker Nabbed," Reuters, April 7, 1998

It sounds like a computer user's worst nightmare: Someone gains access to your personal computer via the Internet and deletes files. Alters money accounts. Destroys information stored on the hard disk. And it all takes just a minute or two.

"Internet Users Fight Back Against Hackers," *The Tampa Tribune*, June 23, 1997

Highlights

1. Even if you are a single Internet user with a dial-up connection, you need to take precautions to protect yourself from security problems online.

2. There are many Web sites dedicated to exposing security weaknesses in computer operating systems and software programs. They include resources like Rootshell and Fyodor's Playhouse. Some of these sites have malicious intent, while others exist for educational purposes.

3. This chapter details five steps that you can take to protect your computer, and your data, from malicious attack through the Internet: use PC firewall software; regularly obtain updates and security patches for your Web browsers; check the security of your e-mail program; use a password management program; and hire a consultant to conduct a security audit of your computer.

Security and the Internet is a complex topic. Link millions of computers worldwide, toss in various technologies from all kinds of companies, and you have the potential for all kinds of problems. Throw in a desire by many people to simply break into systems for the fun of it, and there is some serious momentum happening. Feed into this the reality that the Internet has sped up the software development cycle significantly, with many products rushed to market before they are ready, and you've got the perfect environment for havoc.

Certainly many of us have read about all the security problems related to the Internet. But the challenge for many is to bring what might seem like a faraway or complex problem closer to home. That's the purpose of this chapter. We want to convey several issues to help you become more aware of how security issues on the Internet can affect you directly.

Look no further than some of the mainstream discussion groups on the Internet to understand how security issues are affecting each and every Internet user. Discussions about Internet security have popped up in discussion forums normally devoted to issues like Greek culture and retirement planning.

The *New York Times* drew attention to this trend in an article on e-mail security flaws: "since when did **soc.retirement** become the site of heated debate over bug patches and the accountability of software vendors?" the article asked, pointing out that heated discussions about Internet security are now appearing in places where they would have once seemed out of place.

The most important point that we want to make is this: you don't have to be a large organization with a high-speed Internet connection to benefit from this chapter, or to be at risk online. Even if you access the Internet from home using a plain old dial-up connection, you will find lots of useful information in the pages that follow.

The Culture of Hacking on the Internet

All the technologies, computers, and software that make up the Internet are constantly being probed for security problems and weaknesses. This is why you often see news reports of some new security problems with a Web browser or e-mail program.

If you want to understand the nature of what happens on the Internet from a security perspective, there are a few sites that you can visit. Start off at Rootshell (**www.rootshell.com**). Featured in high-profile stories on hacking on PBS and in various magazines and newspapers, this is one of the primary Web sites used to exchange information about security weaknesses. Visit the site, and you can find a chronological listing of security exposures that have been found with respect to certain computer operating systems, programs, and Internet services:

Choose any of the dates from the homepage at Rootshell, and you will get an extensive listing of security problems discovered during that month:

```
rootshell.com - exploits - Netscape
File  Edit  View  Go  Communicator  Help

Bookmarks    Location: http://rootshell.com/view.cgi?199807

  Back   Forward  Reload   Home   Search   Guide    Print  Security   Stop
```

COMPUTERWORLD
Click here for FREE issues.

Connect from cr943611-a.wlfdle1.on.wave.home.com [24.112.72.92] (Mozilla/4.05 [en]C-DIAL (Win95; U))logged.

rootshell archive for 199807	
7/1/98 ioconfig	IRIX 6.4 ioconfig exploit making use of system calls without full paths.
7/1/98 aspads.txt	By appending ::$DATA to .asp URLs you are able to download the ASP source code from Microsoft web servers (IIS). Vendor patch.
7/2/98 winhackgold.zip	Winhack Gold is a program for Windows that scans blocks of IPs for open file shares that you can access. This is the same program as featured in Newsbytes. Click here to see if your computer is vulnerable. Windows users may wish to download Legion by Rhino9 which does not require a UNIX machine.
7/6/98 qpopscan.sh	Qualcomm Popper scanner shell script for finding vulnerable servers.
7/6/98 netscapetbl.txt	Netscape 3.x and 4.x DoS by using nested tables inside the span tag.
7/6/98 qscan.c	Yet another QPOP scanner. This one is written in C.
7/6/98 smurflog-1.0.tgz	Smurf Logger 1.0. Logs smurf attacks and the broadcast address being used.
	Real Player 5.0 Killer. Allows you to crash users when they are using RP with a HTTP

http://rootshell.com/archive-j457rxiqi3gq59dv/199807/aspads.txt.html

```
Start   Pegasus Mail   rootshell.c...   Microsoft Wo...   Paint Shop P...                    7:13 AM
```

Most of what you read here will seem very technical if you don't have a computer background, and, in particular, if you don't work in-depth with operating systems like Unix or Windows NT. You don't need to necessarily understand everything you read here, but you will get a sense of the culture: people are continually trying to discover new security problems online.

Spend some time browsing Rootshell, and you will get a good idea just how many security problems can be identified in a short period of time. People contribute new items to Rootshell from around the world—and what exists here is probably just a small sample of the many new security exposures that are found on an ongoing basis.

Take a look at the third item from the top on the screen above: it refers to a program, Winhackgold, that can be used to automatically scan your Internet service provider and determine if there are any users who have not properly secured their computers. And the second item from the top reports on a well-known problem with Microsoft's Internet Explorer.

In Rootshell you can examine each item for a detailed description of the risk and how someone could maliciously exploit the problem:

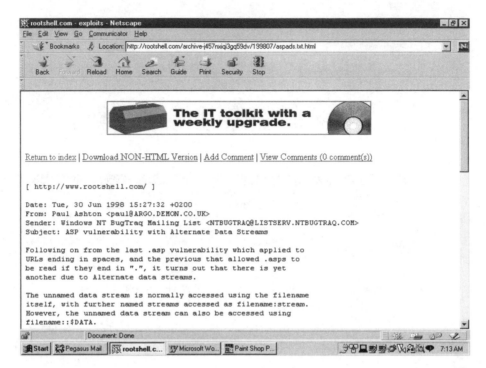

Because they are accessible to the general public, systems like Rootshell allow anyone on the Internet to learn security problems that have been identified on the Internet and therefore to take advantage of them.

Now wander over to Fyodor's Playhouse (**www.insecure.org**), a Web site that also details "exploits," or security problems, that have been found in a wide variety of computers, programs, operating systems, and Internet applications. It makes for fascinating reading and will probably scare the heck out of you. Once again, we ask you not to read it to understand it all, but simply to appreciate the extent of security problems that are identified:

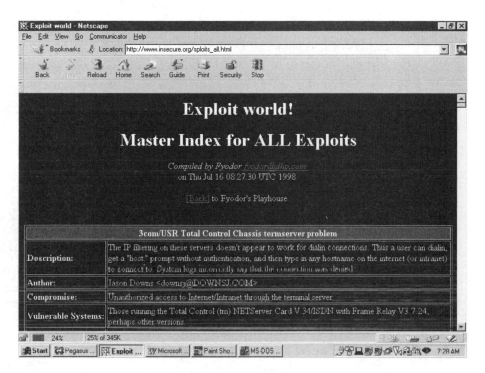

These two sites just scratch the surface of what is available online; there are countless Web sites, USENET newsgroups, mailing lists, and information resources dedicated to sharing information on new security exposures and risks related to the Internet.

What drives this trend toward the discovery and sharing of security exploits? Several things. First, there is an entire culture on the Internet dedicated to finding security problems online. There are some within this community who do so for entirely honourable purposes: they simply want to explore the technological world around them and have no intent of doing real damage. To explore this "hacker culture," visit L0pht (**www.l0pht.com**), one of the most famous online groups dedicated to exploring the Internet and technology:

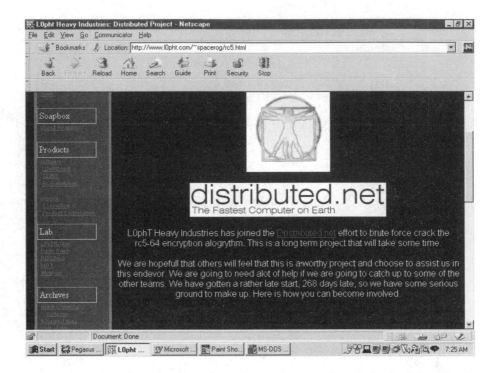

L0pht seems dedicated to the task of simply exploring the outer limits of risk with technology. At the time we visited, the "L0phtites" were encouraging others to participate in a massive global effort to break a new encryption method through "brute force computing." You can visit the site, download some software, run it on your own computer, and then upload the results—in effect, becoming part of a worldwide effort trying to crack a secure encryption code.

Why are they trying to do this? Simply because L0pht wants to prove that it can be done. The group doesn't seem terribly destructive.

Active Matrix Hideaway (**www.hideaway.net**) is another excellent site dedicated to "honourable hacking." They note on their homepage that "we seek knowledge, not robbery and destruction":

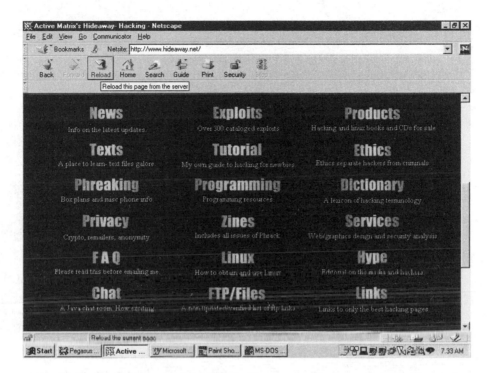

The concept of "hacking" systems just to learn has been around a long time. But just as there are "honourable" hackers, there are hackers who delight in causing problems, doing damage, accessing private systems, and crashing computers. Explore this world further, and you will discover many who have dishonourable and destructive intentions.

Many of them fall into the anti-Microsoft category, which seems to be becoming rampant on the Internet. You can easily find a large number of sites that focus on security problems within Windows 95/98 and Windows NT (particularly the latter), such as the Unofficial NT Hack FAQ (**www.nmrc.org/faqs/nt/index.html**):

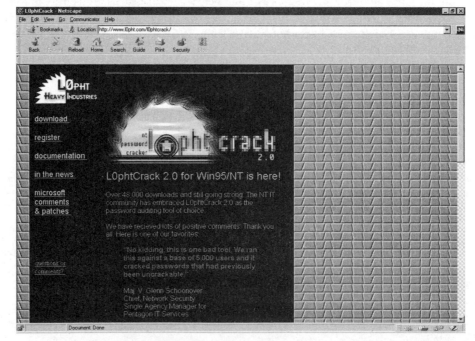

Read this document and you will be fascinated with what people are discussing. As you do so, keep in mind that similar documents exist for all kinds of other software, not just Microsoft's.

But the NT situation does bear special attention. Scan the Internet, and you will find that you can easily download software programs that help you crack a Windows NT system or read "encrypted" passwords on Windows 95/98 systems. One of the programs is L0phtCrack, which is easily downloaded from the L0pht Web site:

What does this have to do with the Internet? Everything, since Microsoft, like all the other software companies, is trying to integrate the Internet into all of its software.

It is almost a running online battle: as the hacker community finds problems in Microsoft software, Microsoft responds online within its security site (**www.microsoft.com/security**):

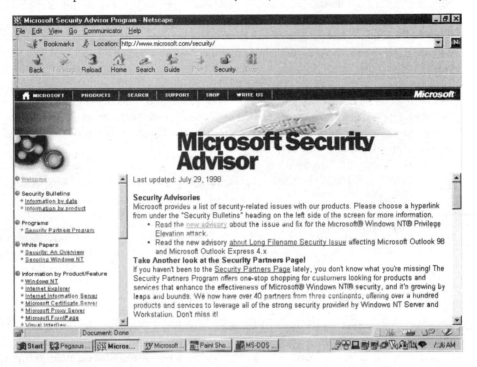

The homepage for Fyodor's Playhouse features the following quote: "History has taught us: never underestimate the amount of money, time, and effort someone will expend to thwart a security system. It's always better to assume the worst. Assume your adversaries are better than they are. Assume science and technology will soon be able to do things they cannot yet."

What does this mean to you? It means that you must recognize that the technology, systems, and software that you use with the Internet are constantly being assessed and probed, with the result that you could experience security problems one day.

You need to be security conscious and aware and must ensure that you do what is necessary to protect yourself online.

Unlike a Password, Your Face Cannot Be Stolen

Want a glimpse at the future of Internet security? Visit **www.miros.com**, where you can learn about a revolutionary technology called TrueFace Web. This is face-recognition technology used to control access to Web sites. As long as a person has a video camera attached to his or her computer, TrueFace can compare the person's "live" face with a previously recorded face image. If the two faces match, TrueFace will allow the person to access the Web site. As video cameras become more commonplace on home and office computers, this type of technology could eventually replace the use of passwords and user IDs on popular Web sites.

Assessing Our Own Computer For Security Problems

After going through all the material on hackers and security problems, one of the authors of this book decided to check out his own computer system to see if he was at risk. He first visited the Rootshell site mentioned above, through a dial-up connection to the Internet. On the main screen there was a button that said, "Check if your file sharing is secure against attacks like Winhack Gold." We were stunned by what we found after we clicked on this button.

Choosing this item causes a program to be run on the Rootshell Web site that determines if you have a security risk with your Windows configuration. This program figures out the IP address (the numbers assigned to a computer when it connects to the Internet) of your computer, and then it in effect queries your computer to determine if the Windows feature known as "file and printer sharing" is turned on.

Having this feature turned on is quite common, especially if you use a laptop at work to access the local area network in your office, and then use that computer to connect to the Internet at home at night.

Why is this risky?

- If you have a computer that is linked to a local area network using Microsoft Windows or an Apple Macintosh, you or your network administrator may have installed a feature on your computer called "file and printer sharing." In addition, if you use a computer to dial up to the Internet from home, you may have installed the "file and printer sharing" capability when setting up your connection to the Internet.

- "File and printer sharing" does just that: when installed, it lets you share your computer files and any printer attached to your computer with other people. This means that when your co-workers browse the corporate network, they are able to see some of the files on your computer. In a corporate organization, this is often done for the express purpose of allowing teams to work together. For example, you create a document and tell your co-workers exactly where to find it—the drive and the file directory—on your computer.

- However, if "file and printer sharing" is turned on and you connect to the Internet, it means that people on the Internet can also access your files and computers—a major security risk.

In our case, the Rootshell program was able to determine that indeed our computer had the "file and printer sharing" turned on. It then figured out the names assigned to our hard disks and attempted to crack the passwords on them. We found out that one of our hard disks wasn't protected by a password (we thought that it was), so the site was able to determine the directories on that hard disk :

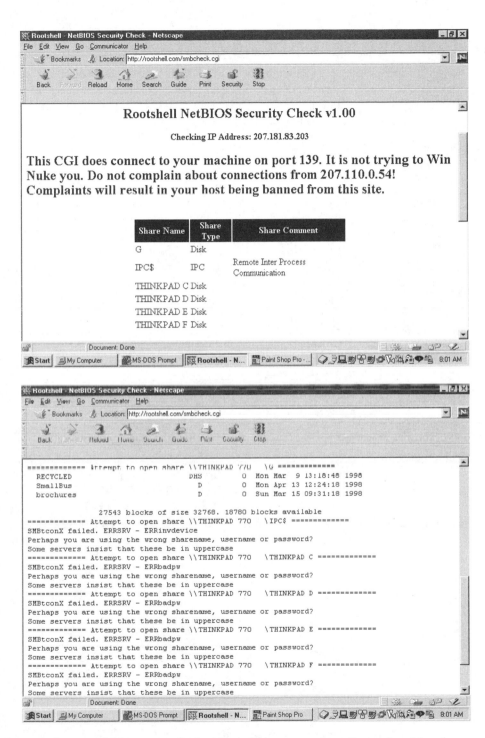

The Rootshell site could have gone further. It could have started reading and writing data to and from our hard disk. It could have been set up to do all kinds of nasty things.

We thought we were protected, but were not.

tip Internet Security Advisories

The Computer Emergency Response Team (CERT) at Carnegie Mellon University provides one of the most comprehensive security monitoring services on the Web. While most of the information is highly technical in nature, CERT's Web site (**www.cert.org**) provides an archive of Internet security bulletins dating back to 1988.

Hacking on Our Own

Determined to see how difficult it was to find other systems that suffered from similar security problems, we decided to do a bit of hacking on our own. We downloaded a program called Legion from one of the hacker sites mentioned above. This program is similar to the Rootshell program in that it sees if "file and printer sharing" is turned on.

With Legion, you give it a block of IP numbers, most often those used by your Internet service provider. Legion then tests these IP numbers to see if there are any computers using them that might be accessible in the same way through the ISP you are currently connected to.

Legion merrily charged off to see which systems we could work our way into. It found a few; obviously, people who aren't cognizant of the risks with their machines. (We had warned our ISP that we were running this test and that we did not have a nefarious intentions.) We could have tried, at this point, to access any files on those computers.

Discovering Even More Risks

At the time we were trying this out, we were in the process of installing Windows 98 for the first time. We were curious: were there potential security problems here too?

We realized that yes, we had subjected ourselves to an unknown risk. We were advised, by testing our computer at the Consumer.net Web site (**www.consumer.net**), that our computer was running a Web site.

The program on the Consumer.net Web site will conduct an analysis of your Internet connection. It is similar to the Rootshell program in that it figures out the IP address of the computer connected to it. (Remember, every time you dial into or connect to the Internet, you are assigned an IP number.) It then checks to see if that particular computer has a Web server (a Web server is software that is used to place a Web site on the Internet). In our case it quickly figured out that yes, we did have a Web server, and it let us know our IP number:

```
Domain System inverse mapping provided by.

NS0.INSNET.NET          194.177.160.2
NS1.INSNET.NET          194.177.170.2

ADDRESSES WITHIN THIS BLOCK ARE NON-PORTABLE

Record last updated on 23-Aug-96.
Database last updated on 29-Jul-98 16:14:29 EDT.

The ARIN Registration Services Host contains ONLY Internet
Network Information: Networks, ASN's, and related POC's.
Please use the whois server at rs.internic.net for DOMAIN related
Information and nic.ddn.mil for MILNET Information.

No match in European database.

No match in Asia-Pacific database.

Are you running a web server on your machine?

Yes. Headers Received:

HTTP/1.1 200 OK
Server: Microsoft-IIS/4.0
Date: Thu, 30 Jul 1998 13:46:02 GMT
Content-Type: text/html
Set-Cookie: ASPSESSIONIDFFFEVXNF=LFKNIMDAACMEOJLDDPPDMLFF; path=/
```

Start   Privacy Analysis of y...   Paint Shop Pro   9:46 AM

This came as a surprise, because we didn't realize that we were running a Web server. But then we realized that when we installed Windows 98, we had installed the option called Personal Web server, a program that allows you to create your own personal Web page and make it available to others in your office.

This capability is being used in many companies. It allows employees to find out information from other employees or to access some of the information they choose to make available on their own personal Web site. We had installed this on our network to make information from one of the computers on our network available to someone else on the network.

But there is a risk with this Personal Web server capability: if you have a Personal Web page on the laptop computer that you use at work, and then take your laptop home at night and connect to the Internet, someone on the Internet could easily access the information you make available on your Personal Web server. If the information on your personal Web site is private, or contains corporate secrets, then you could be at risk of unauthorized access.

We immediately wondered whether this page was accessible to anyone in the world through the Internet. To find out, we typed into our Web browser the temporary IP address assigned to us on our dial-up connection, and to our astonishment, there was our personal home office Web page, available to the world:

Even worse, we had configured this Web page—intended only for use within the home office—to allow "directory browsing" to allow access to various files on any of our hard disks.

The Personal Web server feature included in Windows 98 is a useful feature: you can place a link on your Web site that allows a visitor to that Web site to browse through the directories on your hard disk. This is useful to us because we want to access files on that computer from other computers on the network in our home office.

But clearly there was a very serious risk here: if someone managed to find our personal Web server while we were connected to the Internet, then he or she could easily access any of the files on that computer.

We tried out the theory. From the Internet we typed into our Web browser our temporary IP number, followed by the letter assigned to one of the hard drives on our computer. To our surprise, there were all of our computer files, accessible to anyone in the world with a Web browser:

```
207.181.99.175 - /DriveC/ - Netscape
File  Edit  View  Go  Communicator  Help

  Back  Forward  Reload  Home  Search  Guide  Print  Security  Stop

  Bookmarks   Location: http://207.181.99.175/DriveC/

  Internet   New and Cool   Look Up   Netcaster
```

207.181.99.175 - /DriveC/

```
[To Parent Directory]
  02/07/98   7:34 AM          17038  980630NEW02 CI-DONATE30.htm
  02/07/98   7:34 AM           1069  980630NEW02 CI-DONATE30.txt
  27/07/98   5:01 PM             60  AUTOEXEC.001
  07/07/98   2:43 PM            267  AUTOEXEC.002
  28/07/98  11:08 AM            335  AUTOEXEC.BAT
  27/07/98   5:53 PM              4  AUTOEXEC.DOS
  28/07/98  11:08 AM            267  AUTOEXEC.M01
  02/07/98   3:23 PM          <dir>  back
  23/07/98  10:41 AM          <dir>  christa
  11/05/98   8:01 PM          93880  COMMAND.COM
  07/07/98   4:45 PM            155  CONFIG.001
  27/07/98   5:01 PM            192  CONFIG.002
  24/06/98   8:31 AM             50  CONFIG.DOS
  27/07/98   5:53 PM            157  CONFIG.SYS
  14/07/98  10:25 AM          <dir>  CSTemp
  07/07/98  12:20 PM            224  DBLSPACE.INI
  07/07/98   6:41 PM         491215  drudma.exe
  08/07/98   9:19 AM          <dir>  effects
  27/07/98   4:49 PM          <dir>  eSafe
  08/07/98  11:35 AM          <dir>  Galleries
```

```
Start     207.181....   Paint Shop...   PWS Quic...   Personal ...                9:52 AM
```

After seeing this, we turned off the Personal Web server in a hurry.

What is the risk here? Imagine this:

- You have installed Personal Web server on your laptop and have made "directory browsing" available to your co-workers on that personal Web server.

- You take your computer home at night, and dial into the Internet.

- A hacker on the Internet tries several IP numbers that are used by a particular ISP to see if there are any personal Web servers available. The hacker discovers the IP address for your computer, which is linked to the Internet through a dial-up connection, and can access your personal Web server.

- Once into your personal Web server the hacker sees that you have the directory browsing feature included on your Web site, getting full access to every file on your computer.

Should you use Personal Web server? Perhaps. It can be a useful feature. But be very cautious about using the directory browsing feature when doing so, and be cautious when dialing into the Internet from home; in fact, consider turning off the personal Web sharing capability (temporarily at least; it is easily done).

So sometimes significant security problems occur simply because you set something up to do something and don't realize the implications of what you have done.

Many people who work in organizations, both small and large, are using the Personal Web server found on Windows 98 or the Personal Web server programs available on Macintosh computers as a means of sharing business documents and other information with their co-workers through the corporate network to which they are linked while at work.

But then at night they take their laptops home and dial in to the Internet. They still have their personal Web server available, putting themselves at risk. Suddenly, their machine is open to anyone with a little bit of smarts about the Personal Web sharing feature.

Grim Statistics

According to the FBI's National Computer Crime Squad, less than 15% of all computer crimes are detected. And only 10% of these are reported.

How to Protect Your Computer and Your Data From Attack

Given the security risks that we have illustrated in the preceding pages, what steps can you take to protect yourself?

Step 1: Use a PC Firewall

After reading about our experiences above, now you understand why a firewall for your PC might be necessary. Throughout 1999, you are bound to see more coverage given to the concept of the PC firewall.

A firewall is a software program that protects your computer or network from unauthorized access while you are connected to the Internet. It works by applying a series of rules to the connections that come to your computer or network from the Internet or with respect to your connections to the Internet. These rules define what visitors can and cannot do when trying to access your computer or network and what individuals on your computer or network can do when trying to access information on the Internet.

A firewall may have rules in place that will restrict all inbound access, thus providing very good protection against attack from the outside world (assuming the firewall itself can't be hacked, and some have been). In the case above, a personal firewall can keep a personal Web server from being available to the world when you dial in to the Internet.

Or if you want to make a Web server available to the world on your network, a firewall can be set up with a rule that permits any inbound visitor from the Internet trying to reach your Web site to reach only the computer on your network that hosts your Web site, or to only access the specific program on your machine that is running your Web site.

Firewalls are a technically complex topic, and we can't hope to completely describe what they do. But in a nutshell, they define what is permitted in terms of who is trying to come into, or go out of, your computer system or network. Suffice it to say, they are one of the primary ways of protecting computers when linked to the Internet.

Firewalls have traditionally only been used by large and medium-sized companies with permanent connections to the Internet. But given the increasing number of security exposures occurring on the Internet, it is becoming essential for individual Internet users to install firewalls on their personal computers. As a result, you may want to consider installing a firewall, even if you are a single user accessing the Internet through a dial-up connection.

Even Microsoft recognizes the importance of the PC-based firewall. In August 1998, a well-known hacker group, Cult of the Dead Cow, released a tool that they indicated (subject to some debate in the security community) could compromise any Windows 95/98 computer linked to the Internet. In response, Microsoft noted on its security page that users should protect themselves by "insulating themselves from direct connection to the Internet with proxy servers and/or firewalls wherever possible," among other things. (A proxy is not exactly the same as a firewall, but also provides rules with respect to security.)

Signal 9 Solutions, a Canadian company, sells a personal computer firewall for Windows 95/98 systems for about $50. You can download an evaluation version of Signal 9's PC firewall software at **www.signal9.com.** Installation of the program is straightforward; indicate the type of connection that you have to the Internet:

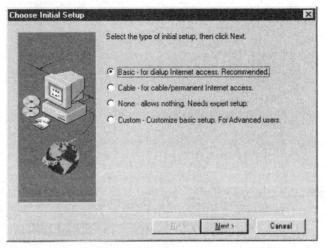

follow a few other steps, and you're done.

You are now protected against unauthorized access. The program is technically complex: what you see on the screen when it is running isn't necessarily user-friendly:

And if you want to edit the "rules" that come with the program (so that you can allow a connection in through PCAnywhere, which we look at later in this book), then you must become quite familiar with TCP/IP addressing:

But the program does work well. We went back to the Rootshell site that we discussed earlier, and Rootshell was unable to access our computer as it had before. The firewall effectively blocked it, even though we had the Windows "file and printer sharing" feature turned on:

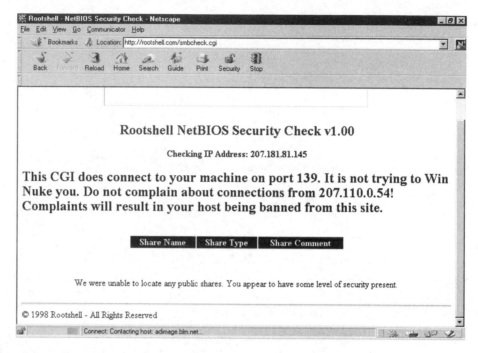

PC-based firewall programs are becoming a reality, even though their need is still being debated. Our experiences convinced us that we wanted to do something to provide an element of protection. One company in the business of developing firewall software for users of the Internet commented in the *Globe and Mail* that the "biggest challenge is not keeping hackers at bay but convincing individual computer users that they need firewall protection at all."

What about Macintosh computers? Is there a similar risk? Visit some of the hacker sites above, and you can find all kinds of security exploits with Macintosh systems. Hence people in this community need to be security cognizant as well.

tip PCSecure

PCSecure is another personal firewall product to consider. You can download a free evaluation copy at **www.pcsecure.com/SBI_Mall**.

Step 2: Always Download the Latest Fixes and Updates For Your Web Browser

If you examine a site like Rootshell, you will see that many of the security problems that are emerging on the Internet are weaknesses discovered with the Netscape and Microsoft Web browsers. Usually, as soon as a security problem is identified, each company releases a patch to its browser, or a completely new version of the browser, to deal with the problem. So it pays to remain cognizant of the security problems appearing with these browsers and ensure that you are working with the most recent version.

Similar problems occur with other software that you might be using for e-mail, IRC, USENET newsgroups, or other purposes. Hence you should always check the Web site of the developer or vendor to see if those programs have had problems as well.

Step 3: Check the Security of Your E-mail Program

When you think about Internet security, the image that first comes to mind is that of a hacker breaking into your computer through the Internet. While that risk shouldn't be overlooked, neither should you overlook security weaknesses in your e-mail program. Vulnerabilities have been discovered in most of the major e-mail programs that would allow someone to send you an e-mail message that would end up erasing files on your hard drive. We strongly recommend that you visit the Web site of your e-mail program to find out whether you need to take any precautions to safeguard your computer from malicious e-mail messages.

tip Where to Get Security Updates For Your Web Browsers and E-mail Programs

Both Netscape and Microsoft have set up Web pages to publicize the latest security holes that have been discovered in their browsers and e-mail programs. These Web sites also provide files that users can download to fix the problems that have been identified. Microsoft's security page can be accessed at **www.microsoft.com/security**. For information on security problems affecting Netscape's browser and e-mail software, visit **home.netscape.com/products/security/index.html** or **home.netscape.com/products/security/resources/notes.html**. If you use Eudora as your e-mail program, security updates can be found at **www.eudora.com**.

Step 4: Do Not Use the Same Passwords Repeatedly

Another thing to think about when it comes to Internet security is password security. If you are a frequent user of the Internet, then you know that you can quickly accumulate lots of passwords that you need to access various sites. For example, you may need passwords to access online newspapers, research databases, members-only sections of Web sites, other e-mail accounts you may own, and custom news services.

For security reasons you should never use the same user ID and password for more than one Web site. After all, someone at that site, such as an employee of that company, could use your password and user ID to see if you have used that for other services on the Internet.

In addition, the user ID and password that you use to connect to your Internet service provider should not be reused on Web sites. To understand why, think about all the keys that you have on your key chain. Now imagine if you could use the same key to access everything: your car, your house, your office, your mailbox, your safety deposit box, etc. While this would certainly be convenient, it increases your risk substantially. If you lost that one key, the person who finds it would have access to almost everything you own. However, if you have different keys for different purposes, losing one key wouldn't be as catastrophic.

On the Internet you reduce your risk substantially if you use different user IDs and passwords for different purposes. That way, if someone were to find out one of your passwords, she wouldn't have access to all of the Web sites that you subscribe to.

However, this is easier said than done. Keeping track of all of your passwords and user IDs can quickly become a daunting task. And then there's the problem of finding a secure place to store them all. Most people tend to scrawl them down on a piece of paper, which quickly gets lost.

If you try to commit all of your passwords to memory, it's easy to forget which password is associated with which Web site.

There is a way to manage your Internet passwords and minimize the risk that you will forget them or someone will steal them: use a software program that manages passwords. Some of the most popular password management programs are listed below.

PASSWORD MANAGEMENT PROGRAMS

Password Manager	**www.celcoserv.com**
Password Keeper	**www.execpc.com/~sbd/**
PassMan	**www.ijen.com**
Web Confidential (Macintosh)	**www.web-confidential.com**

To see what these programs can do, let's take a look at Password Manager. You can specify multiple accounts, providing the user ID, password, and Web site for each:

Simply click on any of the items, and you will be taken to the site. You can also set up the program so that it provides the user ID and password to the site directly for you.

Access to the program is itself restricted through a special password that you provide. In this way, you can be sure that someone doesn't access the program and make off with all of your passwords. And keep in mind that just because these programs protect access to your passwords with a password, you shouldn't assume that they are unbreakable. When it comes to security, trust no one and nothing;

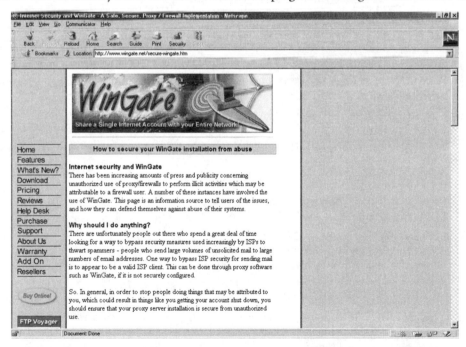

Step 5: Consider a Security Audit

One of the authors has a home network linked permanently to the Internet through a cable modem. The network includes four Windows computers, a Macintosh, and a couple of Unix servers. It's protected—or so we believed—through WinGate, a Windows-based proxy/firewall program, a program that is also useful to connect more than one computer to the Internet. (We wrote extensively about WinGate (**www.wingate.net**) in our 1998 Canadian Internet Handbook.)

But preparing this chapter made us rather concerned. Had we done enough to protect ourselves, even though we had put in place a firewall? We decided to find out.

Learning About Security

The first thing that we did was take an extensive look at whether there were any security concerns with the firewall program we used.

There were. We had never looked before, but found that the WinGate site had extensive information on known security holes that would exist in the program if configured in a certain way:

We followed the recommended procedures to plug this gap, and we now visit the WinGate site regularly to learn whether new potential problems have been posted. Second, we read the documentation in-depth, several times, to ensure that we understood what we were doing in configuring our firewall.

This is important: if you are going to get involved with a program that promises to provide security, make sure you take the time to understand it, and ensure that you follow recommended procedures to maximize its security potential. On an ongoing basis visit the Web sites of any Internet security products you use to keep yourself up-to-date on any security holes that have been discovered in the programs.

A Security Audit

The second thing we did was arrange for two security tests. There are many organizations that are becoming involved in what is loosely referred to as "ethical hacking." These companies will arrange for some of their computer staff, many of whom are familiar with the relentless security exposures with particular computer hardware and software related to the Internet and other technologies, to attempt to break into a system or to probe its weaknesses.

Computer Security Canada (**www.csci.ca**) and IBM Canada (**www.can.ibm.com**) are two of many organizations that provide ethical hacking services. We asked each of them to probe and to test our home network and firewall, to see what they could learn, and let us know whether we were subject to any type of risk.

CSCI went first, and within a day, gave us a FAIL grade. What did they find? Lo and behold, we thought we had turned off "file and printer sharing" on our firewall machine, but we had not. A standard probe by them found the vulnerability. The risk? Someone with a little bit of smarts could have accessed our firewall machine and perhaps opened up our firewall to permit any type of access to our computer. We quickly shut it down.

They also made us aware of a potential risk in which our domain name could be "hijacked" and redirected somewhere else. We were still learning about this issue at the time we finished writing this chapter.

IBM was next. They tested and probed our system over a period of a few days. We could see the many things they were trying within a few of the logs generated by our firewall and Web server. They tried both well-known and relatively unknown and obscure attacks to see if they could break in through the Web server. They also tried "denial of service" attacks to see if they could shut down our network or any of the computers on the network from afar. Then they tried to compromise the setup of the firewall itself.

We had long conversations with the IBM security specialist, David Gamay, each and every day, to understand what he was trying out. The educational part of the exercise was worth its weight in gold.

And it paid off. We were given a clean bill of health; our network is reasonably secure.

What Do You Get From a Security Audit?

We had a big sigh of relief at this point. But a long conversation with Gamay at IBM Canada made us aware that such a sigh of relief is but a momentary one. Why? Having a security test done provides an understanding of your security as of a point in time. As soon as you change your configuration, add new software, or do something else, you are potentially subject to risk again.

CSCI had stated this in its report:

Passing a security audit does not guarantee that a site is fully secure against every kind of electronic penetration. Given the overwhelming increase in the number of Internet attacks from worldwide sources and increased sophistication of novel attack methodologies that emerge daily, penetration techniques often outstrip the ability of electronic audits to detect all of them. Passing an electronic audit does, however, usually demonstrate that a certain level of due diligence has been executed to secure the site.

What to Look For in an Ethical Hacker

Our experience with the security audit convinced us that this is something that anyone with a type of Internet investment beyond merely surfing the Web with a dial-up connection should explore. If you have a dedicated, 24-hour connection to the Internet or if you have linked a network to the Internet, you should strongly consider such an audit. The cost ranges from several hundred to several thousand dollars, depending on the service that you choose. In particular, keep in mind that many companies will provide a custom quote of the cost of such an audit, based on the estimated time they will dedicate to the test, the complexity of the audit, and many other factors. Hence it is impossible to give a precise cost for any given situation.

While the cost of a security audit may seem expensive, it can be a small price to pay when you consider the cost of undoing the damage that a hacker can inflict on your computers.

There are many ethical hacker businesses; it has become a serious business. So if you decide to go this route, there are certain criteria to consider in selecting an ethical hacker:

- **Track record.** How long have they been in the business? What is their experience?

- **Clients.** What clients have used them in the past? Are references available?

- **Methodology and tools.** Do they describe their methodology? What tools do they use? What process will they follow? You should expect to be educated on what they are doing as they do it.

- **Resource and liability.** Are they willing to provide some type of guarantee with respect to what they have done?

- **What do they do to keep up-to-date?** How do their staff keep up-to-date on the many security issues that are emerging?

You can learn more about IBM Canada's ethical hacking services at **www.can.ibm.com**:

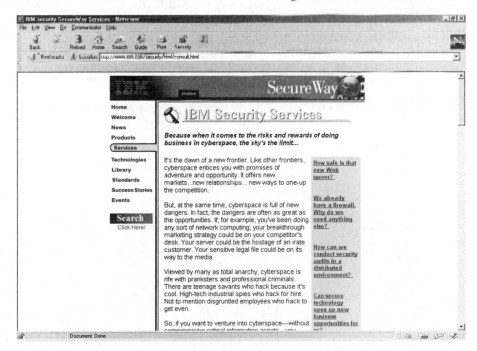

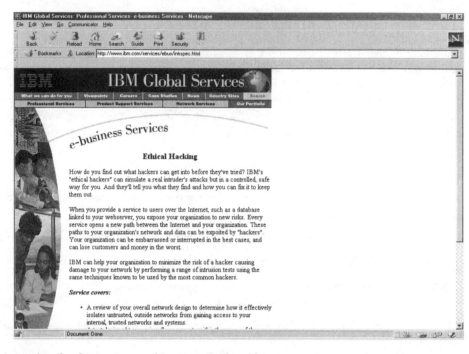

The site makes for fascinating reading in and of itself.

And you can learn more about Computer Security Canada and their services at **www.csci.ca**:

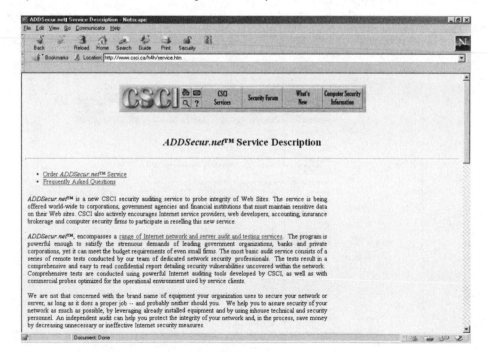

Being Security Conscious Is Key

Finally, above all, recognize that security related to the Internet is nothing less than a state of mind.

There is a basic fact that you should come to expect by using the Internet: your computer or network will be constantly subject to probes while you are online, particularly if you have a dedicated connection to the Internet such as through a cable modem, but even if you have a dial-up connection to the Internet. Gamay tells us that, with the special software he runs, he can see "probes" being made against his machine when he is dialed into the Internet, which are obviously being done with the purpose of trying to find any openings or weaknesses.

This means that you must be security conscious at all times and must keep up-to-date with security issues. Ensure that you always have the latest browser, Web server, or other software, since such programs are regularly updated to solve various security problems that have arisen. You must monitor the Internet to understand what new security risks are emerging that might affect you, and, in essence, you have to commit to keeping up-to-date with security issues. Recognize that change is the enemy: as soon as you change something on your system, you might be putting yourself at risk again.

Based on our own experiences and what we learned throughout the security audits that we underwent, a security audit can be an invaluable exercise in both learning about security and understanding the very risk that you might be up against.

Finally, it should be pointed out that no computer or computer network can ever be completely immune from attack through the Internet. The suggestions offered in this chapter will help you to substantially reduce your risk of falling victim to computer crime, but you will never be able to eliminate the risk completely. Perhaps most importantly, never let your guard down. As George Colony, the President of Forrester Research (**www.forrester.com**), puts it: "think of computer security as a guerrilla war that will last forever."

Improving Your Productivity on the Internet

If you have been using the Internet for a few years, you have probably settled into a fairly comfortable routine. You know what to do and how to do it. But you may not necessarily be completely productive while you are online. In this section we offer practical guidance on how to become more productive on the Internet.

In Chapter 8, "Practical Productivity Tips," we take an extensive look at the many tools, tips, and techniques that you can use to enhance your productivity online. There's a flood of new, innovative software being released for the Internet, and we profile some of the most useful tools that we have discovered.

One of the most common complaints of Internet users is that it isn't fast enough. Is there anything more frustrating than waiting for a Web page to load? So in Chapter 9, "Speeding Up Your Internet Connection," we take a look at a variety of methods that you can use to deal with the speed issue. This includes an assessment of the new high-speed technologies now available in Canada as well as a number of practical methods to speed up a modem-based connection to the Internet.

Many surveys indicate that e-mail is one of the most used Internet applications. But many e-mail users may not be really taking advantage of its capabilities if they don't know how to archive and access old electronic mail, a topic we cover in Chapter 10, "Knowledge Management."

Do you travel and take the Internet with you? If you do, then Chapter 11 is for you. In "Videophones and Remote Internet Connectivity" we show you how you can keep in touch with the folks back home or at the office through the Internet by using remote connectivity software and online videoconferencing. Both technologies have matured rapidly, making them a serious method of ensuring you stay in touch while you are on the road.

One of the most effective ways of improving your productivity on the Internet is to take advantage of the many search programs that have become available, a topic we examine in Chapter 12, "Just-in-Time Knowledge Using Search Accelerators." Type your search, and have these programs check multiple search engines for you!

Finally, in Chapter 13, "Knowledge Monitoring," we walk you through some of the newsclipping services that are available on the Internet. Using such tools, you will be able to keep on top of specific issues, companies, and topics that interest you.

chapter eight

Practical Productivity Tips

It doesn't matter whether you are new to the Internet or an experienced Web veteran. You can always use something that will make your online experience faster, easier and less confusing.

"Essential Internet Utilities Make Your Life On the Web A Lot Easier For Not a Lot of Money," *Dayton Daily News*, January 27, 1998

Highlights

1. Customize search engines to meet your information needs.

2. Create your own starting page in your Web browser.

3. Automatically "redial" busy Web sites.

4. Use a cache browser to easily find Web sites that you have previously visited.

5. Automate the process of filling out forms on the Web.

6. Monitor your favourite Web pages for any updates or changes.

7. Synchronize your bookmarks.

8. Unzip files directly from your Web browser.

9. Protect yourself against incomplete downloads.

10. Browse multiple Web sites simultaneously.

11. Capture Web pages and turn them into a presentation.

12. Share Web pages with friends and relatives.

For any given situation online, there is probably a special software application or online tool that can help you work smarter, faster, and more productively. The Internet has become a hotbed of development, with the result that there is a constant stream of new Internet-related programs being developed by individuals and organizations around the world. In addition, Web directories, search engines, and other Web content developers continuously add new capabilities to their sites, trying to stay one step ahead of the competition.

Consequently, there are many useful tools online that can increase your productivity. We can't hope to provide a complete index of such applications; to do so would be like trying to take an inventory of the number of wheat fields in Saskatchewan. But after reading this chapter, you will have discovered several new techniques for making your online experiences more productive and more enjoyable.

Our Own Unique Productivity Tools

We are in a unique and wonderful position: our careers are defined by the Internet. Unlike other people, we can devote a lot of time and energy to examining many of the tools and applications that have become available.

Throughout this book we give our perspective of many of the tools that we use. But there are many others that don't seem to fit in other chapters but have helped us to become more productive, so we take a look at some of them here.

1. Use the Personalization Features Offered By Search Engines

Most major search engines and directories now offer some type of personalization capability. By using this feature, you can set up your own version of a search engine or directory that contains only the sites, search categories, news, or other information that is relevant to you.

Let's look at an example, specifically, with the Excite search engine (**www.excite.com**). The first thing you need to do to take advantage of Excite's personalization capability is to register with the service. Keep in mind that by asking you to register, search engines and directories are seeking information that will help them build a profile of their visitors. The search engines use the demographic data they collect to sell advertising on their Web sites.

Once you have registered, you can begin to customize your personal page by choosing a "greeting" and by choosing the information categories that you would like to see on your custom page. This helps avoid many of the topic categories found in Excite that might not be relevant to you:

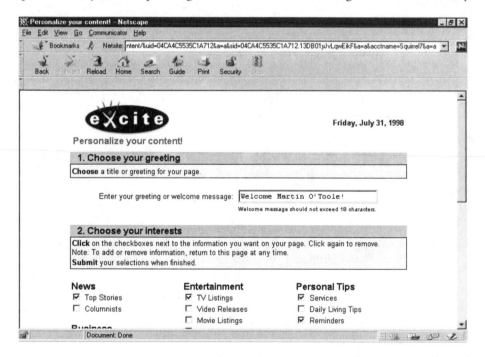

You can also specify the order in which the topics you choose will appear on the page:

One of the most powerful features in Excite and many of the other customizable search engines and directories is that you can have your page display "saved searches." This allows you to set up a number of predefined searches that will examine content on the Web, USENET, or within news sources available on that search engine or directory. The searches will be available to you every time you access your custom Web page, thus providing an effective means of keeping on top of issues or developments that are important to you.

Within our Excite custom page we have set up three custom searches, as seen on the screen below. The first two searches will look in the Excite "NewsTracker" service for any articles about "competitive intelligence" or "identity theft." The third examines USENET to see if our book is mentioned anywhere. Once we have done this, we will get a customized Excite page that features any items that it has found:

You can also use your personalized page to track specific news stories that interest you. For example, Yahoo!'s personalized information service, called My Yahoo! (**my.yahoo.com**), allows you to choose the types of news headlines that you would like to see on your custom page:

Once you have set up your choices, you get a customized Yahoo! page with only the information that you want:

Of course, My Yahoo! isn't restricted to letting you set up customized news; you can also set up your personal page to provide quick access to your favourite Yahoo! search categories. In this way, you can build a "customized Yahoo!" that features only the specific Web directory categories and listings that are important to you:

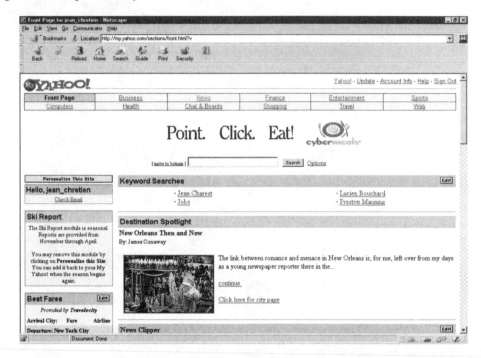

For example, if you are soon to find yourself in new career circumstances and regularly check career counselling categories to link to career placement companies, you can build a customized directory of those Yahoo! directory items:

If you spend some time exploring the personalization features of the major search engines and directories, you will see that there is a lot of flexibility. We suggest that you dedicate some time to setting up a customized version that will help you to work smarter and faster.

But keep in mind that there is a potential downside. From the perspective of the search engines and directories, personalization is all about creating marketing profiles. These services will sell to advertisers special advertising capabilities in which they can reach individuals only interested in particular topics.

So we find that with such services, you often end up seeing a lot of advertisements and "sponsored" areas on your customized Web page, more than you might see when using the regular search engine or directory.

tip Don't Lose Your Downloads

Download Butler (**www.lincolnbeach.com**) is a useful program with a built-in unzip utility to help you manage the files that you download from the Web. Once you have downloaded a zipped file, Download Butler will remember where on your computer you last extracted the file to! In addition, it will associate a Web address with each file you download so that you can find the Web site again at a later date.

2. Create Your Own Default Web Page

Another technique that you can use to improve your online productivity is to create your own default Web page that is displayed as soon as you start your Internet browser. Both Netscape and Internet Explorer are set up to display their own Web sites when you start the browser. However, why not change the default starting page to a page that contains links to the sites that you most often visit on the Web? One of the authors has such a page, and it provides quick access to many of his favourite Web sites:

To create your own personal starting page, you will need to be familiar with basic HTML. Just create a list of your favourite Web sites in your favourite HTML editor or any text-based editor (e.g., Windows Notepad, if you are using Windows 95/98), and save it using whatever file name you like. The file name then becomes the "page" name that you will use to customize your browser:

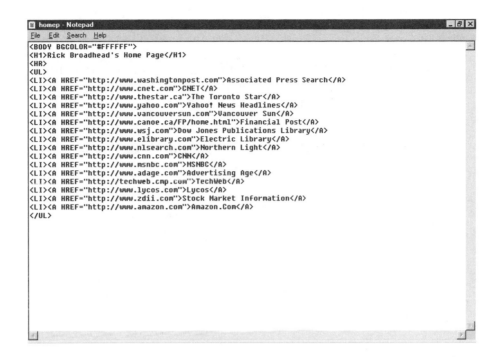

```
homep - Notepad
File  Edit  Search  Help
<BODY BGCOLOR="#FFFFFF">
<H1>Rick Broadhead's Home Page</H1>
<HR>
<UL>
<LI><A HREF="http://www.washingtonpost.com">Associated Press Search</A>
<LI><A HREF="http://www.cnet.com">CNET</A>
<LI><A HREF="http://www.thestar.ca">The Toronto Star</A>
<LI><A HREF="http://www.yahoo.com">Yahoo! News Headlines</A>
<LI><A HREF="http://www.vancouversun.com">Vancouver Sun</A>
<LI><A HREF="http://www.canoe.ca/FP/home.html">Financial Post</A>
<LI><A HREF="http://www.wsj.com">Dow Jones Publications Library</A>
<LI><A HREF="http://www.elibrary.com">Electric Library</A>
<LI><A HREF="http://www.nlsearch.com">Northern Light</A>
<LI><A HREF="http://www.cnn.com">CNN</A>
<LI><A HREF="http://www.msnbc.com">MSNBC</A>
<LI><A HREF="http://www.adage.com">Advertising Age</A>
<LI><A HREF="http://techweb.cmp.com">TechWeb</A>
<LI><A HREF="http://www.lycos.com">Lycos</A>
<LI><A HREF="http://www.zdii.com">Stock Market Information</A>
<LI><A HREF="http://www.amazon.com">Amazon.Com</A>
</UL>
```

Next, configure your Web browser so that it calls up this page whenever you start your browser, or select the "Home" button on your browser's menu bar. You can do this in Netscape 4.0 by choosing "Edit," then "Preferences." In the "Navigator" area of the window that appears, you can indicate the page that you want to use as your start page:

If using Netscape 3.0, select "General Preferences" under the "Options" menu. Under "Startup," type the location of your custom homepage in the box that appears below "Browser Starts With." In Internet Explorer 3.0 select "Options" under the "View" menu, then select the "Navigation" tab. You can change your starting page in the area labelled "Customize." In Internet Explorer 4.0 select "Internet Options" under the "View" menu, then select the "General" tab. Here you can change the page you use for your homepage.

You can even import your bookmark file, and then edit it within the Web editing program that you use. Provide a link to all the important sites that you regularly visit; then every time you start your Web browser or click on the home button in the browser, you will be taken to your custom start page:

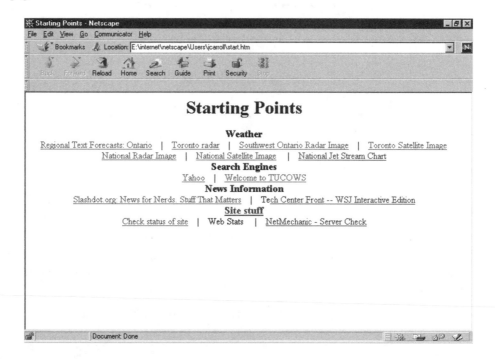

Not surprisingly, there are programs on the market that make it easy for you to create your own starting page. One of these is StartGen from Braindance (**www.braindance.com**). StartGen allows you to quickly and easily develop a customized start page for your Netscape or Microsoft Web browser. The sample starting page StartGen provides includes a number of predefined sites, mostly consisting of various search engines:

When you have finished choosing the items you want to appear on your custom Web page, it will automatically generate that page and set it up within your browser as the default homepage:

You can easily add additional Web sites to your custom start page by providing their Web address and a description:

Once finished, you have a handy little start page configured within your browser that you will see every time you start the browser or when you press the "Home" button within your browser.

3. "Redial" Busy Web Sites While You Work on Other Tasks

How many times have you tried to access a Web site or an FTP site only to find that you can't get in because the site is too busy? We find that this happens often with Web pages related to some breaking news story or "live" Web broadcast and will happen with FTP sites that contain very popular programs or files.

Rather than checking back again and again, try JackHammer (**www.sausage.com/jackhammer**), a great utility that will keep trying a busy Web site or FTP site for you until it gets through. You can work on other tasks while JackHammer works quietly in the background. Think of it as a "redial" service for the Internet.

How could you use such a program? Imagine that you are trying to buy Spice Girls tickets online for your daughter, and the ticketing site is very busy. No problem. Simply set up JackHammer to monitor the ticketing site for you:

The program keeps attempting to access these sites, and when it does gain access, you are notified by way of a box that pops up on your screen.

tip Print More Productively

If you are using a Hewlett Packard printer, consider using HP's Web PrintSmart software (available at **www.hp.com/peripherals2/webprintsmart/index.html**). This software will allow you to take pages from several different Web sites and then print them as a single document with consistent formatting. The software will automatically add a Table of Contents to the file and provide a convenient index of all the Web links that appeared on the Web pages you have chosen.

4. Keep Track of Previously Viewed Web Sites

Another problem that we and many others have when using the Internet is forgetting where a particular Web site is located. How many times have you wanted to go back to a Web site that you visited before but you can't remember the address and didn't bookmark it? Fortunately, there are a few ways to get around this problem.

As you probably know, when you surf the Web, your Web browser usually keeps a copy of the pages that you visit on your own hard drive.

If you go back to those Web sites again and the specific pages that you looked at before have not changed, your browser will obtain a copy of the page and the images on it from your hard drive rather than from the Internet. This saves you a lot of time when surfing and is why you will often find that a Web site seems faster when you visit it a second time.

This process of storing Web pages on your hard drive is called "caching," and the area of your hard drive that stores these copies is called a "cache." This means that on your computer there are copies of many of the Web pages that you have previously visited. Exactly how many are stored there will depend on the settings in your browser; if you have not adjusted the settings, then they will be the default settings on your computer.

You can view your cache settings in both Netscape and Internet Explorer.

If using Netscape 3.0, select "Network Preferences" under the "Options" menu. In Netscape 4.0 choose "Preferences" under the "Edit" menu and then double click on the "Advanced" option that appears on the left-hand side of the window. Then select "Cache":

If using Internet Explorer 3.0, select "Options" under the "View" menu, and then choose the "Advanced" tab. Next, choose "Settings" in the "Temporary Internet files" box:

If using Internet Explorer 4.0, choose "Internet Options" under the "View" option, then select the "General" tab. Under the section "Temporary Internet Files" choose "Settings" to view the amount of disk space being used.

Your browser's cache can be a powerful tool if you know how to extract information from it, particularly if you want to return to a Web site that you had visited recently but can't remember the address. This is where a program called a "cache browser" can be very useful. A cache browser indexes all the information within your browser's cache and allows you to browse through a list of previously visited Web pages. Some cache browsers will also allow you to browse those Web pages while you are not connected to the Internet. Most cache browser programs allow a great deal of flexibility in specifying how much information you can store in your cache.

Secret Agent (**www.ariel.co.uk**), one of many cache browsers that you can download from the Internet, takes just seconds to set up. Once it has been installed, you can search for particular words or phrases within your cache:

You can find quite a few cache programs for both Windows and Macintosh systems in TUCOWS (**www.tucows.com**). Look in the "Cache Viewers" category within the "Browsers and Accessories" section.

POPULAR CACHE BROWSERS

UnMozify	**www.evolve.co.uk**
WebCache	**alpha1.fsb.hr/~dzorc/webcache.html**
Secret Agent	**www.ariel.co.uk**
Netscape/Internet Explorer Cache Explorer	**www.mwso.com**

In addition to using a cache browser, you should make yourself familiar with the "history" list within your Web browser. The history list contains a lengthy list of the sites and Web pages that you have recently visited. If you are using Netscape 3.0, select "Window," then "History." Within Netscape 4.0 you can access your history list by selecting "Communicator," then "History":

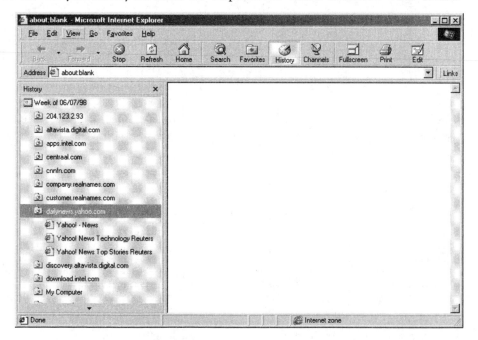

If using Internet Explorer 3.0, select "Go," then "Open History Folder." Within Internet Explorer 4.0 you can find your history list under the "Explorer Bar" found under the "View" menu:

Both Netscape and Internet Explorer allow you to control the length of time that Web addresses remain in your history file. It's generally a good idea to keep all the Web addresses you visit for at least 2 to 3 weeks, since you never know when you're going to want to look up a site that you recently visited.

There are specialized programs that you can download from the Internet which take the "history" concept one step further. Consider the program called WebTree (**www.paw-print.com**), which allows you to build a "map" of the Web sites that you have visited. The program keeps track of your activities as you use the Web and makes it very easy to find any of the Web pages you have recently visited:

In addition, the program will examine your cache every few minutes and add Web sites to the list; it also keeps a much more extensive and far better organized list than what you get with the history command in either browser.

5. Fill Out Online Forms Automatically

One thing about the Web today: you will become sick and tired of filling out forms.

Many Web sites ask that you fill out a form in order to download a file or gain access to a special area of the site. Since most of these forms ask for the same type of personal information (e.g., your name, mailing address, e-mail address), you can save yourself a lot of time by using a program called a "form browser." These programs allow you to store personal information about yourself in a file and then quickly transfer any of your stored information to an online form without having to retype it.

A good example is FormBot (**www.connect-pal.com/formbot**). Within FormBot you have a choice of two kinds of "templates": a Web template, with information that you might enter into a form such as your name, address, etc., and an access template, for the storage of common user IDs and passwords for Web sites that you frequently access:

ConnectPal FormBot organises your information for web data into two categories. Web Template and Access Template. Web Template holds your general information (first name, last name, email address, street, etc) in one intuitive and simple to use interface. Through this interface, you can then copy and paste the data into those web forms without the need to repetitively type in the same information over and over again. The Access Template holds your username and password for password protected sites. ConnectPal FormBot has the capability to scan your current webpages and auto display a dialog box with your pre-defined username and password for that site without you having to remember which password is for which web site.

Please choose type of template to create :

◉ Web Template

◯ Access Template

[Next >>]   [Cancel]

You can create different templates for the different types of forms you frequently encounter:

Name of Web Template :   General Web stuff

Editing Web Template Values

List of Template Values :

Sampson
Martin
123 Anderson Str
St. Catharines
New Brunswick
514.1212.1212

Enter Template Value to Add :

[Add Value]

[Delete Value]

[Modify Value]

[Up] [Down]   [Clear Template List]

Input Mode
◯ None
◯ Space
◉ Carriage Return/Line Feed

[OK]

[Cancel]

[Help]

You can specify that each item above be entered in the form with either a space, no additional information, or a "Carriage Return/Line Feed." You would normally select the latter, so that each line in your template is entered into the form you are filling out on a separate line, thus filling out the form in entirety:

An Input Mode dictates the appearance of the values when pasted onto a text field. There are three (3) input modes, namely "None", "Space" and "Carriage Return/Line Feed" or CRLF for short. Each input mode specifies which character(s) would be inserted in between Web Template Values. For Input Mode "None", no character would be inserted. For example, when the Web Template Values "Firstname" and "Lastname" are chosen together and pasted onto a text field in a web form, the exact strings being pasted would be "FirstnameLastname". With Input Mode "Space", the exact strings pasted would be "Firstname Lastname" (Note the space character between the firstname and the lastname). Similarly, CRLF would place each value on a new line. Hence, the CRLF input mode is useful for multiline descriptions.

To store web values which are multiline in nature, create a separate web template with the Input Mode as "Carriage Return/Line Feed".

Please select Input Mode :

     ○ None   ○ Space   ● Carriage Return/Line Feed

[<< Back] [Finish] [Cancel]

Visit a Web site, see a form, select the template that contains your information in the right order, press a key, and the form will be filled out for you.

POPULAR FORM BROWSERS

FormBot	**www.connect-pal.com/formbot**
Dropit	**www.spinnerbaker.com/dropit.htm**

6. Monitor Web Pages For Changes

You probably have a number of Web pages that you regularly visit to see if there have been any updates. There are a number of programs that will help you automate this task so that you don't have to do the checking yourself. NetLookOut (**www.primenet.com/~ckennedy/software/lookout**) is a good example of what is possible. You can import into the program a listing of Web sites and addresses from your bookmark file and add additional sites manually. You then simply tell the program to check to see if the sites have changed since you last visited them, and within a few seconds you will have a summary:

Description	Status	Last Checked	Last Changed
Check All	Reset All	New Web	New FTP	New Gopher

Description	Status	Last Checked	Last Changed
Internet	No change	Fri Jul 31 14:36:...	Fri Mar 21 15:25:...
Yahoo! Comp...	No change	Fri Jul 31 14:36:...	Mon Jul 20 09:3...
TB's Video Site	Checking...	Fri Jul 31 14:36:...	Mon Jul 20 09:5...
Codec Central...	Checking...	Fri Jul 31 14:36:...	Mon Jul 20 09:5...
MPEG . ORG ...	Host unavailable	Fri Jul 31 14:36:...	Mon Jul 20 09:5...
Online Store	No change	Fri Jul 31 14:36:...	Sun Jul 26 17:4...
rootshell.com -...	Checking...	Fri Jul 31 14:33:...	Tue Jul 28 20:0...
Internet Prote...	Checking...	Fri Jul 31 14:33:...	Tue Jul 28 20:1...
1st quarter (Ja...	No change	Fri Jul 31 14:36:...	Tue Jul 28 20:1...
Welcome to ...	No change	Fri Jul 31 14:36:...	Tue Jul 28 20:3...
Canadian Plus...	Checking...	Fri Jul 31 14:34:...	Tue Jul 28 21:0...
TotalNEWS: a...	Host unavailable	Fri Jul 31 14:34:...	Tue Jul 28 21:0...
TROPICAL P...	Host unavailable	Fri Jul 31 14:34:...	Fri Jul 31 13:26:...

Please register!

Simple little utilities like this help you to work better, by saving you time and energy in keeping up-to-date with the information and sites that are important to you.

POPULAR WEB SITE MONITORING PROGRAMS

BookMarx	**www.msw.com.au/bwolf/index.html**
NetLookOut	**www.primenet.com/~ckennedy/software/lookout**

7. Synchronize Your Bookmarks

If you are like many Internet users, you use both Netscape Navigator and Internet Explorer. Using two different Web browsers, however, leads to a frustrating problem: you end up compiling one set of bookmarks in one browser and a completely different set of bookmarks in the other browser. Wouldn't it be convenient if you could synchronize your bookmarks so that regardless of which Web browser you're using, you have quick access to both sets of bookmarks? A handy program called SyncURLs will help you do this. Run the program, and it will take both your Internet Explorer bookmarks and your Netscape bookmarks and organize them in a single file. You can then export the merged file back to both of your browsers. Next time you use either Netscape or Internet Explorer, you have access to the same set of bookmarks. SyncURLs can be downloaded from the Hotfiles Web site at **www.hotfiles.com**. Just do a search for "SyncURLs."

8. Unzip Web Files With Ease

If you frequently download software from the Internet, then you know that most files are in "zip" format. In order to install the software, you have to "unzip" the file you downloaded. This means that you have to use an "unzip" program once the file has been downloaded to your computer. This extra step doesn't take long, but it is inconvenient when you are in a hurry. If you do a lot of downloading from the Internet, then check out NetZip (**www.netzip.com**), a useful program that simplifies the process of downloading zipped files. With NetZip you can download and unzip files without ever leaving your Web browser. NetZip starts automatically whenever you start to download a zipped file. The file is automatically uncompressed, and all the files are displayed within your Web browser for easy access:

tip Save Time With Zip Files

A program called Browse and Zip (**www.canyonsw.com**) will allow you to view the contents of a zip file without having to download the entire file from the Internet. It is available for both Netscape and Internet Explorer.

9. Protect Yourself From Incomplete Downloads

Have you ever been in the middle of downloading a large file from a Web site, and then were disconnected for some unknown reason? It happens to us all the time, and it's extremely frustrating because you have to start downloading the entire file from the very beginning. To put an end to this kind of misery, consider using a program like Bullet Proof FTP (available at **www.bpftp.com**). Bullet Proof FTP allows you to resume downloading a file if you get disconnected for almost any reason. For example, if you have downloaded 75% of a file, and your modem accidentally gets turned off, Bullet Proof FTP will resume the downloading right where you left off and will get the remaining 25% of the file, saving you lots of time and aggravation.

POPULAR PROGRAMS THAT WILL RESUME INTERRUPTED DOWNLOADS	
Bullet Proof FTP	**www.bpftp.com**
CuteFTP	**www.cuteftp.com**
FileHound	**www.allaboutgames.com/albinofrog**
GetRight	**www.headlightsw.com**

10. Browse Multiple Web Sites Simultaneously

While browsing the Web, you will sometimes need to have several Web sites on your screen at the same time. For example, suppose you come across an interesting article on Yahoo! while doing a search on some music-related topic. While reading the article you want to see if a particular CD that they mention is available on the Internet, and you would also like to see if anyone has written any books about this particular musical group. Is there an easy way to look at all of these Web sites at the same time?

Katiesoft Scroll (**www.katiesoft.com**), despite its rather bizarre name, is a unique product that allows you to view and control up to four Web sites simultaneously. It can be used with both Internet Explorer and Netscape Communicator:

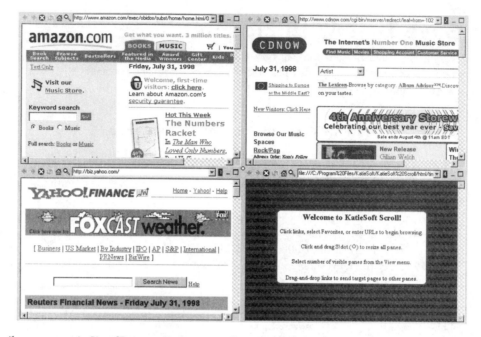

A similar program is SimulBrowse (**www.sea-glass.com**), which works only within Internet Explorer. It places tabs at the bottom of your Web browser for up to 15 sites that you are concurrently accessing:

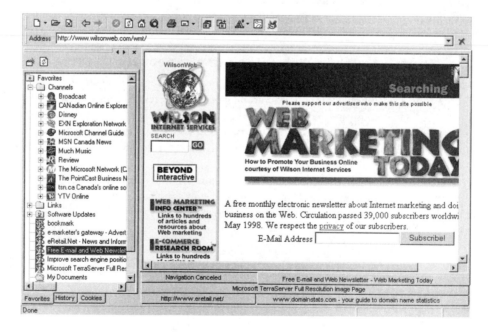

Two simple and straightforward applications. It's often the small things that can help you to work better.

11. Capture Web Pages and Turn Them Into a Presentation

This is one of those brilliant ideas that comes along that makes us ask, Why didn't we think of that? Catch the Web (**www.catchtheweb.com**) is a program that allows you to grab Web pages, store them in an archive on your computer, and convert the stored pages into a structured presentation that you can e-mail to someone or make available through your Web site.

When you install Catch the Web, there is a small push-pin that appears in your Web browser. If you want to capture a Web page for the program, just drag the pin onto the page within your Web browser:

Then you can assign the page a title and some descriptive information:

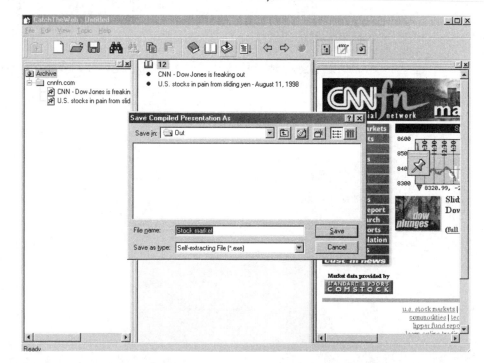

Once you have captured several, you can assemble them into the order that you want them to appear within your presentation, and then save it as a presentation file. This causes the Catch the Web program to compile a compressed file that contains all the Web pages that you have captured, including graphics. You can then e-mail this file to someone or store it on your Web site so that others can download it:

When someone downloads the file or receives it by e-mail, he or she simply double clicks on it to run it. This causes the Web pages and graphics within the file to expand to their normal form. The recipient can load the "starting" Web page into his or her Web browser:

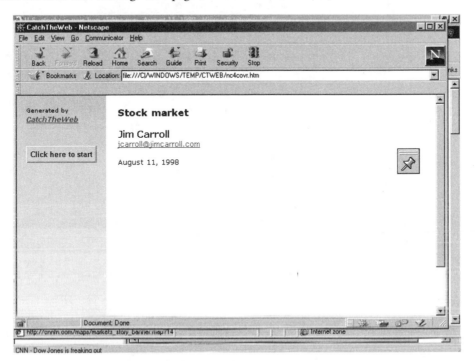

and then view each page within the presentation:

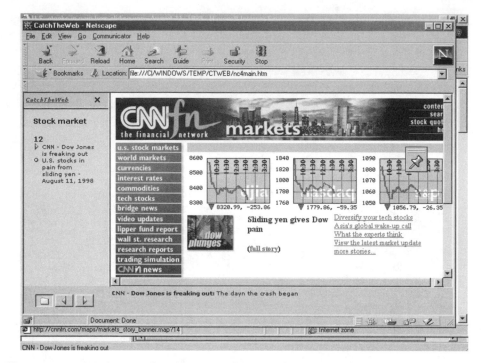

A brilliant program! We're sure that this one will be a winner and will lead to all kinds of innovative uses.

tip One Program Does It All

Have you ever tried to listen to a sound or video clip on the Web, and then discovered that you don't have the right program installed on your computer? Because different Web sites use different programs to deliver audio and video content, most Internet users end up downloading a different program for each of the different file types they want to play. Microsoft's Media Player addresses this problem by allowing you to use a *single program* to access many of the most popular types of audio/video content on the Web. You can download it from **www.microsoft.com/windows/mediaplayer/default_other.htm**.

12. Share Web Pages With Friends and Colleagues

One of the most interesting programs we have found is Hot Off The Web (**www.hotofftheweb.com**), a fascinating little utility that is fun to use. It lets you grab copies of Web pages, annotate them, and then print them or e-mail them to someone else.

You can grab a Web page within Internet Explorer in seconds. The page is then brought into the Hot Off The Web program. Then you can add text, pictures, and other information to highlight certain pieces of information on the page. For example, we have added the attention button, arrow, and sign with the cartoon character to draw attention to certain information on this page:

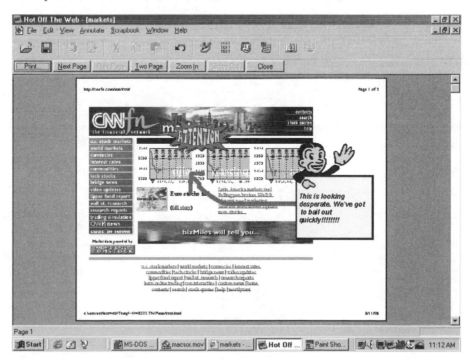

We can then print it in a format that removes all the Web browser information:

or, by selecting another button, e-mail it to someone else.

Keeping Up-to-Date With New Developments

There is a lot of fascinating new software becoming available for the Internet, much of which can help you with your day-to-day productivity as you use the Web. To keep yourself up-to-date on the latest productivity software for the Internet, we recommend that you regularly visit some of the popular software archives listed below.

POPULAR SOFTWARE ARCHIVES

DOWNLOAD.COM (Windows and Macintosh)	**www.download.com**
PC Magazine (Windows)	**www.pcmagazine.com**
TUCOWS (Windows and Macintosh)	**www.tucows.com**
DaveCentral (Windows)	**www.davecentral.com**
ZDNet Software Library (Windows and Macintosh)	**www.hotfiles.com**
SOFTSEEK.COM (Windows)	**www.softseek.com**
SlaughterHouse (Windows)	**www.slaughterhouse.com**
5Star Shareware (Windows)	**www.5star-shareware.com**

chapter nine

Speeding Up Your Internet Connection

The Internet disappoints at least as many people as it dazzles. A major reason is speed, or the lack of it.
"Getting the Web Up to Speed," *Star-Tribune* **(Minneapolis-St. Paul), July 5, 1998**

Highlights

1. High-speed Internet access technologies such as cable modems, ADSL, and satellite access will speed up your connection to the Internet, but the speed improvements these technologies provide are relative.

2. Browser accelerators work by fetching Web pages while your modem is idle. They can be link-based, history-based, or use a combination of both technologies.

3. Search accelerators work in this way: while you are looking at one of the results produced after a search, the search accelerator fetches the next page in the list of search results. Naviscope is an example of a search accelerator.

4. There are programs available now, for example, TweakDUN, that will help you optimize your Windows 95/98 settings so that you can browse the Web faster.

5. Many Internet users have reported noticeable speed improvements by using a Norwegian-developed Web browser called Opera.

6. Many Internet performance problems can be identified and fixed by using an Internet diagnostic tool such as Net.Medic.

7. Tools like interMute and AdsOff! speed up your Web browsing by allowing you to filter out banner advertisements, pop-up windows, and background music from the Web pages you visit.

8. You can speed up your Internet connection by increasing the size of your hard drive and your browser's cache, boosting the amount of RAM on your computer, and turning off the graphics in your Web browser.

There probably isn't a day that goes by when you don't get frustrated with the Internet. No doubt you have experienced delays waiting for Web pages, files, or programs to download.

Help is here! There are a number of ways to speed up your access of the Internet. Some are relatively expensive, while others are not. What you can do really depends on your budget.

In this chapter we review practical ways to speed up your use of the Internet.

1. Use Cable Modem, ADSL, or Satellite Technology

Our most basic recommendation is this: if you can afford some of the new higher-speed alternatives that have become available for home-based users of the Internet, and they are available in your area, upgrade without delay.

Regular telephone lines can only support connections up to 56 Kbps. But three major competing technologies, and soon to be four, are already providing high-speed access to Internet users out of their homes across Canada. The three current major technologies are cable modems, ADSL, and satellite technology; the upcoming fourth technology is a wireless Internet service.

Speed Improvements Are Relative

One thing to keep in mind is that you should be cautious about the speed improvements that come with such technologies. Access is definitely faster with any of these technologies. However, you will still probably run into problems with certain Web sites and using the Internet at a certain time of day.

There have been some reports in the media of some individuals who are very frustrated with cable modem access to the Internet; it seems that in some cases the speed you get depends on the location of your neighbourhood. But to be fair, the cable companies are upgrading their cable networks across the country, so it should come as no surprise that there can be variation in terms of the speed of the connection.

But what is also evident from the early experience of many users of a high-speed Internet service is that they easily develop unrealistic expectations of what "fast" means. You certainly get a faster connection to the Internet, but that won't help you if you are trying to access a site on the Internet that is simply busy or has a slow connection to the Net. It doesn't help you much if it is 4:00 in the afternoon, there has been a major news story, and so many people are trying to get into the CNN Web site that it is just plain slow.

Hence you have to keep things in perspective when gauging "how fast" a service is. There is a big difference in speed when using the Internet at 4:00 a.m. compared to 5:00 p.m.

Cable Modems

In our own case, one of the authors has been using the WAVE (**www.wave.ca**) cable modem service for over a year.

It has been reliable, fast, responsive, and makes the speed of a 56 Kbps modem seem excruciatingly slow in comparison. With the price having dropped almost everywhere in Canada to $39.95 per month, high-speed Internet access is more affordable than ever before. Because WAVE is now part of the @Home network (**www.home.net**) in many parts of Canada, even faster speeds are possible. @Home runs its own high-speed Internet network that allows its customers to connect to Internet sites faster than over the traditional Internet network. @Home is able to deliver this increased speed for a number of reasons. One reason is that they store copies of popular Web sites on their network so that the information doesn't have to travel as far to get to @Home users. Another is that companies can connect their Web sites directly to the @Home network so that @Home users have direct access to those sites without having to go through the regular Internet network.

Let's put things into perspective: when we used a 56 Kbps modem to download a file, we were getting speeds of about 5 Kbps. On our WAVE @Home connection, we have seen speeds of up to 80 Kbps. Others report faster speeds still as the "cap" on the service is raised to provide even better access.

Visit the WAVE Web site at **www.wave.ca**, where you can check with your local cable company to see if cable modem access and/or @Home service is available in your area.

Another benefit of a cable modem connection is that you can set up your own Web server or other Internet servers, since you have your own full-time dedicated connection to the Internet. One of the authors uses his cable modem service to set up his own Linux server on the Internet. He uses this server to make his promotional videos available to Internet users, a topic we discuss further in Chapter 15, "Adding Audio and Video to Your Web Site."

There seem to be a lot of cable modem users who are doing the same type of thing.

ADSL

ADSL (asymmetric digital subscriber line) is the high-speed Internet service being deployed across Canada by Canada's telephone companies. ADSL works on your existing telephone line and requires a special type of modem called an ADSL modem. It provides speeds of up to 2.2 Mbps when downloading information from the Internet. You can see whether ADSL service is available in your area by visiting the Sympatico High-Speed Web site at **adsl.sympatico.ca** (Alberta residents should connect to the TELUS PLAnet Web site at **www.telusplanet.net**):

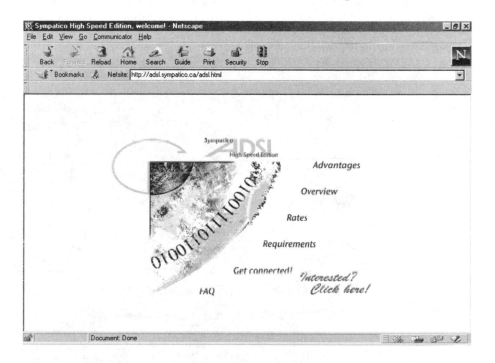

You may have heard that Sympatico has been accused of "unfair trade practices" by other Internet service providers who have not been able to offer the service at similar costs. You may be wondering what this allegation is all about.

Reports are that Sympatico is selling ADSL access for a fee that is far below cost. The industry buzz is that it costs $200 to $250 per month to support an ADSL connection, yet the Sympatico High Speed ADSL service is sold for $69.95 per month. The other Internet service providers argue that if another ISP such as Netcom wanted to sell ADSL access to the Internet, they would have to purchase ADSL connectivity from the phone companies and invest in the necessary hardware. This means that they would have to price their ADSL service at $200 to $300 per month simply to break even.

Sympatico has responded to these charges by saying they are absorbing the loss in order to compete against the WAVE cable modem service that we described above. They also argue that the market price of a cable modem connection bears no relation to the actual cost of that connection. Hence, they argue, there is no unfair competition.

Critics charge that because they are part of the Stentor group of major telephone companies, Canada's long distance and regular telephone users are subsidizing high-speed Internet access and that this represents an unfair form of competition. And in 1998, a group of Internet service providers filed an unfair competition charge with the federal government against Sympatico and Bell Canada.

By mid–1998, ADSL was available in only a few select communities across Canada. However, you can expect wider deployment throughout 1999.

Satellite Access

If you live in a remote area not serviced by cable modem or ADSL access, you can check into satellite Internet service, available from various companies including Telesat. In fact, you can learn about satellite access at the Telesat Web site, **www.telesat.ca**.

We experimented with Telesat's satellite-based Internet service in 1998. The current satellite dish used by Telesat (shown below) is somewhat larger than those used by television-based satellite services such as ExpressVu or StarChoice:

Satellite Internet technology involves a mix of low- and high-speed communications. It is based on the premise that most of the time you are retrieving a lot of information from the Internet, but aren't sending large volumes of information to the Internet. Hence information from the Internet is sent to you through a very high-speed Internet connection using the satellite dish, but anything you send back (such as e-mail or when you click on a link to go to a new Web page) is sent through a modem. So you still need a dial-up connection to the Internet, which could make the service cost-prohibitive if you live in a rural area that doesn't have a local ISP. (However, given that most of Canada's long distance phone companies have gone to a flat rate telephone plan on evenings and weekends, the economics have improved considerably.)

Our experience with the Telesat service was good: it is almost as fast as a cable modem when retrieving information from the Internet. The fact that the connection back was through a regular modem didn't seem to make much of a difference, except when we were sending files from our computer up to our Web site and sending e-mail.

Setting the service up was straightforward.

First, we set up the satellite dish. Next, we installed in our computer a special card that came with the satellite dish. This card allows for the interaction between our computer and the satellite dish. Then we connected a transmission cable (looks like the cable wire that connects to your TV) to the satellite dish and to the special card.

Next, we installed the software for the service onto our computer. Once this was done, we pointed the satellite dish in the right direction to get the best signal. You do this by first selecting your location from a list of Canadian cities:

This gives the direction your dish should be pointed (i.e., longitude—east/west, and latitude—north/south). The manual that comes with the dish will help you figure out the best place in the sky to first aim the dish. Using a compass as the starting point, we turned the satellite dish until close to the correct position. Then, while aligning the satellite dish, we ran a program that provides audio and visual indications of how good a job the user is doing:

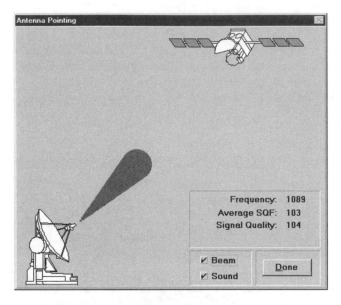

Once that was done, we dialled in to our ISP (any ISP can be used, although Sympatico is the default) and completed the connection:

Wireless Internet Technology

Finally, wireless Internet access is being developed for release in various areas of Canada in 1999. One of the companies offering the service is Western International Communications (WIC), a company best known for the radio and television stations they own.

You can learn more about WIC's wireless Internet service, called Connexus, at the WIC Web site (**www.wic.ca**). The service was in limited testing in 1998, but WIC promises deployment soon in major metropolitan areas. A small radio transmitter/receiver is connected to your computer, and the high-speed Internet connection is supported by radio transmission.

2. Use a Browser Accelerator

The second thing that you can do to speed things up while online is try out one of the many browser accelerator programs that are available on the market. You can also use these accelerators with the high-speed Internet technologies we just described.

A browser accelerator is a tool that makes Web pages appear to load more quickly in your Web browser. These programs will work over your existing Internet connection, regardless of its speed. How do they work? There are two types of browser accelerators: link-based and history-based.

A link-based browser accelerator works by "fetching" all the Web pages that are linked to the one you are currently viewing. If you decide to click on one of the links on that Web page, it will load more quickly because the entire page has already been downloaded to your hard drive. The advantage? Faster access. The disadvantage? It wastes bandwidth, since it spends a lot of time downloading pages that you may never view.

A history-based browser accelerator takes a different approach: it learns the sites that you like to visit frequently, and it regularly fetches those Web sites and stores them on your computer for faster access.

Both link-based and history-based browser accelerators work by fetching Web pages while your modem is idle. While you are busy reading a Web page, the accelerator program operates in the background, fetching other Web pages that you are likely to want to visit. There are many of these programs available; it has become a competitive market. Many of these browser accelerators offer both link-based and history-based fetching.

POPULAR BROWSER ACCELERATORS

PeakJet (link-based and history-based)	**www.peak-media.com**
Surf Express (history-based)	**www.connectix.com**
NetSonic (link-based and history-based)	**www.web3ooo.com**
NetAccelerator (link-based)	**www.imsisoft.com**

We tried one of these programs, Surf Express. We simply installed it and it went to work automatically in the background. We used it for a few days and found that over time, at least 43% of the Web pages that we viewed had already been obtained by Surf Express, making them load noticeably more quickly:

It can be very useful to utilize the features as seen above, to understand how many pages they are successfully caching. If you find they aren't caching many pages, you can modify the settings in the program to increase the number of pages they will cache.

Most of these programs offer a fair degree of flexibility in configuring how they work. PeakJet, for example, allows you to specify the size of the cache, if you want to use link-based caching at all (what it calls LookAhead caching), and whether you should use history caching (which it calls Freshener caching):

And all the programs will let you specify how much disk space should be devoted to caching, an important feature, since the amount of hard disk space that is available will vary depending on who is using the program:

There are other useful features in these programs as well. For example, Surf Express allows you to undertake a search of the cache that it builds, thus allowing you to easily find Web pages that you previously visited but couldn't locate (an issue that we discussed in Chapter 8, "Practical Productivity Tips"):

3. Use a Search Accelerator

In addition to browser accelerators there are also search accelerators, which are programs that will help you speed up your Internet searches. There are two different types of search accelerators:

• search accelerators that query several search engines simultaneously and filter the results;

• search accelerators that fetch additional pages of results before you click on them.

An example of the latter is Naviscope (**www.naviscope.com**). During installation, you tell the program what types of pages it should fetch (i.e., those marked "next" or "more") and how many pages of search results you want it to fetch and store on your hard drive:

Naviscope Setup & Registration

Browsers | Prefetch | MTU/RWIN | Logging | ◄ ►

☑ Delay prefetches while real pages are coming in

Naviscope will prefetch all links which contain the phrases listed below. Use a comma to separate the phrases from each other.

next

Maximum number of prefetched pages that Naviscope will hold (as new prefetches are made old ones are removed to make room).

10

Help | Cancel | OK

The drawback of this program is that you need to manually configure it for each search engine you plan to use. This can be tricky, because search engines use different symbols and labels to identify the links that lead you to the next page of search results.

These programs can have a dramatic effect on the way you use the Internet. We have devoted a separate chapter (Chapter 12, "Just-in-Time Knowledge Using Search Accelerators") to the first type of search accelerator, the programs that allow you to search several search engines simultaneously.

tip Browse the Web Using Index Technology

A software program called Quickscape allows you to browse Web sites and search the Web faster than if you were using a traditional Web browser. Quickscape displays Web sites in an easy-to-read index format, eliminating the graphics and descriptive text that you normally get on the Web. Simply click on the link you want, and Quickscape will retrieve the page using a conventional Web browser, either Netscape or Internet Explorer. When you search the Web using a popular search engine like AltaVista or Lycos, Quickscape will display your search results in index format, allowing you to quickly scan and visit Web sites without annoying graphics or other information on your screen. You can download a trial version of Quickscape at **www.qscape.com**.

4. Tweak Your Windows 95/98 Settings

If one of the high-speed Internet access technologies that we previously discussed isn't available in your area yet, what else can you do to speed up your Internet connection? If you are using a modem, you can improve the speed by "tweaking" your Windows 95/98 settings. (In some cases, you might be able to use these methods if you have a high-speed connection to the Internet, but the results won't be as significant; they may not even be noticeable.)

This method isn't necessarily for the faint of heart, but if you are technically oriented, don't mind learning, and are willing to try it out, you can change your dial-up settings to such an extent that you will get some speed improvements.

POPULAR MODEM-TWEAKING PROGRAMS FOR WINDOWS 95

TweakDUN	**www.pattersondesigns.com/tweakdun**
iSpeed	**www.hms.com**
MTUSpeed Pro	**www.mjs.u-net.com**

Most of these programs are simple to use. A good example is TweakDUN. Once installed, you get a screen that looks like this:

If you wish, you can set each item yourself, or you can choose the "Auto" button; this will change certain Windows settings so that the next time you dial in to the Internet, you should notice some speed improvements.

How does it work? Visit the TweakDUN site for an explanation; it's complicated, but worth a look:

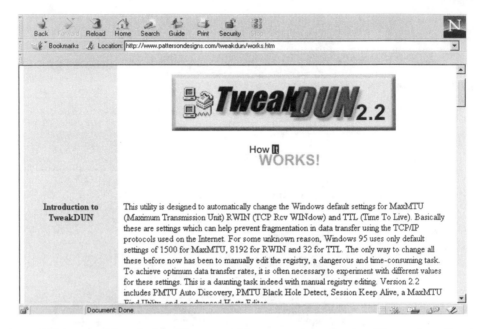

Does it work? Yes; we did notice significant speed improvements after installing and configuring the TweakDUN software.

5. Use Another Browser

With the release of new software from Netscape and Microsoft in 1998, a lot of attention was given to the fact that Web browser programs are becoming larger and larger. It seems that as efforts are made to stuff Java, ActiveX, and all kinds of other capabilities into browser programs, performance has been sacrificed for features.

Since most people seem to be using Netscape or Microsoft Web browsers, it's easy to forget that alternatives exist. One of the best so-called "alternative" browsers is a program from Norway called Opera (**www.operasoftware.com**). Although Opera doesn't support some of the popular Internet technologies like Java, the program's speed makes up for its shortcomings. You can think of Opera as a stripped-down, no-frills Web browser that still provides many of the features found in Netscape and Microsoft browsers. We have used Opera on various computers and have come to appreciate it for its speed, particularly on older, slower computers that can't easily run the Netscape and Microsoft browsers.

If you visit Opera's Web site (**www.operasoftware.com/press.html**), you will see some of the glowing reviews that the program has received. Clearly, they're on to something:

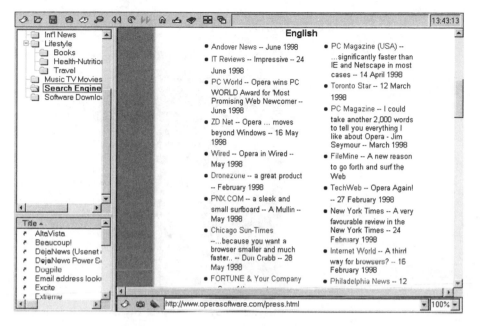

There is debate within the Internet community over whether Opera is faster than other browsers. Our suggestion? It seems worthwhile enough that you should try it out and decide for yourself.

6. Use Diagnostic Software

It is possible that your connection to the Internet is plagued by speed problems, and you don't even know it. Of course, in order to take corrective action, you need to identify the source of the problems. There are many diagnostic programs that can help you assess and correct problems that are affecting the speed of your Internet connection. If you take the time to learn how to use these programs, you will get a better understanding of how various things can affect the speed you get when online. These factors include the time of day, the Internet service provider you are using, the site you are visiting, your modem, and the overall level of congestion on the Internet. Many of these programs offer recommendations to help you fix speed problems, and some, like Net.Medic, will fix the problems for you.

POPULAR SPEED-MONITORING PROGRAMS

AnySpeed	**www.pysoft.com**
Net.Medic	**www.vitalsigns.com**
VisualRoute	**www.visualroute.com**
DU Meter	**www.hagel.threadnet.com**

Net.Medic is one of the best speed-monitoring programs that we have used. Once the program is installed, it gives you a running view of the speed of your Internet connection and how well you are doing in terms of speed when visiting various Web sites:

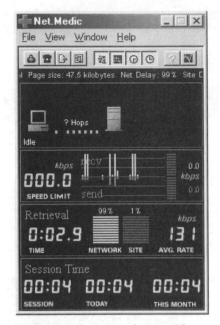

You can use this window to judge how well you are doing with a certain Web site compared to other sites in terms of speed, which will help you to appreciate that some Web sites are slower than others. Over a period of a few days or weeks you will get a good sense of how the speed of your Internet connection varies with the time of day.

You can also access a number of reports, such as this one, which gives an overview of the speed that you have achieved on connecting to various Web sites:

And this one, which details an overview of problems that have occurred with specific Web sites or pages:

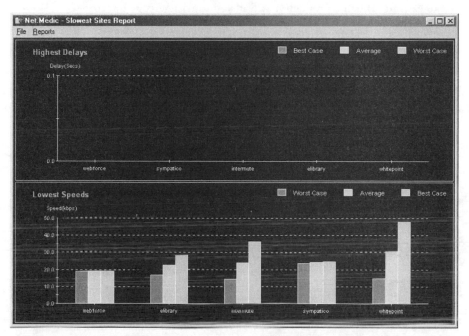

In addition, you can obtain a health summary report of the types of problems that have occurred with your Internet connection. Sometimes, this information can be useful if you are trying to resolve problems with your modem or other problems you may have with your Internet connection:

We highly recommend that you use a program like Net.Medic to gain insight into how the speed of your connection to the Internet can be affected by a number of different factors. The information you learn from such a program may lead you to change your Internet service provider, change your browsing habits, fix your modem, or take other steps to improve the speed of your Web browsing.

7. Filter Unwanted Content

You have probably discovered that one of the most obnoxious types of Web sites that you have visited is the one that insists on "playing a tune" when you first visit it or provides a lot of Java applications, advertisements, or animation that can take forever to load.

Some people haven't yet realized that the key to effective Web site design is the no-frills approach, so that pages load quickly. To avoid all the extra "junk" that can come from such sites, consider using a Web filter, a program that blocks certain types of information from appearing on Web pages.

POPULAR INTERNET FILTERING PROGRAMS

interMute	**www.intermute.com**
@Guard	**www.atguard.com**
Web Free (Macintosh only)	**www.falken.net/webfree**
Ad Wiper (Internet Explorer users only)	**www.webwiper.com**
AdsOff!	**www.intercantech.com**

A good example of such a program is interMute (**www.intermute.com**), which eliminates advertisements, animated images, background music, and more from Web sites. The program is fully customizable, in that you can define the types of information that you would like to restrict:

The program is set up to automatically exclude advertisements that are placed on Web sites by some of the major advertising companies as well as to exclude images that contain the common "tagging" used to identify them as advertisements. The list that determines how to exclude advertisements can be updated at any time simply by clicking a button, allowing the program developers to add new advertising companies to the list. You can only get this updated list if you register and pay for the program. And you can add your own items to the list, thus ensuring that online advertising companies in Canada are blocked from sending you advertisements. You can also tell the program to block images that contain certain letter patterns in their HTML code that identify them as advertisements:

Does the advertising filtering work? You bet. We visited the Canoe Web site, which has an ad in the middle of the page for their financial service:

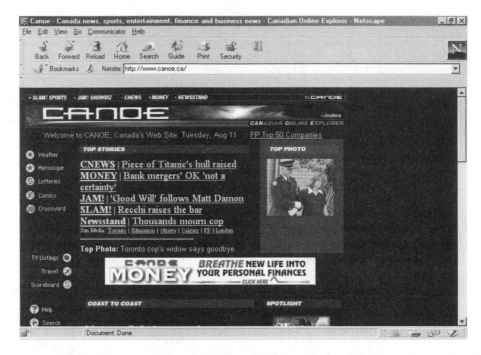

Then we installed interMute, and the ad disappeared. We were hooked and have been using the program ever since. Because programs like interMute block out certain types of content from Web pages, they have the effect of speeding up your Internet browsing:

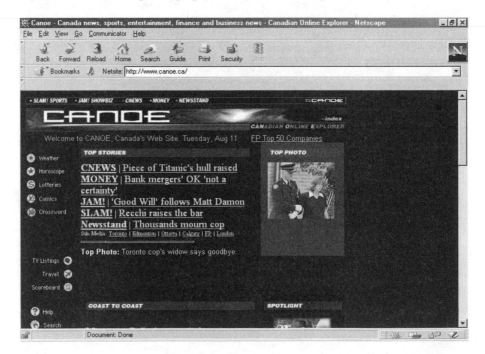

8. More Techniques For Faster Internet Surfing

There are even more things you can do to speed up your Web browsing:

- **Increase your RAM.** RAM (random access memory) is the internal memory in your computer. Increasing the amount of RAM can make a huge difference in your use of the Web. One of our computers was equipped with 8 MB of RAM and was very, very slow in terms of accessing Web sites. Once the computer memory was increased to 32 MB, the speed increase was dramatic.

  RAM is very inexpensive; hence it is one of the easiest and least expensive things you can do to speed up your Internet connection.

- **Turn off the graphics when browsing the Web.** If you really want to move around the Web quickly, turn off the graphics. You will simply see a box where any pictures used to appear.

  In Netscape 3.0 you can do this by selecting the "Options" menu and then deselecting "Auto Load Images."

  In Netscape 4.0, you choose "Preferences" under the "Edit" menu, select "Advanced," then deselect "Automatically load images."

  In Internet Explorer 3.0 select "Options" under the "View" menu, select the "General" tab and then deselect "Show pictures."

  In Internet Explorer 4.0 select "Options" under the "View" menu, select the "Advanced" tab, and locate the "Show Pictures" item. Deselect it.

  Once you have done this, you will still be able to display selected graphics on a Web page. If you are using Netscape with the images turned off and you want to see a specific graphic, click your right mouse button on the image symbol and select "Show Image." If you are using Internet Explorer, click your right mouse button on the image symbol and select "Show Picture."

- **Increase the size of your cache.** We described the cache in our section about browser accelerators above and in Chapter 8, "Practical Productivity Tips." You can speed up your use of the Internet by increasing the size of your cache. A larger cache means your Web browser can store more Web pages on your hard drive, thus giving you faster access to a greater number of Web sites.

  In Netscape 3.0 select "Network Preferences" under the "Options" menu, select the "Cache" tab, and modify the size of your browser's disk cache.

  In Netscape 4.0 select "Preferences" under the "Edit" menu, click on the "Advanced" option twice to reveal the dropdown menu, click on "Cache," and modify the size of your browser's disk cache.

  In Internet Explorer 3.0 select "Options" under the "View" menu, select "Advanced," and select the "Settings" box under "Temporary Internet Files." Use the slider (it appears under "Amount of disk space to use") to control the size of your disk cache.

For Internet Explorer 4.0 select "Internet Options" under the "View" menu. Under the "General" tab you will find "Temporary Internet Files." Next, select "Settings," then use the slider (it appears under "Amount of disk space to use") to control the size of your disk cache.

- **Increase the size of your hard drive.** Increasing the size of your cache is only as useful as the size of your hard drive. In other words, the larger your hard drive, the larger your cache can be, and the more Web pages you can store. The cost of hard disk storage has dropped significantly; hence adding more hard disk storage can make a difference in the speed of access to the Web.

- **Increase the speed of your modem.** Finally, if you can afford it, you should upgrade your modem to the fastest speed possible, currently 56 Kbps. Before doing so, however, check with your Internet service provider to ensure that they support 56 Kbps access. Most do.

Summary

As you have seen throughout this chapter, you have a lot of control over the speed of your Internet connection, much more control than you probably thought. Whether it's tweaking your Windows 95 settings or switching to an alternative browser like Opera, there are lots of options that you can experiment with. Although some of the methods we have described produce better results than others, each technique, in its own way, will help make your Web browsing more productive.

chapter ten

Knowledge Management

...by 2000, e-mail users will number 107 million. These users generated more than 812 billion messages in 1994, and this year they'll hit the Send button 2.7 trillion times. By 2000, that figure will explode to 6.9 trillion messages a year.

"Stop the E-mail Madness," *Windows*, **October 1, 1997**

Highlights

1. Round out your Internet research skills by learning how to archive your e-mail messages and Web sites.

2. There are many useful programs now available that permit you to do this, such as AskSam, SurfSaver, PaperMaster, and WebSnake.

In addition to learning how to better take advantage of the information resources of the Internet, you may want to explore how you can enhance your research activities by building your own research archives. For example, have you thought of the wealth of information that can be found in all the e-mail that you have sent and received? Do you find that there are Web pages or sites that you have seen in the past that you wish you had kept? If the answer is yes to either question, then we suggest you start thinking about how to electronically archive some of the information that you generate and access online.

E-mail Archiving

One of the authors, Jim Carroll, keeps many of the e-mail messages that he sends and receives. He has been doing so since 1984, and as a result, now has some rather large files containing hundreds of thousands of messages. Some 15 years' worth.

tip E-mail Archiving

Should your organization be more serious about archiving your e-mail? You may want to order the Message Retention Toolkit, a publication available from the Electronic Messaging Association (**www.ema.org**), which represents e-mail software developers as well as major users of e-mail systems. The publication "shows how to tailor the right retention policy for your enterprise and avoid legal liability for years to come while making messaging technologies a tool for operational efficiency." It promises to help you "learn ways to ensure that important information is retained while unnecessary information is deleted."

While much of this information might be useless, there is a lot that is extremely useful. As Jim wrote in his book, *Surviving the Information Age*,

> *Years ago, I purposefully set out to try to master the skill of "turning information into knowledge." I've done several things that have convinced me that I've managed to turn myself into a true "knowledge worker."...Much of what goes back and forth through my electronic mailbox involves little things: arrangements for meetings, thank you messages and many letters and documents that I*

have typed that have little lasting value. But scattered throughout all the messages and documents, there is some information that is useful.

Way back in 1984, I decided that it was important to keep most of my e-mail and documents, regardless of how useless such information might be. So I have now amassed some pretty large computer files containing hundreds of thousands of messages, documents, reports, letters and other information.

This has become an invaluable knowledge tool. If I am working on a book, a news or magazine article, a client seminar or a consulting project, I can be pretty certain that buried in all of that information is a nugget directly relevant to what I am doing. I use several programs to help me locate specific pieces of information buried within those files, turning them into an invaluable resource.

I've taught myself to recycle my own information and to extract knowledge from my own electronic database, and that, I think, is a good skill to have in the information age.

AskSam (**www.asksam.com**) is the program used by Jim to manage, access, and search this massive collection of e-mail messages. The program, which can be used for many different types of databases, includes a built-in Internet e-mail archive program. Using this, you can easily import all of your old e-mail messages and then search the resulting database for messages that contain certain words or phrases. You can import e-mail as plain text, which means that you can use the program with just about any e-mail program that allows you to save your e-mail as text messages. In addition, it will allow you to import messages from the Eudora e-mail program directly:

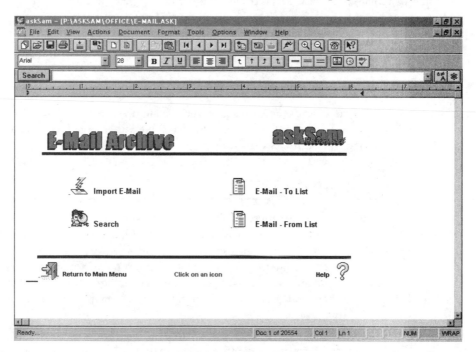

How can this be useful? Say you remember writing or receiving an e-mail message on "Internet usage policies." Simply type the words "usage policies" into the search box, and you will see the first message that contains both of these words anywhere in the message. You can also do a search for an exact phrase:

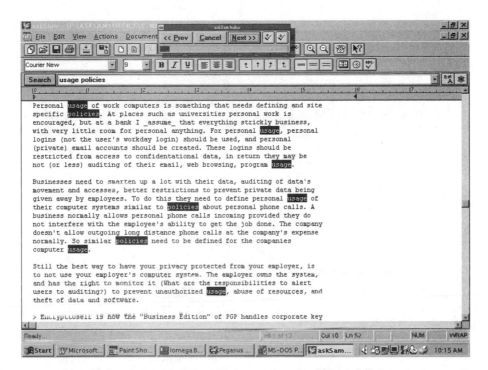

If there were other messages matching the search, pressing the right arrow key shown on the small box at the top of the screen lets you see them one by one.

What if you are looking for the e-mail address of someone with whom you communicated a few years ago? Just type in the name:

You can also generate a list of all the TO: and FROM: fields of your e-mail messages, which goes into a separate database. This can be useful to search directly if you simply want a listing of everyone that you have ever sent e-mail to or from:

The highlight of the program is the text search capability. Since it builds a special index of all the words that a database contains, you can type in a search phrase and find information extremely quickly. Worthwhile? We think so.

AskSam, although unique, isn't the only program that allows you to archive and search your e-mail. Check out AltaVista Discovery as well, which is available through the AltaVista Web site (**www.altavista.digital.com**). Based on the same technology as the popular AltaVista search engine, the program indexes not just your e-mail messages, but everything found on your hard disk.

E-mail Reliability

A 1997 study by Inverse, an organization that studies the reliability of the Internet, found that "91 per cent of all e-mail sent arrived at the intended destination within 5 minutes" and that "attempts to access a mail server to send or receive an e-mail message were successful about 95 percent of the time."

When you install the program, it appears, by default, at the top of your Web browser:

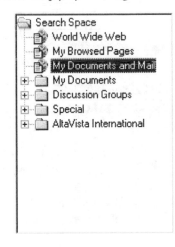

You can use the program to query documents on your computer, AltaVista itself, Internet news-groups, and other information sources simply by selecting the items you want to search from the list:

The program will set itself up so that it goes off and indexes every file that is found on your computer. Should you find it doing this right away and it is interfering with your work, you can go into the program and configure it so that it runs at night.

Once it has indexed your computer, you can do a search for any word or phrase within the files on your system. In this case, we have done a search for any files that contain the words internet, strategic, and planning. AltaVista Discovery has returned a list, similar in layout to what you get when you use the AltaVista Web site, that contains the files found on our computer that match the search phrase:

Assessing the Effectiveness
of Your Web Site

Protecting Yourself Online

**Improving Your Productivity
on the Internet**

Enhancing Your Web Site

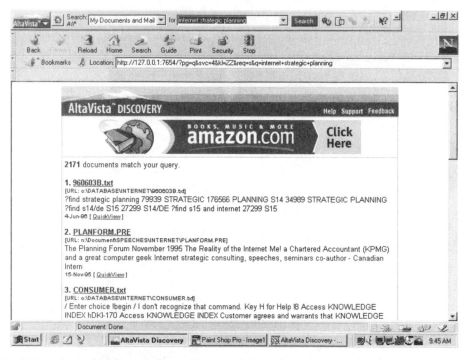

AltaVista Discovery includes a number of "viewers" that allow you to see the content of a file
without having to load the program used to create the file. On this screen we are looking at a
Lotus Freelance presentation file which was included in our search results:

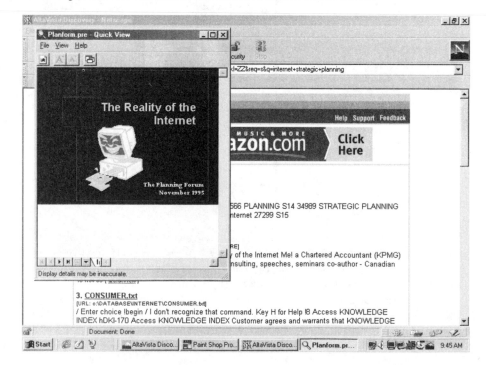

And here we are looking at a Microsoft Word document:

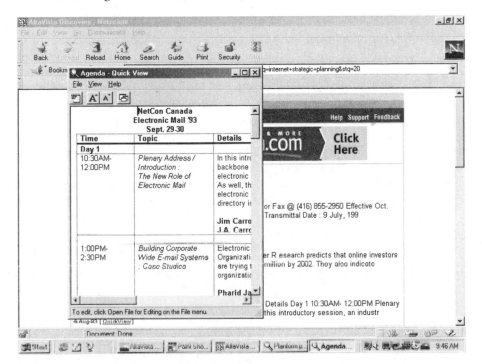

You can specify the types of documents that should be included when AltaVista indexes your computer and which hard drives should be examined:

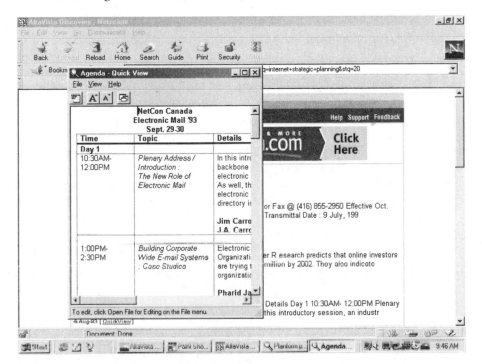

All in all, the program is convenient, straightforward, and certainly priced right: it's available for free from the AltaVista Web site and is definitely worth investigating.

Capturing and Archiving Web Pages

The second thing you may want to do is keep a copy on your PC of the various Web pages or even Web sites that you have visited. However, before you think about doing this, remember that there may be copyright issues to think about here. While the whole area of trademark and copyright law on the Internet is still evolving, the fact is that you could be breaking the law if you download and save in your archives a Web page that is from a site that specifically restricts you from doing so. Hence we suggest that you proceed with caution here.

However, there are now some programs that permit you to "grab" a certain Web page, or even entire Web sites, and store it on your PC. Some of these programs then permit you to do a keyword search of what has been stored. The AskSam program mentioned above allows you to archive Web pages that you saved to your computer and search within these pages. But it isn't always a straightforward process. As a result, AskSam developed SurfSaver, a program that allows you to grab a page simply by clicking a button. You can then store that page, images and all, to your PC.

When visiting a Web page that you would like to store, you just click the right mouse button for a menu of options, and choose "SurfSaver Save"; you will see that option listed in the box that comes up, as seen below. This immediately saves a copy of the page, images and all, to your computer:

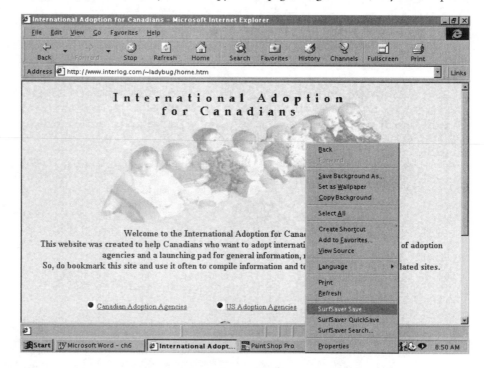

You can then assign the page to any of a number of different folders (you can create any number of folders that you like):

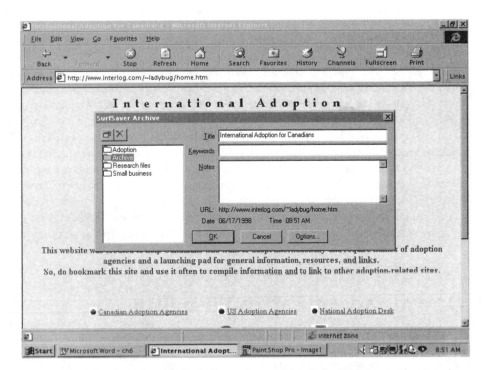

At any time you can initiate a search for information within all the Web pages that you have stored:

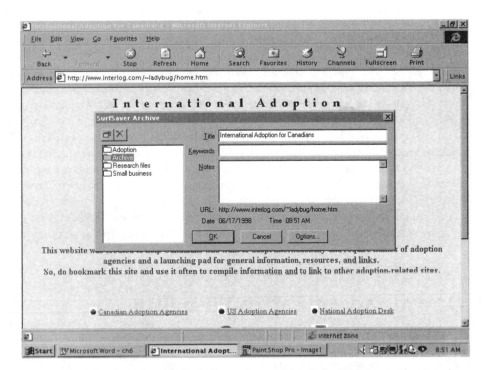

We found this to be a very useful tool to build an archive of useful Web pages.

Another program that offers similar capabilities is PaperMaster from JetFax Inc. (**www.documagix.com**). This program places a button on the tool bar within your Web browser. When you want to save that page, simply click on the button, and a copy will be stored on your hard disk. You can then place that saved page into any one of an unlimited number of filing cabinets that you create, and you can search for information by keyword from throughout those cabinets. It operates similarly to SurfSaver.

You can also look into a program like WebSnake, which we mention briefly in Chapter 12. It has the handy feature of being able to download an entire Web site to your PC. It certainly works as advertised; as we mention in Chapter 12, we instructed it to download the entire TDBank site, consisting of some several thousand pages, and it did. You can use a program like this to build your own archives of particularly important Web pages concerning a topic that interests you.

For a comprehensive listing of such programs, you can visit the TUCOWS (**www.tucows.com**) site and look at the "Offline readers" category found under the "WIN95/98" heading, or search for the topic "offline browsers."

tip Download an Entire Web Site

In addition to a tool like SurfSaver, which lets you download selected Web pages, you can use a variety of tools that let you download an entire Web site:

WebZIP	**www.spidersoft.com**
WebSnake	**www.anawave.com**
SiteEater	**www.sfs–software.com**
WebVCR	**www.netresultscorp.com**
Teleport Pro	**www.tenmax.com**
Grab-a-Site	**www.bluesquirrel.com**
WebFlyer	**www.webflyer.com**
WebCut	**www.webcut.com**
Second Site	**1automata.com**

A Category to Watch

There aren't a lot of e-mail archiving programs available, so AskSam is definitely worth looking into. Programs like SurfSaver also seem to be few and far between. However, we expect that over time, these software categories will see a lot of growth, as people and companies come to realize the value of archiving this information. We definitely suggest that you examine both types of tools to get a good idea of how you might begin to archive your own electronic knowledge files.

chapter eleven

Videophones and Remote Internet Connectivity

While most big companies have elaborate setups to allow employees to access parts of the office computer network when they're home or out of town on business, individual users can do much the same thing with just a couple of modems and a bit of software.

"Remote Access Software Makes Connecting Machines Less Far-Fetched," *Chicago Tribune*, June 22, 1998

In the past 18 months, several companies have bravely moved into the consumer videophone market, fortified by a new international technical standard for video calling, more powerful computer chips and the prospect of high-speed home Internet links.

"Videophones Evolve, Slowly," *The New York Times*, July 16, 1998

Highlights

1. Remote access software allows you to access your home or office computer from another location. Videoconferencing software allows people in different locations to see and hear each other in real time.

2. To use remote access software or to engage in videoconferencing with another Internet user, you need to know the IP address of your computer or the computer you will be connecting with.

3. There are many software programs that you can download from the Internet to help you determine your computer's IP address. Some of these programs, called IP posters, will post your IP address to a Web site where it can be retrieved by anyone who wants to videoconference with you.

4. Remote access software can be used to access a computer attached to a corporate network, a computer that is permanently connected to the Internet, or a computer that is temporarily connected with a dial-up connection.

5. Remote access software can also work over a regular telephone line. No special hardware is required. Remote access is easiest when the computer you are connecting to is permanently connected to the Internet and a firewall is not being used.

6. Videoconferencing software has improved dramatically over the last few years, but the quality of the session will depend on the speed of your connection to the Internet.

7. Be cognizant of potential hardware and software conflicts when using videoconferencing software.

Many people do a lot of travelling as part of their job, but many also work out of a home office. If this is you, then chances are you use a laptop computer.

There is also a very good chance that you use your laptop to check your e-mail, transfer files, and send other information to the office or use it to access other parts of the Internet, such as the World Wide Web or discussion groups, while travelling.

If you fall into either of these categories, then we think you may be interested in looking at these two types of products: remote access and videoconferencing programs.

Remote access programs let you link two computers together, for example, the one you use while out of the office to a computer you use in the office. When travelling, you can use a remote access program such as pcANYWHERE to access your office computer from your laptop. The connection can be done through a telephone call, which may involve long distance charges, or could occur directly through the Internet, with no additional long distance charges involved. When travelling, you can use this capability to retrieve a file that you may have forgotten back at the office or to run an actual computer program on your office PC that you don't have on your laptop.

Another capability that has become very sophisticated within the last year is Internet-based PC videoconferencing. Once you are linked into the Internet, you can use any one of a number of videoconferencing programs with the many small video cameras now available. These programs allow you to connect back to your family or co-workers through the Internet and have a video-conference where the quality of the audio and video is quite respectable.

Since the Internet can be used for the connection, you can undertake either activity for an extremely low cost, particularly if you have a flat rate Internet plan with your Internet service provider. As a result, not only have some wonderful new remote access capabilities emerged, but the economics are absolutely perfect.

Dealing With IP Addresses

To take advantage of either of these capabilities, you need the right software, and in the case of videoconferencing, the right hardware. But one thing that you generally need to know in both cases is the IP address (Internet protocol address) of the computer you are trying to reach.

If you aren't familiar with IP addresses, you will need to be. When any computer connects to the Internet, either on a temporary basis through a dial-up connection (i.e., telephone modem) or on a full-time basis through a dedicated connection (i.e., cable modem, ADSL, or T1 link), it is assigned an IP address. You can think of it as the equivalent of a telephone number for a computer while it is connected to the Internet. An IP address is a fundamental component of TCP/IP, the protocol that makes the Internet work and that allows computers around the planet to plug together.

Determining the IP address of the computer you are trying to connect to can sometimes be challenging, depending on how the computer is configured and how it connects to the Internet. So the first thing we need to do in using remote access or videoconferencing programs is to help you understand how to figure out the IP address of the computer you are trying to reach.

Figuring Out the IP Address of the Computer You Want to Reach

Computers that access the Internet through a dial-up modem connection will likely get a different IP address each time they connect. This is because ISPs have a bank of IP addresses and assign them on an as-needed basis to people dialling in.

Computers that are permanently connected to the Internet usually have an IP address that doesn't change for a long time. In fact, the only time it might change is when the computer or cable modem is restarted. At that point, the cable company will reassign an IP address, which might be different.

There are a number of computer programs that you can use to figure out the IP address of a computer that is connected to the Internet. Remember, it is the IP address of the computer you are trying to reach that you need, not the address of the computer you are currently using, in order to use a remote access or videoconferencing program.

Here are some situations where you need to know the IP address of a computer you wish to access from another location:

- If you have a cable modem or other permanent connection to the Internet, you can find out the IP address of the computer linked to that connection before you leave on your business trip. You then provide that information to the remote access or videoconferencing program on the computer you are travelling with, so that it knows how to reach your computer.

- If you want to have someone contact you through a videoconference program, you need to find out the IP address of your computer when it is linked to the Internet, and tell the person trying to reach you that IP address. If you want to reach him, he has to tell you his IP address.

- If your office computer connects to the Internet through a modem, and you want to access it from home or while travelling, you will likely have to have someone in your office dial in to the Internet and then advise you of your office computer's IP number once it is connected to the Internet.

IP Programs

As we mentioned above, there are several programs that will determine the IP address and that you can download from the Internet and install on your computer. For Windows systems one such program is Local IP. You can find this program at **home.sol.no/~tmanneru/localip.html** (if it has moved, simply do a search for the phrase "local IP" in AltaVista (**www.altavista.digital.com**), and you are bound to find it. It provides a little window that tells your current IP address once you have connected to the Internet:

For Macintosh systems there are a number of similar programs available. We use MacTCPWatcher, which provides a screen with our IP address. You can find this program at the TUCOWS site (**www.tucows.com**).

IP poster programs go one step further: they can be set up so that they actually upload a page to a Web site advising others of the IP address. At the TUCOWS site, look in the "Internet Tools" section, then in "IP Posters."

POPULAR IP POSTING PROGRAMS

AutoIP	members.lsol.net/smiller/autoip
DynamIP	DynamIP.home.ml.org
Here	www.cris.com/~beers/here

AutoIP provides a good example of how these programs work. When you set up the program, you provide details on how the program can log in to your Web site through FTP:

It will use this information to generate a custom Web page that contains the IP address of the computer connected to the Internet and will generate and upload this page to the Internet each time that computer accesses the Internet. This allows you to make your IP address accessible to others who want to establish a videoconference with you.

Not only that, when you disconnect your computer from the Internet, it will generate a page advising people that there is no IP address, since you are not currently online.

Using an IP Program

How can these Web page posting programs be useful? Imagine this scenario: you are on a road trip to Halifax. You want to contact your husband and kids back in Regina to have a videoconference. You have set up one of the IP poster programs to run every time your home computer connects to the Internet. Your husband dials into the Internet in order to accept a call from you at a pre-arranged time. The IP poster program runs and uploads a Web page to a Web site that you can upload files to, or a publicly accessible FTP site that anyone can post files to.

You take a look at this Web page to figure out the IP address that he has been assigned in Regina and use this to establish the videoconference.

Finding Out Your IP Address Online

Finally, you don't necessarily have to use a computer program to find out your IP address. Simply visit this Web site at Stanford University: **www.slac.stanford.edu/cgi-bin/nph-traceroute.pl**. It will run a program called Traceroute, which will link back to you over the Internet, advising you of the IP address that you are using. In this case, your husband would visit this site and tell you the IP address that it provides.

Now that you know how to get the IP address of the computer you are trying to reach, or your own IP address, let's look at some of the programs that you can use for remote access and Internet-based videoconferencing.

Remote Access Over the Internet

There are a number of different remote access programs available, the main ones being pcANYWHERE by Symantec Corporation (**www.symantec.ca**) and LapLink by Traveling Software (**www.laplink.com**). The concept behind these programs is that you can use them to access another computer linked to the Internet, run programs on that computer, or access files on that computer. Hence this is an extremely useful application if you are travelling and want to go back to your home or office computer to get some important files or run a program on that computer.

The remote access program itself must be loaded and running on the computer you are using (e.g., your laptop) as well as on the computer you are trying to connect to (e.g., your desktop at home or at the office). No special hardware is required for these programs. The connection can be made using a modem directly without the Internet being involved (which might involve a long distance call) or by two computers connected to the Internet (either using a modem, ADSL, or cable modem).

It can be a real advantage in certain situations to be able to access files and run programs on a computer as if you were sitting in front of that computer instead of being miles away. However, you must be conscious of security; one thing to remember when using these programs and if you are connecting to a network is that you will be able to access all the files on the various computers that are connected to the network. Hence your network administrator may not permit you to use such a program.

One of the authors has been using pcANYWHERE to access his main home office computer while travelling across North America. This comes in handy when he needs to grab a computer file that he forgot to take with him or to run a program back at the home office that wasn't available on the laptop computer he travels with.

He does so by dialling in to the Internet from wherever he is, using an Internet service provider like Netcom Canada, which provides access across North America. Once connected to the Internet, he loads pcANYWHERE and simply tells it to connect to the home office PC. In a second or two, the program provides the screen of the home office desktop computer as simply another window on his laptop PC:

From here, he can do anything he would normally do on his home office desktop PC from the comfort of his hotel room or wherever he might be.

He uses a 56 Kbps modem while travelling, and, as you might expect, using the remote computer isn't as fast as if he were right there. But pcANYWHERE has proven to be very reliable, fast enough for what he needs to do, and certainly a lifesaver in a few situations when he really needed a certain file.

What makes this particularly worthwhile is that his main home office computer is connected full-time to the Internet using the Rogers @Home cable modem service (**www.wave.ca**).

Methods of Using pcANYWHERE

pcANYWHERE can work in a variety of ways, but the underlying premise is the same. The computer that you are trying to reach acts as the "host" computer, and the computer you are using to reach the host computer is the "remote access" computer. Both computers have the pcANYWHERE program installed, but each computer is configured in a different way. In configuring the computers, you establish a user ID and password. When the remote access computer that is running pcANYWHERE contacts the host running pcANYWHERE, the host will verify the user ID and password that it has been provided and, if valid, will accept the connection.

The easiest way to set up a connection is using a regular telephone call. This is a straight modem-to-modem connection, with no linking through the Internet. Using the remote access computer (make sure it is plugged into a telephone line), you run pcANYWHERE telling it the telephone number to dial. The computer then dials the phone number. The host computer at that telephone number answers the call, checks the user ID and password, and if valid the two computers are connected. However, if you are making a long distance phone call, you could end up spending a bit of money for this type of remote access. So you may prefer to use the Internet to establish the connection from the remote computer to your host computer.

There are three scenarios in which you may connect through the Internet:

- You have a single computer connected full-time to the Internet through ADSL or a cable modem. This is the easiest configuration to work with for a program like pcANYWHERE.

- You have a single computer that you connect to the Internet using a dial-up connection on an as-needed basis. This is the most common situation for many users of the Internet in Canada, but it isn't necessarily easy to use pcANYWHERE in this configuration.

- At home, you have a local area network with a dedicated connection to the Internet through ADSL or a cable modem, with all the computers on the network sharing access to the Internet through what is known as a proxy server/firewall. Or at work you have a corporate local area network to which your desktop computer is linked, and a proxy server/firewall is in place. pcANYWHERE will work in this situation. It is more complicated, because you have to configure the proxy server/firewall to permit a connection from the outside world through pcANYWHERE. Your corporate network administrator may not allow you to do this.

Complexities of Connecting Using the Internet

You can use pcANYWHERE in each of the above scenarios, but each will differ in terms of complexity of configuration. One of the complexities involves finding out the IP address of the host computer. While you can use a program like pcANYWHERE with a dial-up modem, the program really shines when you have a cable modem or ADSL connection to the Internet, or when your desktop computer is on a corporate network that is linked to the Internet on a full-time basis.

This is because the host computer will have a permanent IP address (or one that changes infrequently) and is connected to the Internet all the time. The only thing that you need to do is make sure that the host computer is turned on and is running the pcANYWHERE program.

On the other hand, if your host can only connect to the Internet using a modem, then you will have to arrange for someone (perhaps at your home or office) to go to the computer to establish a connection to the Internet and start the pcANYWHERE program so that you can access it. Or you will have to set up your host computer to automatically dial in to the Internet and load the pcANYWHERE software. This may not be practical or possible, which adds another layer of complexity to using this type of program.

To understand how you can use a package like pcANYWHERE on the road, we will first take a look at the situation in which you are travelling with a laptop and want to access your home (or office) computer which is attached to the Internet full-time through a cable modem. We look at this case first because in many situations, a cable modem user has a dedicated IP address that rarely, if ever, changes.

Setting Up a pcANYWHERE Connection Over the Internet With a Cable Modem Connection

Say the IP address of your desktop computer, the host, which is linked to the Internet using a cable modem, is 192.168.199.7. (This is a fictitious address; we aren't using our real IP address here.)

You set up your host computer to accept an incoming connection, by providing information on the computer protocol that you will use (in this case, TCP/IP) and establishing a user ID and password that will be used from your remote computer. You also put in place various security options, which we describe below.

Once the host program is set up and configured, it waits for an incoming connection that comes from the Internet. This means that it can accept a connection from your remote computer at any time, as long as the right user ID and password are provided. Note that it will only accept a connection from another pcANYWHERE program. You will see that it is "waiting" for a connection:

On your remote computer, you must first set up the system to place a connection to your host. To do this, you provide the IP address of your host computer, the user ID and password that you have set up, and various other options, depending on the way you have configured the security options for the system. Once it is set up, you can connect automatically at any point without having to access this information again:

You then dial in to the Internet and run the pcANYWHERE program to connect. In a few seconds, you will see the exact screen that appears on your desktop computer at that moment in time:

At this point, you can do anything that you could do if you were actually at the desktop computer. You can start and run programs, move files around, print something—anything. You can also invoke the pcANYWHERE file manager program. This is a convenient program; it lets you quickly and easily browse through the directory of your desktop computer, accessing files and copying them to your remote computer. This comes in handy when travelling and you have forgotten an important file:

Nothing could be easier.

You can set up pcANYWHERE so that it loads and is ready to go any time you start Windows. What we usually do is run it and configure it to start with Windows when we are about to go on the road, rather than running it all the time. (If your computer doesn't automatically start up in Windows, i.e., you boot it up in DOS, ensure that you reset this so it does start in Windows.)

There are other options that you can specify; for example, you can have pcANYWHERE restart your computer after you have done a remote session, which can sometimes be a worthwhile thing to do to ensure that there are no stability problems with your system. In either situation, you need to have configured your computer to automatically start Windows when it is restarted.

Security Options

Given that you are linking your desktop computer to the world, it isn't surprising that you'll find a lot of security provisions within pcANYWHERE, as well as a number of other options:

You can set up a number of different remote users within pcANYWHERE, providing each user with an ID and password. Each user can have a different profile that allows him or her different levels of access to your system:

New Caller Wizard

What will the caller's login name be?

    FROM AWAY

What will the caller's password be? (If left blank, the caller will not have a password.)

    xxxxxxxxxx

Confirm the password:

    xxxxxxxxxx

    < Back   Next >   Cancel

You can also specify, for each and every user, the type of access they are provided to files on your system, in particular, whether they can only read files or write to files, as well as whether they can access other computers on your network, if you have one:

Drive Access

Floppy drive access
  ○ No access   ○ Read only   ● Full access

Local fixed drive access
  ○ No access   ○ Read only   ● Full access

Network drive access
  ○ No access   ○ Read only   ● Full access

CD-ROM drive access
  ○ No access   ○ Read only   ● Full access

    OK
    Cancel

You can also build a log of connection attempts so that you can see if someone is trying to access your computer; lock someone out if he tries with an invalid password a certain number of times and encrypts (scramble) the transmission during the connection:

Using pcANYWHERE Through a Dial-Up Connection

It's easy to use a program like pcANYWHERE with a full-time connection, but as we said, it is a little more complex if the host computer accesses the Internet using a modem connection. For it to work, your host computer must be connected to the Internet. How can you do this? Several ways:

- You can dial in to the Internet with your host computer before you leave on your trip, and then leave your computer connected to the Internet for an extended length of time. This is probably impractical for many people, and in most cases, your Internet service provider would end up disconnecting your computer from the Internet after several hours of inactivity.

- You can ask someone at your home/office to connect your host computer to the Internet at the time when you need to access it from your remote location. This is the most likely situation.

- You can set up your host computer with a scheduling program that causes it to dial in to the Internet on a regular basis; then you access it with your remote computer during those scheduled times. This is also a workable solution.

To do the latter, you can try a program like NetLaunch, which allows you to configure a schedule defining when your Internet connection should occur; you can also specify which programs should be run when it dials in. This allows you to set up a system in which your computer dials in to the Internet for a few minutes each hour and runs pcANYWHERE. If you did this on a regular basis, say the first five minutes of every hour, you would at least know that you could dial in with pcANYWHERE during those times of the day. You can also set NetLaunch so that it automatically runs an IP posting program that uploads the current IP address of the host machine to your Web site:

You can find NetLaunch at **www.primenet.com/~simpson/software.html**. If it has moved, a search within Yahoo! (**www.yahoo.com**) or AltaVista (**www.altavista.digital.com**) should locate it for you. AutoIP, mentioned earlier, can also upload the current IP address of the host machine to your Web site.

Using pcANYWHERE Through a Corporate Network

Finally, if you want to use a program like pcANYWHERE on the road to access your desktop computer which is located on a corporate network, and the corporate network is linked to the Internet, you will have to talk to the folks responsible for your network. It is quite likely that the organization has a firewall in place to prevent unauthorized access to the corporate network from the Internet, and they may not want to support an inbound connection from a program such as pcANYWHERE.

One of the authors uses pcANYWHERE through his local area network at home, since it is connected to the Internet using a cable modem. Since he has installed a firewall/proxy server to protect against unwanted access, the firewall has been configured to allow inbound pcANYWHERE calls, as long as the appropriate user ID and password are provided.

If you want this type of connection, we suggest that you talk to your corporate network administrator. It will work, but it depends on whether they will allow it.

Videophones and Videoconferencing Through the Internet

In one of our earlier books, the *1997 Canadian Internet Handbook*, we examined some of the programs that were available at the time that allowed you to make a "telephone call" through the Internet. We weren't too impressed; they seemed flaky and unreliable, and the quality was marginal at best.

Today, the technology to communicate with others on the Internet, either by voice only or by voice and video, is much more mature, due to improvements in the software, hardware, and the emergence of 56 Kbps modems and higher speeds of access. Many companies are now producing "videophone" products that allow two or more people to hear and see each other "live" on the Internet. We had the opportunity to work with a few of these videophone products, and we are impressed with what we have found. To videoconference over the Internet, you will need video-conferencing software plus the following hardware:

- **To send and receive audio:** microphone, speakers, sound card.

- **To send and receive video:** video capture card, video camera.

If your computer was purchased within the last few years, it probably came with speakers, a microphone, and a built-in sound card. You may, however, need to obtain the video capture card and video camera, although many newer computers come bundled with these components. Some videoconferencing products include the camera and video capture card. This is the case with the Intel Create and Share Camera Pack, which we review below. However, other videoconferencing products, like VDOPhone (also discussed below), only supply the videoconferencing software.

You should also be aware that some video cameras have the video capture card built in. In this situation, all you need to do is plug the camera into a port at the back of your computer. Otherwise, you may have to manually install a video capture card in your computer and then attach the camera to it. The situation will depend on what package you buy and what hardware you already have installed on your computer. Before buying any videoconferencing package, read the system requirements carefully, and make sure that you have all the necessary pieces of hardware.

If you are interested in experimenting with videoconferencing over the Internet, take a look at the Intel Video Phone software, which comes with the Intel Create and Share Pack (**www.intel.com/createshare**). It is one of many PC-based videoconferencing packages that you can buy. The package includes videoconferencing software and hardware for your computer as well as a tiny video camera, seen below:

The videoconferencing software takes just a few seconds to install:

Intel A/V Configuration Wizard

Welcome to the Intel A/V Configuration Wizard.

This wizard helps you configure your system for use with Intel visual communication products.

Please close all other programs that play or record sound or video. Then choose one of the following options:

- ○ Configure Audio
- ○ Configure Video
- ● Configure Both Audio and Video

Help

< Back | Next > | Cancel

It will run a series of tests to make sure that it can play sound, record your voice to transmit through the Internet, and pick up a picture through your video camera:

Speaker Test

Click Start Playing.

This wizard repeatedly plays an audio file of a person speaking. Adjust the speaker volume to a comfortable level. Click Next when you are satisfied.

If you do not hear any audio, click Help.

Start Playing

Low   Speaker Volume   High

Help

< Back | Next > | Cancel

When you start the software, you will see a picture of yourself on the screen if you are sitting in front of the camera:

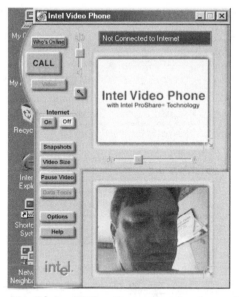

When you want to call someone with Intel Video Phone, you simply provide his or her e-mail address, telephone number, or TCP/IP address. You will most likely use the latter. If you use an e-mail address, that information is used simply to look him or her up online in order to find the IP address. You can also use a telephone number to contact someone directly without going through the Internet:

Most videophone software programs are integrated into the Web, so that you locate other users of the software and find people to videoconference with. If during the setup process you indicated that you are willing to accept calls from anyone, your name and e-mail address would be added to the list of online users. Whenever you start the videophone software, the listing of online users will indicate that you are online and available to accept a call:

Once you have provided the details of who you want to contact, the software works on establishing a connection. The person you are trying to reach will be notified that he or she has an incoming call, which can either be accepted or rejected:

Once that is done, you're in business! We were up and running within a matter of minutes, so our opinion on this technology has definitely changed.

tip Videoconferencing Over Regular Phone Lines

In addition to allowing you to videoconference over the Internet, some videophone products allow you to videoconference over regular phone lines without the Internet. Perhaps the person you want to connect with isn't on the Internet. However, remember that this type of videoconferencing can be expensive if the person you are calling isn't in your local calling area. If you want to videoconference over regular telephone lines, make sure your videophone software (and the videophone software the other person is using) supports the H.324 standard. This standard allows a videophone product from one manufacturer to accept calls from a videophone product from a different manufacturer For your modem to work properly with an H.324-compliant videophone product, your modem must support the new V.80 modem protocol. Older modems do not support this protocol, but some of the newer modems do.

We also experimented with VDOnet's VDOPhone software (**www.vdo.net**), one of the leading software videoconferencing programs. Unlike the Intel Create and Share Camera Pack, however, VDOPhone doesn't come with everything you need. For example, you have to supply your own camera and the appropriate video capture card. We found that VDOPhone worked with the camera that came with our Intel Create and Share Camera Pack as well as a variety of other cameras.

The program provides a very good example of how easy and straightforward it has become to install videoconferencing software on your computer:

The first thing you can do when setting it up is indicate whether you are willing to accept calls from anyone, or if you want the ability to "screen" them, thus indicating who you are willing to take calls from:

Assessing the Effectiveness
of Your Web Site

Protecting Yourself Online

Improving Your Productivity
on the Internet

Enhancing Your Web Site

VDOPhone Setup Wizard - Session Preferences

How do you want to handle incoming calls?

Screen all incoming calls

Greeting Message :

Hi there and good day, eh?

Help   Default   < Back   Next >   Cancel

There is a screen where you can conduct tests to make sure that the audio—both listening and talking—is working correctly:

VDOPhone Setup Wizard - Audio Devices

Choose the audio recording and audio playback devices you
want to test:

☐ Enable Hardware Compression

Audio Devices

Recording   Windows Multimedia's Selection

Playback   Windows Multimedia's Selection

Help   < Back   Next >   Cancel

VDOPhone Setup Wizard - Audio Configuration

Press the Record button and speak into your microphone.
Stop speaking and press the Stop button.
Press Play and listen to your recording, using the slider below
to raise or lower volume. If necessary, repeat test adjusting
your distance from the microphone.

Recording volume:

Playback volume:

Playback
progress

Help   < Back   Next >   Cancel

Then the program tests your video configuration to make sure that it can get a picture:

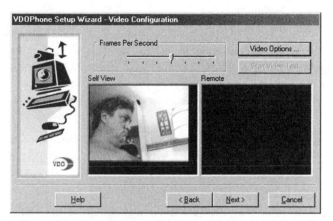

Once this is done, you're ready to start videoconferencing!

State-of-the-Art Today

What can you expect in terms of quality with such technology? First, the size of the screen will be somewhat small; most programs provide a resolution of 320×240 or smaller, so you will see a relatively tiny picture on your screen. Second, the number of frames per second that you can transmit will depend on the speed of your Internet connection. The slower the number of frames per second, the jerkier your video will be. But you don't need to have a cable or ADSL connection to the Internet in order to use the videoconferencing programs we have described. While the quality won't be terrific, they will work over 28.8 Kbps or 56 Kbps dial-up connections.

POPULAR VIDEOCONFERENCING PRODUCTS FOR THE INTERNET

CU-SeeMe	**www.wpine.com/Products/CU-SeeMe**
Intel Video Phone	**www.intel.com/createshare**
Microsoft NetMeeting	**www.microsoft.com/netmeeting**
VDOPhone	**www.vdo.net**
Bigpicture video phone (3COM)	**www.3com.com/bigpicture**
Connectix VideoPhone	**www.connectix.com**

Potential Complexities

From our experience with videoconferencing products, we have found that the technology has matured enough that it is very simple and certainly worth investing in, particularly to keep in touch with friends and colleagues when you are on the road. Nevertheless, there are a number of issues that you should be aware of:

Firewall Conflicts

One of the authors was not able to use the videoconferencing software on his local area network because it was protected by a firewall, a limitation that exists with all videoconferencing software. Hence you can probably expect problems if you try to use such software to communicate with your co-workers back in the office, if they are on a corporate network that is protected by a firewall.

Software Conflicts

Earlier we told you about the emerging standard called H.323, which promises to allow videoconferencing software from one vendor communicate with that of another (as long as both of you are using videoconferencing software that adheres to the H.323 standards). However, since it is still relatively new, we suggest that you stick with one software program for both the sending and receiving ends, and if possible, stick with the same camera.

Hardware Conflicts

You may find that the video camera you've purchased doesn't work with the video card in your computer. We had that problem. Hence before you buy videoconferencing software, make sure that it will work with your computer.

Hardware Opportunities

The upside of learning that the video camera we bought didn't work with our video card was the discovery that our regular Sony video camera would. We simply plugged our Sony Handycam into the Matrox video card that we use for video editing (see Chapter 15, "Adding Audio and Video to Your Web Site") and discovered that it could be used to support a videoconference. An unexpected but welcome surprise.

Summary

If you travel, get a program like pcANYWHERE; it is invaluable. But to really make it work well, get a cable modem or ADSL connection to the Internet, so that the computer you are trying to reach with pcANYWHERE is always available.

As for videoconferencing, we encourage you to try it out should it fit your business or personal needs. A few years ago the concept of a phone call over the Internet, while real, was almost laughable in terms of the quality and complexity of what you were faced with. But what we have seen with online videoconferencing makes it obvious that things have improved for the better.

chapter twelve

Just-in-Time Knowledge Using Search Accelerators

The sheer vastness of the Web can be frustrating...search tools pick up where the search sites leave off.
PC Magazine Utility Guide 98

Highlights

1. Programs called search accelerators (sometimes called offline search utilities) can help you speed up your search for information on the Internet.

2. These programs operate by querying several search engines simultaneously and summarizing the results in a variety of formats.

3. Some programs offer special features, such as conducting searches on specialized databases, downloading the search results onto your hard drive, and scheduling your search to take place on a regular basis, at a specified time each day or a certain day of the week.

The ability to search the Internet for information is improving all the time, particularly if you use some of the programs that are now available to help you streamline your search. These programs, called search accelerators, simultaneously query several search engines for the words or phrases you are searching for. They then summarize the results for you in a simple, easy-to-read format, eliminating any duplications that may have been found.

POPULAR SEARCH ACCELERATORS

Copernic Plus 98	**www.copernic.com**
Hurricane WebSearch	**www.gatecomm.com**
Inforian Quest 98	**www.inforian.com**
Mata Hari	**www.thewebtools.com**
NetFerret	**www.ferretsoft.com**
QueryN Metasearch	**www.queryn.com**
SuperSleuth	**www.promptsoftware.com**
WebCompass	**www.qdeck.com**
WebFerret Pro	**www.ferretsoft.com**
WebSeeker98	**www.bluesquirrel.com**
WebSleuth	**www.promptsoftware.com**
WebSnake	**www.anawave.com**
WebStorm	**www.sharpeware.com**

How Do Search Accelerators Work?

A search accelerator is a separate program that runs on your computer. It acts as an intermediary between you and a number of different search engines on the Web. Type the word or phrase that you are looking for, and the program will go off and check the most popular search engines for any related Web pages. It then lets you examine the results, either on a custom Web page that details the results of the search or within the program itself.

The greatest benefit of these programs is that the results are sorted into a simple, easy-to-use format, allowing you to quickly browse the search results and review only those sites that appear to contain relevant information. Some of the programs will also let you see the first few lines of each relevant page in that site, which helps you to quickly identify those pages that interest you, while others download the entire Web page for you. The result is that you can cover a lot of different search engines very quickly when doing a search, and you can then do a quick scan to find those sites most likely to contain what you need.

Within a short time, you will likely find yourself relying on one of these tools, and you will discover that they greatly simplify the task of searching for information on the Internet.

A good example of such a search accelerator is Copernic 98plus by Quebec-based Agents Technologies. To undertake a search, you simply type the words or phrase you are looking for into the search box on the screen. You can specify whether you are looking for the exact phrase, any of the words, or all of the words together on a Web page. You also choose the category of information you would like to search, in this case, any information found on the Web:

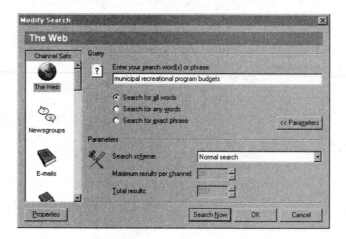

Copernic 98plus reports on its progress as it submits the search to various search engines:

Within a few seconds or more, depending on the complexity of the search and the speed of your Internet connection, Copernic 98plus builds a list of the Web pages that it found and includes the first few lines of text from each page. This helps you to quickly browse through the list to focus on the most relevant ones:

Common Features Found in Search Accelerators

The sophistication of these programs is improving all the time; indeed, we found that the programs we looked at for this year's edition had improved greatly over those available in previous years. But there are still a number of basic features that you will find.

Downloading the Results of Your Search

A great feature found in some search accelerators is the ability to download Web pages that your search has turned up. Why is this useful? Think about this: when you use a search engine on the Web, you see the title of the Web page and, sometimes, a brief description of the page. You scan through the list and identify one that looks interesting. But when you travel there, you discover that the information it contains is of little relevance. In effect, you have wasted time travelling to a Web site.

But if you use one of the software tools that allow you to download the pages that match your search, then you can browse through the results much more quickly, since the information from the page is now stored on your computer.

Both WebSeeker98 and WebCompass allow you to do this. For example, when doing a WebSeeker98 search, under the type of search you specify the "FilterFind" option. This instructs the program to go off and retrieve the actual Web pages for the sites that it finds in its search:

It takes longer, but the results are worth it. On the left-hand side of the screen below is a list of the sites that contained the phrase we were looking for; on the right-hand side is the text from one of the pages. In 5 or 10 seconds you can quickly browse through the text of the retrieved sites, making it very easy to select only those sites that you want.

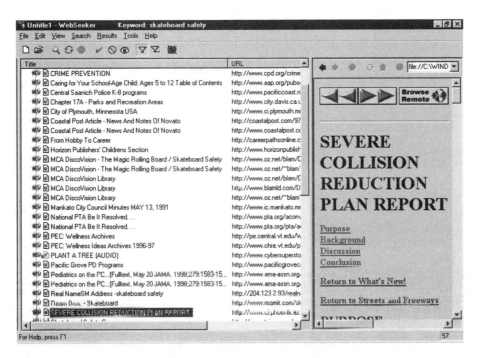

WebSeeker98 also lets you do this another way: it builds a customized Web page for you containing the results of your search, which includes snippets of information from each Web page. Each item is linked to some information now stored on your hard disk, meaning that you can very quickly browse through the list to find the best information.

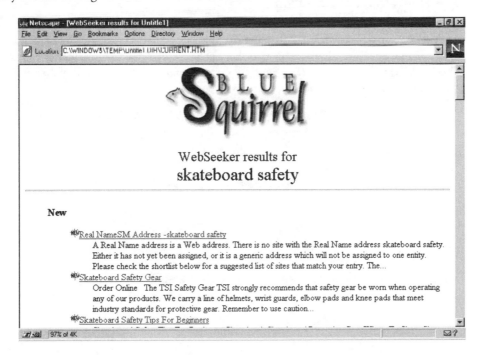

Choose any of the items on this page, and you can view a copy of the actual Web pages that have been downloaded—without the graphics, so that you can search through the information faster.

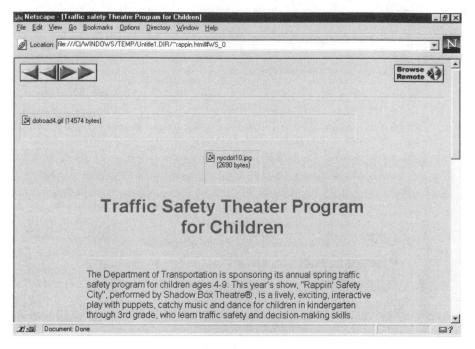

Customizing Your Search Engines

All the programs allow you to select from the list of search engines that they access, and some of them have a more extensive list than others. Some of the programs also organize search engines into various categories. For example, in the WebSeeker98 screen below, we have chosen to search the "Kids" category, which means only two search engines—Disney (**www.disney.com**) and Yahooligans! (**www.yahooligans.com**)—are searched:

Similarly, when you install Inforian Quest 98, you are provided a list (that you can change later) in which you can specify the search engines that should be searched:

As might be expected, some programs offer a more extensive list of search engines than others. Inforian Quest 98, for example, allows you to search within a number of global search engines from Japan, Korea, Germany, France, and many other countries, thus getting away from the typical reliance on mainstream search engines, such as AltaVista (**www.altavista.digital.com**). This can be extremely useful if you are doing geographic- or culture-specific research:

With WebCompass and WebSeeker98, you can add your own search engines to the list.

Our only disappointment? Few of the search engines used Canadian-specific systems, such as Yahoo! Canada (**www.yahoo.ca**) and AltaVista Canada (**www.altavistacanada.com**).

Goto a New Search Engine

A new search engine appearing at the time we wrote this chapter, goto.com (**www.goto.com**), promises to help you concentrate on simply searching the Internet and avoids many of the advertisements and other features that clutter other search engine sites.

Scheduling Your Searches

Most of the programs can be instructed to run a search at a predetermined time. This can be useful if you want to program a search for, say, 4:00 a.m., when the Internet might be least busy in your area. WebCompass goes one step beyond simply scheduling: you can program WebCompass to update the results of your search on a regular basis.

Eliminating Advertising

One final benefit of some of these programs is this: in some cases, Web page advertising disappears! At least you don't see it in your search results. Instead, you view straightforward, concise summaries of search results. In some cases, however, you do have the option of seeing advertisements if you wish. WebSeeker98, for example, will let you choose to see advertising on the pages that it retrieves:

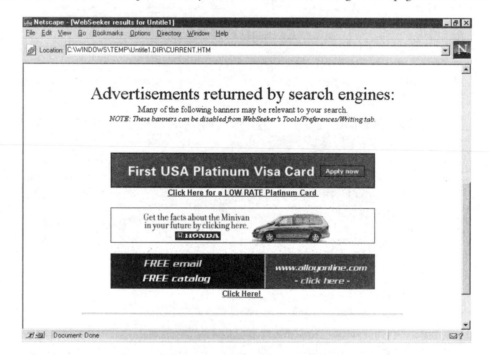

What Search Accelerators Do Not Solve

Before you begin to use the tools described in this chapter, it's important to understand that search accelerators do not solve several of the major problems associated with searching for information on the Internet. You will still encounter irrelevant, out-of-date, and inaccurate information. And you will still be frustrated by pointers to sites that no longer exist. These programs do not make those challenges disappear; they simply make them more manageable. Depending on what you are looking for, in some cases they may simply help you find junk on the Internet that much quicker.

All in all, search accelerators are great for serious researchers and casual Internet users alike. Trial versions of most of the programs we review in this chapter are available on the vendor's Web site. Many of these programs will automatically upgrade themselves through the Internet, so that you know you are using the most recent version.

tip Keeping Current

There is a constant stream of new search accelerators being developed. To keep on top of them, look at the Search Tools category in Yahoo! at **www.yahoo.ca/Computers_and_Internet/ Software/Reviews/Titles/Internet/Search_Tools/**.

Select Search Accelerators

Copernic 98plus

We liked this program a lot! It's fast, responsive, does a good job in retrieving information, and sports enough flexibility that you can undertake some pretty sophisticated and extensive searches.

The program allows you to search for exact phrases, all occurrences of various words within a page, and any of your search phrases within a page, thus providing a lot of flexibility in the way you search.

After running your search, you can instruct the program to simply retrieve a listing of results or to actually go ahead and download the Web pages that it found.

By downloading the pages to your PC automatically, you can speed up how much time you spend browsing the results to focus on relevant pages. Of course, downloading them will obviously take longer, so you will likely use this feature only if you have the time to wait, are about to head out for lunch, or are leaving the office for the rest of the day.

You can also choose to run your search, click on the results that look the most interesting, and then download only those Web pages (or "documents," as Copernic 98plus refers to them) that are relevant:

If you run a search but do not choose to automatically download the results, you will find that one of the most useful features of the program is its "validation" feature. In this case, you can instruct the program to determine whether the Web pages that were found by the various search engines actually still exist:

This helps get around the frustration we all feel when going to access a Web page that was indexed within a search engine and included in the list of results by Copernic 98plus, only to discover that it has disappeared.

Copernic 98plus has more useful features: you can keep copies of your searches so that you can refer back to them, rerun them, and even modify what you are looking for at any time; you can organize your saved searches into folders, thus helping you to organize information into topics that you research on a regular basis.

In addition, when searching, you are not restricted to the usual list of search engines such as AltaVista (**www.altavista.digital.com**) and Infoseek (**www.infoseek.com**). In fact, the program allows you to run searches within a number of specific categories, as can be seen on the left of the search screen below, including searches for telephone numbers, business news, e-mail addresses, sports information, and more:

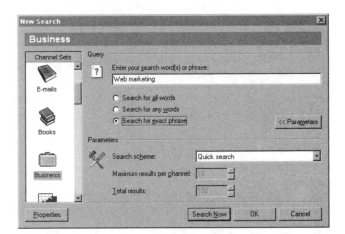

When Copernic 98plus does such a category search, it avoids the mainstream search engines and instead relies on systems that are dedicated to that topic. For example, we went looking for information about "tourism guides" for "New Hampshire" and got a very concise and useful list of results:

When Copernic 98plus does such a category search, it avoids the mainstream search engines and instead relies on systems that are dedicated to that topic. For example, we went looking for information about "tourism guides" for "New Hampshire" and got a very concise and useful list of results:

Looking behind the scenes, we found that Copernic 98plus accomplishes such a feat by relying on a select list of travel-related search engines (which it refers to as "channel sets"):

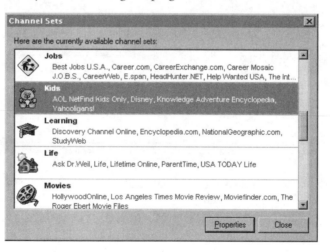

You can examine any of these search categories, or "channel sets," to get an idea of the specialized information searches that you can do using the program:

There are some very specialized searches that you can do using this capability, such as looking for jobs posted on popular job boards for a particular city. In just a few short seconds, we were able to retrieve a listing of "year 2000" related jobs in the City of Toronto:

The only thing that we didn't like? Given that the program was developed by a Canadian company, it does little in terms of searching Canadian-specific information resources. In particular, the version we explored didn't use AltaVista Canada, Yahoo! Canada, or any other Canadian search systems. The disappointments didn't end there: when we chose to do a search of job listings, it didn't use any of the sophisticated Canadian career sites online, the news search didn't access any Canadian news sites, and so on.

Obviously, many software companies in Canada must focus on the opportunities south of the border, because all too often that is the only way to make any money. But we don't think it is a lot to ask that the obvious U.S.-centric focus of the program be tweaked a bit to include some useful Canadian content. We have no doubt that this situation will be corrected in future releases. But all in all, we think Copernic 98plus is one of the most useful Internet utilities you can find.

Inforian Quest 98

Like Copernic 98plus, you can use Inforian Quest 98 to run a search that focuses on specific categories such as entertainment, news, and technology. In doing so, you will find that one of the most fascinating aspects of this particular program is the extent of specialized search engines that you can use for your search. For example, you can focus on specific countries, ski-related information, television-related information, and many other categories. You can even do a search within a search engine that is devoted to acronyms.

For each category, Inforian Quest 98 maintains a list of the search engines that it looks at, as seen with this list of sources referenced when doing a search on Chinese topics:

Clearly, this is a program designed for an international market; not only can you research various global search engines, but you can choose to run the program in either English, French, German, or Spanish:

Inforian Quest 98 is useful if you need to find very specific country information or other specialized searches, but it is not as extensive in terms of features as Copernic 98plus. Hence we recommend it if you have specialized global research needs.

NetFerret

NetFerret, by FerretSoft, has a "family" of seven utilities:

- WebFerret and WebFerretPRO for searching the World Wide Web.

- EmailFerret for finding e-mail addresses.

- FileFerretPRO for locating files on the Internet.

- IRCFerret for finding people in Internet chat forums.

- NewsFerret for retrieving USENET news articles (USENET is a collection of tens of thousands of discussion groups on the Internet).

- PhoneFerret for finding telephone numbers.

All the programs are simple, straightforward, and to the point. For example, in the screen below we are using EmailFerret to search a number of Internet Web sites for e-mail addresses:

And below, we are searching a variety of telephone directory Web sites for phone numbers. Unfortunately, the program wasn't capable of searching for online Canadian phone directories:

These utilities, which run as separate programs, are quite worthwhile, since they let you do some quick and effective searches on very specific topics.

While the Web search programs, WebFerret and WebFerretPRO, do not offer the sophistication of some of the other programs in this chapter, they do allow you to quickly browse through a list of search results. Simply move your cursor over any retrieved item, and a box pops up with the first few sentences of text from that Web site, which it retrieved while running the search:

WebFerretPRO provides a lot of flexibility in your search, including looking for an exact phrase.

Overall, the NetFerret group of programs, although not as sophisticated as some of the other programs, do offer flexibility and straightforward searching capabilities and are definitely worth a look.

tip All-in-One

In addition to using search accelerators to query multiple search engines simultaneously, try using all-in-one search engines, Web sites that query multiple search engines. Popular all-in-one search engines are MetaCrawler (**www.metacrawler.com**), Dogpile (**www.dogpile.com**), Ask Jeeves (**www.askjeeves.com**), and SavvySearch (**www.savvysearch.com**).

SuperSleuth

Another worthy contender is SuperSleuth from Prompt Software (**www.promptsoftware.com**). This program will search multiple search engines and organize the search results into a concise list, as seen on the left-hand side of the screen:

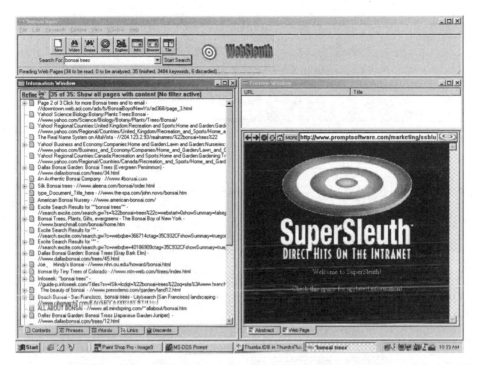

Choose any item, double click on it, and you will see the associated Web page on the right. You can easily navigate within that page within the SuperSleuth program, exploring other Web pages linked to this one, or you can quickly load your Web browser to view the page:

SuperSleuth contains an extensive list of search engines, all of which can be categorized by topic:

The most important feature of this program, and the one that makes it unique, is its ability to "refine" your search terms after running a search. The biggest problem with using a search engine or a desktop search utility is the often massive volume of search results that you can obtain. For example, we did a search for the phrase "Internet strategic planning" and came away with a lengthy list of likely Web pages:

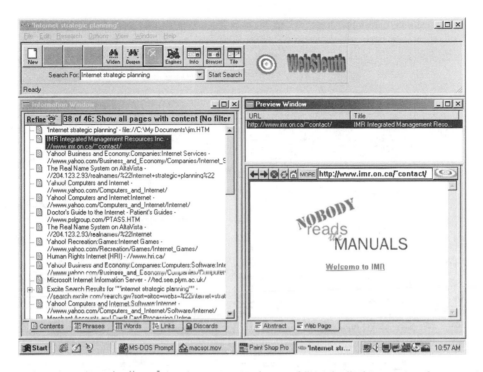

We then chose to refine the list of sites by typing in the word "articles." This restricted our retrieved list to only those that contained references to actual articles about "Internet strategic planning." This refining feature can help greatly in narrowing in on only the most useful information:

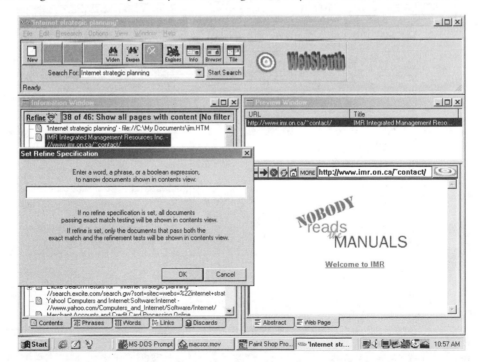

In addition to this feature, you can access a list of words that have been indexed by SuperSleuth in the retrieved Web pages. It can be a pretty extensive list:

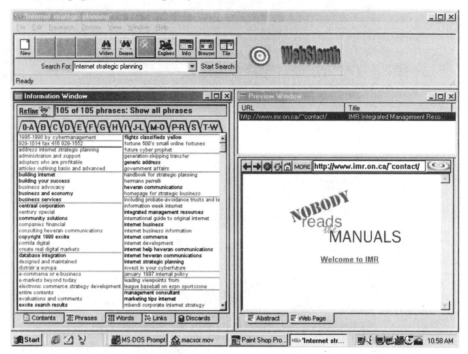

But you can refine this list too, focusing on only those that match a certain word. This is another useful way to focus on the best Web pages, in this case, articles related to "Internet strategic planning":

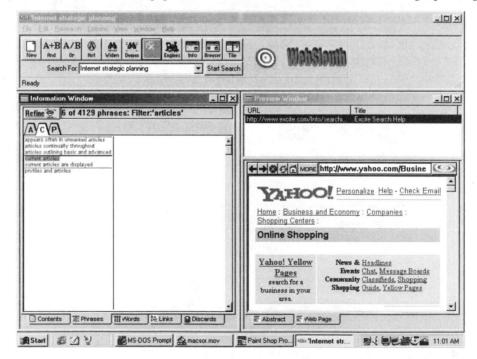

Hence SuperSleuth includes some innovative features that help you deal with the flood of information that you often encounter when searching the Internet.

SuperSleuth Does Super Searches

You can use SuperSleuth to do more than search the Internet; it will search your entire hard disk as well, making it an excellent tool to archive and search your own information. We talked about archiving and searching e-mail in Chapter 10.

WebCompass

WebCompass is perhaps the most sophisticated of all the desktop search software, and has certainly been around for the longest period of time. It contains many of the features found in Copernic 98plus, but does a better job at organizing the retrieved information for you. The program will retrieve your search results and organize them on the right-hand side of the screen. It also retrieves the Web page and places the text that was found at the bottom of the screen. Thus you get a concise view of the results of your search:

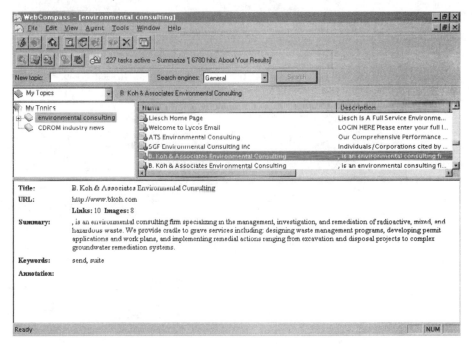

As a result, rather than travelling to each and every Web site, you can quickly scan through the list of what was found, examine some of the content from certain sites, and determine which are useful. Want to see the full Web page of a site of interest? Just double click on any item, and your Web browser will load the page from your hard disk.

WebCompass stands out as a tool when it comes to managing the results of your searches. It allows you to keep many different searches and update them at any time simply by clicking a button; you can also schedule your searches to take place on a regular basis. This allows you to automatically update a particular topic search every week, thus turning WebCompass into a powerful and useful information-monitoring tool:

You can search for the occurrence of any word or phrase in the database of all of your searches. This can be very helpful if you have a number of searches and cannot find a particular document that you remembered reading:

One of the most powerful features of WebCompass is its ability to organize the search results into various categories. For example, we have done a search for any Web pages that contain the topic "environmental consulting." After WebCompass retrieved the results (in this case, several hundred documents), we chose the option "Organize by content." WebCompass suggested a number of subtopics based on its analysis of what was retrieved:

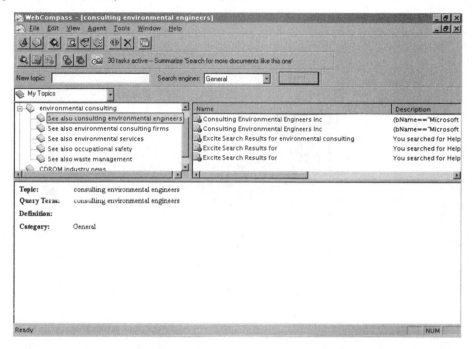

It then filed relevant pages into each subtopic, further assisting you in narrowing in on relevant content.

If you have done a lot of searches within WebCompass and have kept most of them, you may have difficulty finding a particular page that you looked at before. WebCompass has a handy feature that lets you examine every page within every search that you have undertaken:

Perhaps the most useful aspect of this program is that you can add your own search systems. Go into the "Tools" section, and choose "Search Resources." Choose to add an item and provide a name and the Web address of the page that is used to search the archive. Here, we want to add to our search category "Canadian news" the ability to search back issues of the *Toronto Star* (**www.thestar.com**):

Add Search Resource

Enter a name for the new resource and the URL where you normally enter your search query. WebCompass will then show you a copy of the form and ask you for additional information.

Resource name:	Toronto Star back issues
Resource URL:	http://www.thestar.ca
Category:	Canadian news
Username:	
Password:	

Capture   Cancel   Help

WebCompass then leads you through a process in which you can add the search capability within the *Toronto Star* site to the list of "search engines" that WebCompass will use.

We highly recommend this program for the avid researcher; its features and flexibility make it one of the most powerful desktop search programs that you can use.

WebSeeker98

Like WebCompass, WebSeeker98 has been around for several years and is also an extremely sophisticated desktop search program.

WebSeeker98 offers excellent flexibility in how you go about conducting your search. There are three types of searches that you can run in WebSeeker98: InstantFind, CleanFind, and FilterFind:

Start New Search

Keywords | Search Engines

OR   AND   PHRASE   SUBSTRING

success of community networks

Type of Search

Speed

InstantFind - Fastest, removes duplicates.

CleanFind - Faster, removes unavailable sites and duplicates.

FilterFind - Fast, same as CleanFind but indexes results for further refinement.

Accuracy

Find Now
Find Later
Cancel
Help

The first, InstantFind, retrieves a list of matching Web pages (which it refers to as documents) from various search engines, removing any duplicates, while the second, CleanFind, takes the time to verify if the Web pages that were found actually exist. The third option, FilterFind, downloads the relevant Web pages to your PC (excluding images) so that you can browse through the results that much more quickly. Obviously, the CleanFind process takes longer than the InstantFind, and the FilterFind method takes even longer.

You can use these features in various ways. For example, if you have done an InstantFind search, you might discover that a particular Web page does not exist or has been moved:

Rerun the entire search in CleanFind or FilterFind mode, and such irrelevant documents will disappear from your listing. Thus the program provides the same type of "validation" feature as found in Copernic 98plus.

What is also important and useful, and goes beyond what is offered in many other desktop search programs, is the flexibility available for your search. Take a look at the types of searches you can undertake in the screen on page 276: you can do a search based on the use of the operators OR and AND, or you can search for an exact PHRASE. You can even do a SUBSTRING search, that is, looking for AUTOmobile, AUTOmotive, and other similar words.

Once you finish searching, you can browse the results within WebSeeker98 or within your browser program simply by choosing that option:

Like WebCompass, you can also schedule searches to be run on a regular basis, and you can index all the searches that you have run before and have been saved, so that you can find information within those searches directly.

You can also add your own custom search systems to WebSeeker98. For example, say you want to add the ability to search CANOE (**www.canoe.com**), the Canadian Online Explorer site, so that you can search the *Financial Post* and other back issues of various Canadian newspapers. Choose the option within WebSeeker98 to add a Web search engine, and then click on the button to "link" to the site within your Web browser. Your browser program is started, and you are taken to that page:

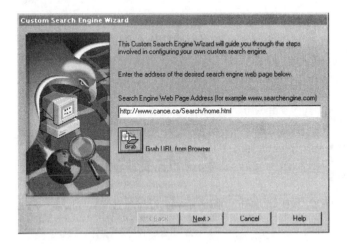

Then WebSeeker98 instructs you to run a search within that page on CANOE, and from this, figures out how to add the search capability at CANOE to your WebSeeker98 program:

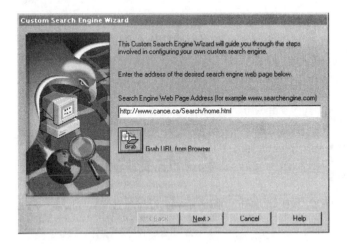

Like many other programs, WebSeeker98 offers a number of different categories that you can search and examines various specialized search engines related to each of those categories:

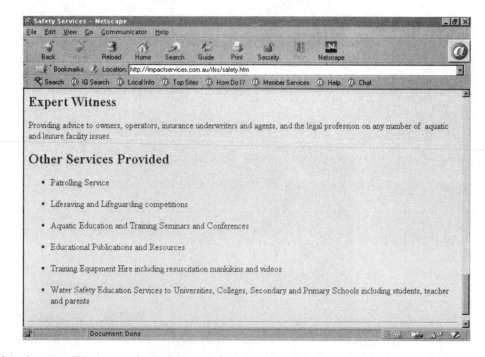

In addition to WebSeeker98, Blue Squirrel offers two other search programs: LegalSeeker98 and TechSeeker98, both of which are based on the WebSeeker98 program. LegalSeeker98 allows you to search some 40 legal search engines, making this a very useful tool for those involved in the legal profession.

For example, we used the legal program to search for an "expert witness" on "swimming pools" and were quickly able to locate a number of relevant resources:

TechSeeker98 will help you find "drivers, software, technical solutions, & product info using 75+ online technical resources." When running the TechSeeker98 program, the search results are categorized into "new" and "old" categories. This helps you to focus on the most recent articles about specific technologies within the computer trade press.

Bottom line? We found the WebSeeker98 and related LegalSeeker98 and TechSeeker98 programs to be more than up to the job, particularly if you want to focus on these two topics, or if you want to be able to customize the searches.

In the *1999 Canadian Internet Directory and Research Guide* we dedicated a few chapters to the topic of how to better search the Internet. The *Directory and Research Guide* is a valuable tool to assist you in finding information on the Internet.

WebSnake

WebSnake is in a class of its own, in that it doesn't use search engines to find information; rather, it locates information for you that exists within the Web site you specify. The program was designed primarily to help you download an entire Web site (which you can do), so that you can read it offline, something we talked about in Chapter 10. But in addition to locating information within a certain Web site, it has another very interesting and useful ability: it searches for e-mail addresses. Say you work in public relations and would like to locate all the e-mail addresses within the Baton Broadcasting system Web site (**www.baton.com**). Simply instruct WebSnake that you would like to do an e-mail search:

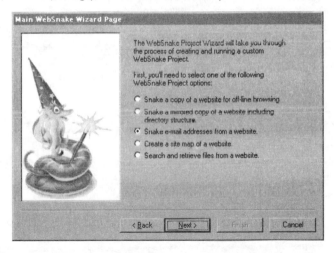

Type in the Web site address you want to search, in this case, **www.baton.com**:

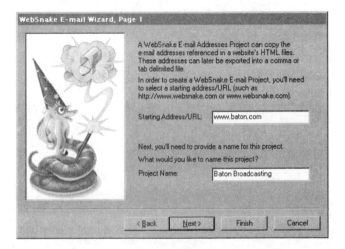

and within a few minutes, WebSnake builds a list based on the information it found by examining each page in that site:

Looking for details about the CEO of Baton Broadcasting? Do a search of the same Web site looking for "CEO" or "Chief Executive Officer." WebSnake will build a listing of Web pages within the Baton Broadcasting Web site containing those words:

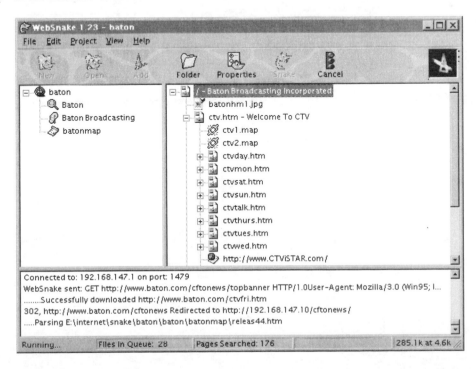

Just click on any of the results, and you will be taken to that page.

Finally, you can use the program to download an entire Web site to your hard drive or create a "map" of the structure of the site:

The program is very powerful in this regard; we once instructed it to download the entire TDBank site (**www.tdbank.ca**), consisting of some several thousand pages, and it did.

Conclusion

As you can see, these programs range from simple and straightforward tools, such as the NetFerret group, which simply search several Web sites and prepare a concise summary of search results, to more detailed tools, such as WebCompass, which allow you to manage the information you gather and conduct some fairly complicated searches.

You may find that there is no "best" program that you will use. Instead, you may use a mix of the programs found in this chapter, since you will likely find that you will need the straightforward features of a program like WebFerret for some "quick and dirty" searching, and you may need the more detailed features of something like Copernic 98plus for your more advanced needs. Since many of these programs vary in price, it is a good idea for you to download a demonstration version of the program(s) you are interested in. By trying out a number of them you will be able to determine which ones are best for your particular needs.

chapter thirteen

Knowledge Monitoring

"It's like someone writes a daily paper for me," she says.

"PC services deliver all the news you see fit to print," *HomePC*, March 1, 1997

Highlights

1. A number of personalized news, or "newsclipping," services are emerging on the Internet.

2. Every day, these services "read" new articles appearing in magazines and newspapers and can either e-mail those that interest you or build a customized Web page detailing those articles.

3. You can use these services to track certain topics, issues, industries, or companies on a regular basis, thus enhancing your knowledge monitoring skills.

In this chapter we look at five personalized news services that can assist you in developing your knowledge monitoring skills. We define "knowledge monitoring" as the ability to use the tools of the Internet to keep up-to-date on a topic or issue that is important to you. Many also call these types of programs "newsclipping" services, but the programs we review here do more than just retrieve up-to-the-minute news, sports, weather, and other information. (These "newsclipping" programs are often called "push services," examples of which are PointCast and Headliner. They can become quite overwhelming after a short time, because the number of news and other articles sent to you can be huge with many of little value.) The services that we are talking about are designed to let you define some very focused and specific search criteria. The programs then automatically and regularly retrieve articles and access Web pages containing articles related to those criteria. There are currently five such services that we think are worthy of your attention.

KNOWLEDGE MONITORING SERVICES

NewsPage	**www.newspage.com**
Inquisit	**www.inquisit.com**
NewsHound	**www.newshound.com**
Infomart	**www.infomart.ca**
InfoGlobe-Dow Jones Interactive	**www.djinteractive.com**

Each of these services differs in the information that they allow you to access, the nature and sophistication of the custom search routine that you set up, the options available to you to access the results of searches, and other features. Cost, for instance. There are essentially two cost categories: straightforward, low-cost services, such as NewsPage, Inquisit, and NewsHound, and more expensive services, such as Infomart and InfoGlobe-Dow Jones Interactive.

Comparison of Different Custom News Services

Cost

Many newsclipping services are available for free, while others charge a yearly or monthly fee. Some fee-based services offer only one package, while others provide a variety of different pricing options to accommodate customers with different needs. Commercial services generally offer more flexibility and customization than free ones. If a fee is charged, find out what it does and does not include.

Method of Delivery

News can be delivered to you by electronic mail or on the World Wide Web. Some services offer both of these options, while others offer only one delivery method. Think carefully about which delivery method you prefer. If you choose to receive news stories by e-mail, and if you are tracking a very popular subject such as politics, be prepared to receive a lot of information. If you are not accustomed to dealing with large volumes of information, a regular stream of e-mail messages can easily overwhelm you. In such cases, e-mail may not be the best choice. However, if you are interested in receiving breaking news as it happens, then e-mail is the way to go, since an e-mail-based service notifies you automatically; with a Web-based service, you have to regularly log in to access new stories. A third method of delivery is to use a proprietary software package that you must obtain from the company supplying the news service.

Sources of News

Personalized news services differ both in terms of the variety of sources they monitor and the number of sources they use. The most popular sources of news are the major news wire services (Associated Press, UPI, Reuters, Business Wire, and PR Newswire) and Canadian press release services (Canada Newswire and Canadian Corporate News). Certain sources may be more important to you, depending on the types of topics you want to follow.

Archives

Some news services offer archives of old news stories to their customers. Here are some questions to ask: Are archives available? Can they be searched? Is there a fee for this service? How much does it cost to retrieve an article from the archives?

Frequency of News Delivery

Some services are more flexible than others here. Determine how frequently your news is delivered to you. For example, is it delivered to you once a day, several times a day, or as it happens?

Access to Full Text

Again, the services differ here. Does the news service deliver the full text of articles to you or only the headlines? If you only see part of the article, can you access the full text version, and how much does it cost?

Value-Added Services

Some news services allow you to receive other information in addition to news stories, such as stock quotes, comics, horoscopes, and birthday reminders. Often these extras are available at no charge.

Depth of Customization

Some news services impose a maximum on the number of topics you can track and/or restrict you to monitoring topics that they have predefined. Other services provide much greater flexibility and allow you to select an unlimited number of topics to follow. So when choosing a newsclipping service, find out to what extent you can customize the delivery of your news stories. Also find out how easy it is for you to change your personal profile should you decide at some point to modify the types of subjects you are monitoring.

tip Newsclipping With Explorer

You can do a rudimentary form of newsclipping in Internet Explorer 4.0. Add a page to your "Favorites," and indicate that you want to be notified when the page changes. Then click on customize. You can ask to be notified by e-mail. This allows you to monitor a particular Web page and stay on top of any changes on that page.

We have a few other general comments about personalized news services:

- Some services will require you to obtain a user ID and password to use when you sign in. There are two problems here: first, if you have a popular name, you will probably find that your choice of username is already gone. (There seem to be, for example, a lot of people out there who have already taken the name jcarroll on most of these services.) Second, with many sites on the Internet now requesting user sign-ons, you will soon find yourself having to remember far too many user IDs and passwords. (Let's see, on this system am I jcarroll, jimcarroll, carrolljim, or j-carroll?) The bottom line is this: if you are assigned a username and password, make sure you write it down and store it in a safe place. You will need this information in order to gain access to the service and modify your profile settings.

- Many of these services use the same information sources: certain news wires and press release wires as mentioned above. There are two problems with this. First, you can quickly become bored with the lack of in-depth content that you get from news wire sources. Second, and perhaps more important, you may find that many press releases are not really news; they are just issues from corporate public relations departments.

   To make good use of these services, you must become adept at defining your search. Define it too loosely, and you will find yourself swamped with a lot of irrelevant information; too narrowly and you will probably miss some of the information that might be useful to you.

NewsPage

Features

- Free search profiles and free access to resulting headlines and article summaries on the NewsPage Web site.

- Pricing of U.S. $3 per month for unlimited e-mail delivery of up to 100 search results. An additional U.S. $3.95 per month allows you to access "premium" articles not available to free subscribers.

- Ability to do searches on words, phrases, specific topics, and companies.

NewsPage offers news from over 600 wide-ranging sources, including newspapers, magazines, and other publications. Canadian content is limited; you can get access to news wire information (mostly press releases) from Canada Newswire and Canadian Corporate News as well as the *Montreal Gazette*. Beyond the limited Canadian content, though, the list of publications available is extensive and impressive; you can view a complete list on the NewsPage Web site (**www.newspage.com**).

You can set up a variety of different searches within NewsPage, receiving news on predefined topics, companies, general news categories or based on search terms that you provide.

The predefined topics method can be very useful; the people at NewsPage have taken the time to place each and every article into one of over 2,500 different predefined news topics. With so many topics available, you will often find yourself doing a search just to see if a particular predefined topic exists. For example, we did a search to see if there were any predefined topics related specifically to conventions and conferences:

We quickly found that NewsPage did have such a topic, and we added this to the list of topics that we wanted to track:

In addition to using any of the more than 2,500 topics, you can also add companies to your search profile:

NewsPage also allows you to search for any words or phrases in articles, thus providing you with the greatest flexibility:

Once you have set up the articles you would like to see, you indicate how you would like to receive them. Keep in mind that e-mail delivery costs U.S. $3 per month. In addition, you can change your subscriber service level. Some articles in NewsPage are free, but others are ranked as "premium" articles. To read them, you must be a subscriber at the rate of an additional U.S. $3.95 per month:

Finally, there are other articles that you can access, which are considered to be "pay-per-view" and carry a charge of at least U.S. $1.

Once you have set up your search topics, they are stored on the NewsPage system. You can return at any time to view an updated Web page that contains any new matching articles. If you have signed up for the e-mail delivery service, you will automatically get a summary of articles that match your search phrase on a regular basis, that is, daily or weekly, with a link directly back to the article location at the NewsPage Web site:

Given that you can do quite a bit with NewsPage for free, and given the sophisticated custom searching capabilities, it is a very worthwhile service to take advantage of. And certainly the cost for e-mail delivery is reasonable, just U.S. 10¢ per day.

Totalnews

Although it doesn't provide newsclipping sources, one of the best news sites on the Internet is Totalnews (**www.totalnews.com**). It aggregates news information from thousands of worldwide sources, allowing you to undertake a very comprehensive news search in just seconds.

Quibbles? The obvious lack of Canadian content. We also often found that much of the "news" information simply consisted of press releases, which devalued the use of the information somewhat. But we certainly view NewsPage as a good starting point to develop your knowledge monitoring and tracking skills.

Inquisit

Features

- Flat fee pricing of U.S. $12.95 per month, U.S. $69.95 per 6 months, or U.S. $129.95 per year.

- Good flexibility in terms of setting up categories and doing searches, including Boolean-based searching.

- The search results are reported in one of four ways; you have the choice of how often your search should run, from one to seven days; and you even have the choice of which e-mail address to receive the search results.

Inquisit emerged from a service called FarCast, which provided newsclippings by e-mail. FarCast also required you to create and manage your custom searches by e-mail, a process that was too cumbersome. Since then, however, the people at Inquisit have made some significant changes to their program.

The Inquisit service excels as a simple, easy-to-use newsclipping service. Simply set up your searches, and you will receive e-mail, on a frequency that you determine, related to the topics that interest you. It also allows you to set up, manage, and modify your custom search routines on the Inquisit Web site (**www.inquisit.com**).

There isn't a lot of Canadian content on the service, short of press releases from Canada Newswire and Canadian Corporate News. But you can draw from a wide variety of publications, such as the *Anchorage Daily News*, the *Boston Herald*, *Consumer Electronics*, *The Daily Telegraph London*, *Financial Planning*, *The Gazette*, *The Jerusalem Post*, *Multimedia Monitor*, *Petroleum Finance Week*, *Reuters North American Business Report*, *The Times of London*, and *The Washington Times*.

tip Keep Focused

When setting up a newsclipping service, it is important to be concise in your search so that you do not receive too much information. In 1997, news systems like PointCast, which delivered a constant stream of updated "customized news" to your desktop, were all the rage. But many have since abandoned such services, simply because they provided too much information. Keep focused on what you are looking for, and newsclipping can be a powerful ally. Be too broad, and you'll lose the opportunity.

Inquisit refers to the custom search routines that you set up as "agents." In addition to your own custom agents, you can also sign up to a number of preconfigured broadcasts on particular topics; more on that later.

You can choose to set up a new agent from the subscriber menu, or you can choose to select from an existing agent within the Inquisit library. The latter allows you to take advantage of agents that have been set up by other subscribers to the Inquisit service:

If you choose to create a new agent, you are presented with a screen that lets you indicate if the agent will scan for news about companies, certain subjects, or stocks or whether the topic is related to sports or hobbies:

If you choose to create a subject agent, you are then asked to provide the search phrases that the agent should watch for. You are provided with a fair degree of flexibility, in that you can set up a search based on Boolean logic. For example, you can stipulate that articles include the words "executive" and "recruiting" and only if they mention the word "remuneration":

Once you have set up your search, you are asked to provide more details, such as the types of information sources that should be examined:

You can then specify how much information should be sent by the subject agent and how often you would like to receive it. There are other options that you can specify at this point too, such as the e-mail address that the information should be sent to and the type of report you would like your agent to send to you:

If you ask to receive the full text of articles, you will be sent that on a regular basis for the days that you specify. If you choose to receive headlines or headlines and summaries only, you will get an e-mail message with only that information, but each article reference will contain a link back to the full text of the article at the Inquisit Web site:

Finally, you are presented with a summary screen related to the agent you have just created:

```
Bookmarks  Location: riberServices.woa/17421000002527000000423220000002203/DeliveryOptions.wo/809420000072203/0/2/hobbes  N

Back  Forward  Reload  Home  Search  Guide  Print  Security  Stop
```

Subscriber Services   **Review Your Agent**

| 1 **Agent name** | 2 **What to look for** | 3 **Where to look** | 4 **Delivery** | 5 **Summary** |

Please review your **Subject Agent** described below.

Agent Name: Executive recruitment
What to look for: executive recruiting and renumeration
                     Anywhere in the article.
Where to look: (News, Business, International, Science)
When to report: (Mondays, Tuesdays, Wednesdays, Thursdays, Fridays)
                     (6am)
What to send: First Paragraph
Where to send: inquisit@jimcarroll.com

☑ Agent Test? By selecting Agent Test your agent generates a report on what it would have
reported during the last 30 days. This report is sent to your primary email address.

[Accept]   [Cancel]

If your agent is not doing what you want it to, have our experts help you fix it.

Need additional custom research? Ask FIND/SVP

```
Document: Done
```

Now, at this point you can run an "agent test." Inquisit will look through the news information it has for the last 30 days and will send you any articles that match the search criteria of your new agent. This is very useful, because it will help you to refine your search if you are getting too little or too much information from your agent.

In addition to setting up your own agent, you can subscribe to any number of predefined information broadcasts on specific topics. Inquisit defines "broadcasts" as "groupings of articles on a predefined topic sent as a headline-only report to everyone who subscribes to that broadcast." Each of these broadcasts contains a number of subcategories:

```
Bookmarks  Location: criberServices.woa/17421000002527000000423220000002203/AccountStatus.wo/833400000063203/4/2/hobbes  N

Back  Forward  Reload  Home  Search  Guide  Print  Security  Stop
```

Subscriber Services   **Broadcasts**

Broadcasts are groupings of articles on a predefined topic sent as a headline-only
report to everyone who subscribes to that broadcast. Unlike our other agents you
cannot see or change the criteria used to select articles.

Each of the following broadcast categories has a number of member broadcasts. We
suggest you select only a few broadcasts at first.

National and International News   Sports
Business and Financial News   Entertainment
Business and Industry Press Releases   Weather Reports
High Technology News   Miscellaneous
Wall Street Today

Done with Broadcasts

```
Document: Done
```

The "Agent Library" service within Inquisit is extremely useful as well. Using this, you can instantly sign up to any of the searches that other subscribers to Inquisit have set up. Once again, you can choose from a variety of different topics:

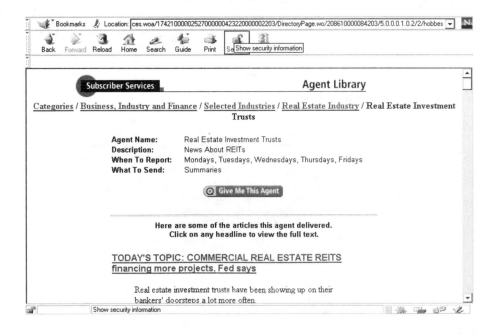

In our example below, we are signing up to an agent that scans for any news related to Real Estate Investment Trusts. Notice that at the bottom of the screen, Inquisit shows you an example of a type of article that will be retrieved by this particular agent:

If you look into the item "This Week's Hot Agents" within the Agent Library, you will get an idea of some of the hot topics that people are interested in. For example, we signed up to this agent for "stolen identity" as soon as we saw it:

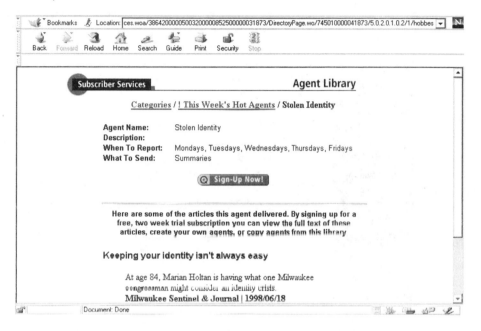

All in all, we found Inquisit to be a fabulous service with a lot of flexibility. Our only quibble would be the lack of Canadian content. However, given that the field of online newsclipping is still relatively new, we suspect that this will be resolved over time.

Personalized News
Want to find other newsclipping services? Take a look at the Yahoo! "Personalized News" category. You'll find it at **www.yahoo.ca/Business_and_Economy/Companies/News_and_Media/ Personalized_News**.

NewsHound

Features

- Flat fee pricing of U.S. $7.95 per month for up to five custom searches or U.S. $59.95 per year.

- The predefined categories, or "term sets," help to narrow your search.

- Search results can be viewed in the NewsHound Web site, sent to your e-mail box as stories, or sent to your e-mail box with the option of viewing them in your Web browser offline.

NewsHound, set up by Knight Ridder newspapers, is similar to Inquisit in many ways and is also sold as a low-cost, consumer-level newsclipping service.

In keeping with the NewsHound theme, the service refers to the process of setting up a customized search as "training your hound." Like Inquisit, you first set up the words or phrases that you are looking for:

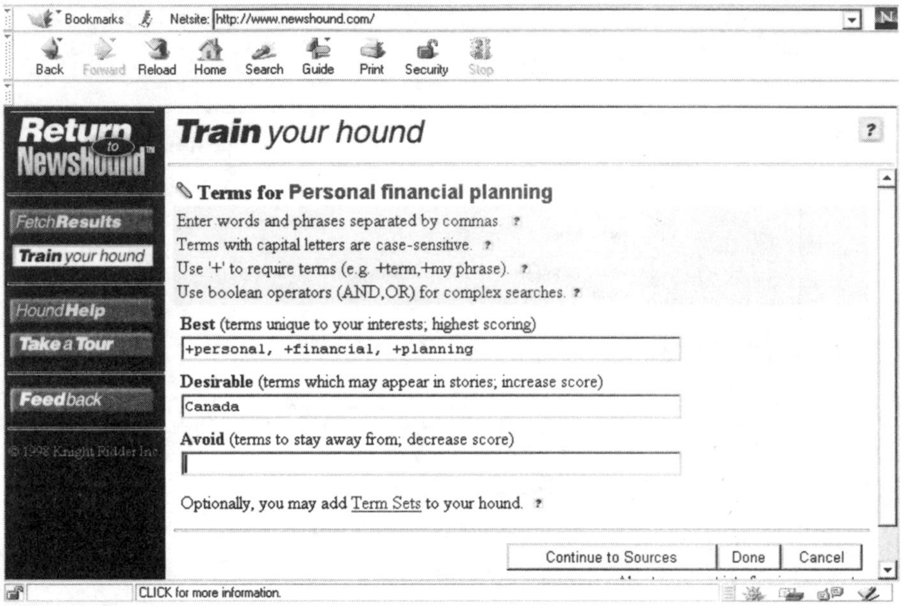

When setting up your search, you can choose to add predefined information categories, or "term sets," to your search:

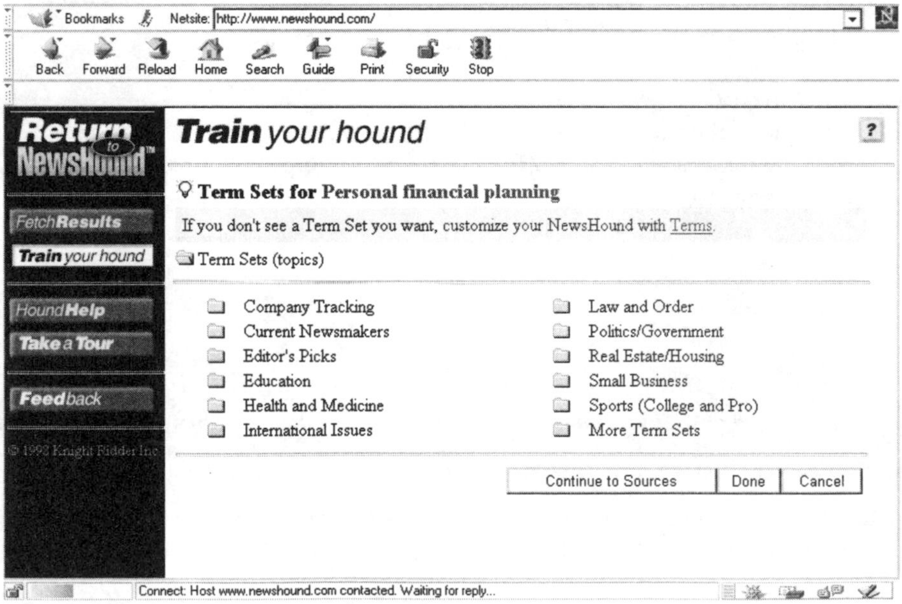

For example, we are selecting the "Small Business" term set for our search; we are able to refine further within the subcategories that show up on the next screen:

You then specify the information sources that you want examined:

and the delivery options. With NewsHound you can choose to have the searches sent to your e-mailbox, or you can view them on the NewsHound Web site (**www.newshound.com**). Should you choose to receive them by e-mail, you can receive the news stories as Web pages (should you be using an e-mail program that supports that capability), which you can then open and view in your Web browser whenever you like:

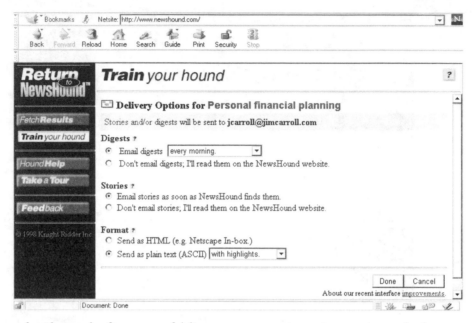

You can also choose the frequency of delivery: every morning, every evening, or both. Unfortunately, these are the only choices. You cannot choose delivery on a weekly or other scheduled basis.

Once you have set up your search, you are provided with a screen that summarizes everything that you specified. Here, you can specify a "minimum score." Each search result returned by NewsHound is "scored," or "ranked," on how it fits your search criteria, with 100 being the best. You can use this "score" to limit how many articles you will see: set a very high score of 90 to 100, and you will avoid many of the articles that were not quite a "perfect" fit to what you are looking for:

On the screen above you can also choose to "test" your search; this shows what types of articles will be found for the search. Like Inquisit, this will help you to refine your search so that it more closely matches what you are looking for:

```
Test Results                                                              ?
✷Return to Perso[fetch results]cial planning                    Go to Minimum Score

SCORE    STORIES RETURNED
57       K&F Financial Consulting Adds Two Principals, Changes Name
         SAN FRANCISCO, June 16 /PRNewswire/ -- K&F, a San Francisco-based financial consulting and
         investment management firm catering to investors with minimum portfolios of $2 million, has added two
         new principals to support its growing clientele. The firm will be renamed Kochis Fitz Tracy Fitzhugh &
         Gott (Kochis Fitz) on July 1, reflecting the addition of principals Michael Fitzhugh and Kacy Gott.

1 of 6644 stories matched your NewsHound profile.
```

We found NewsHound to be as sophisticated as Inquisit, except it did not have the "Agent Library" feature. The only problem is the limited range of news information that is available; if you look at the screen above, which lists newspapers and wire services, you can see the extent of what was available when we began using the service. However, we expect this to change, given that Knight Ridder is one of the largest news organizations in the world.

Infomart

Features

- Flat fee pricing of $350 per month.

- Not as flexible as other services, but a lot of Canadian content, which, depending on your research needs, may make it very useful.

Infomart is a division of Southam Communications, and like the InfoGlobe service from the Globe and Mail, has long been in the business of providing a service that allows serious researchers to electronically search the archives of many major Canadian newspapers, magazines, and other sources for not insignificant fees. Infomart now has a "customsearch" feature that allows you to set up a number of searches, which are run on a daily basis, with access to the search results through the Southam Web site.

Infomart now provides online access to the customsearch service information through the Web. The service is anything but inexpensive; to sign up, you're looking at a fee of $350 per month. Hence this service will be of interest only to larger organizations and serious researchers. But it is flexible when it comes to setting up custom search profiles that allow you to quickly access, each day, a listing of news articles from major newspapers across Canada that meet your search terms. Setting up a new search profile is very straightforward:

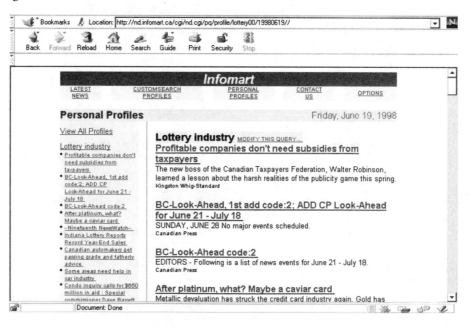

Once you have set up your profile, you can browse through the headlines and then examine all the matching articles:

You don't have all the flexibility provided in some of the other services, such as the ability to search within predefined categories and the ability for more sophisticated Boolean search phrases. Also, Infomart currently does not provide electronic mail delivery of matching articles; however, they hope to add this feature in the future.

Given the Canadian content not available elsewhere, the service is a good source of information if it fits within your budget. From our perspective, given the growth of inexpensive, flat fee information services like NewsHound and Inquisit, we expect that it will only be a matter of time before the cost for a service like this drops significantly. After all, information market realities will make that a necessity. You can get more information about the Infomart service at 1–800–668–9215 or on the Infomart Web site (**www.infomart.com**).

tip Use a Search Profile

There are many "newsclipping services" that promise to provide customized news but that really just allow you to choose news from various limited categories. Use such a service, and you will quickly be overwhelmed with news. It is our opinion that the truly useful newsclipping services are the ones that let you define a search profile by using keywords, unless there are several thousand predefined categories or topics available.

InfoGlobe-Dow Jones Interactive

Features

- Pricing is $79 per month plus $12.95 per CustomClip per month plus $3.95 per article viewed.

- Although expensive, the service contains by far the broadest range of Canadian news information.

Dow Jones has been in the information business long before many had ever even heard of a modem. Through the last two decades, one of the services it has offered to the business world is the Dow Jones Interactive Service, which allows access to the full text of some 75 million articles from over 5,500 publications within its Publications Library. The Publications Library includes many of Canada's leading news and business publications, including most of the major newspapers published in Canada. Originally accessible with a modem only, the service has been available on the Internet for the last few years.

You can get more information about the InfoGlobe-Dow Jones Interactive service at 1–800–369–7466 or at the Dow Jones Web site (**www.djinteractive.com**).

InfoGlobe-Dow Jones Interactive has the following six components:

- **Business Newsstand.** Access to the current issues of leading business publications such as the *Wall Street Journal*, the *Washington Post*, the *Los Angeles Times*, the *Financial Times*, *Barron's*, *Forbes*, and *Fortune*.

- **Publications Library.** A searchable database of 5,500 publications and over 75 million articles. Searches can be narrowed by industry, publication type, and geographic region.

- **CustomClips.** An electronic newsclipping service that monitors newspaper, magazines, wire services, and other publications for company or product names or other keywords that you specify. You will be notified automatically by e-mail when articles appear that match the information you are looking for.

- **Company and Industry Center.** Thousands of in-depth company, industry, and country reports.

- **Historical Market Data Center.** Access to more than 20 years of historical pricing information on securities, dividends, and exchange rates.

- **Dow Jones Business Directory.** Free reviews and ratings of top business sites on the Internet.

The newsclipping section of this service is called CustomClips. You can take full advantage of the sophistication of the InfoGlobe-Dow Jones Interactive service by setting up a search that looks for articles that have been assigned to predefined topics:

You can also set up CustomClips that look for particular words or phrases or that examine certain information sources. For example, you can set up a search that will look for any new articles that are related to the topic of "executive recruitment," by looking for these words anywhere within articles. And if you want a Canadian-specific search, you can choose to add a field to the search that restricts the source only to Canadian publications:

You can even set up your CustomClip so that it examines only Canadian newspapers or specific industry publications and news sources, or a mixture of sources.

Indeed, there is so much flexibility in the way that you can specify which information should be "clipped" that you can develop some highly refined searches, allowing you to avoid a lot of irrelevant material.

Of course, this comes with a price; it costs $79 per month plus $12.95 per month per CustomClip that you set up, plus $3.95 for each and every article that you look at. Hence, once again, this is a product that is clearly targeted toward the serious researcher or corporate executive with a budget to spend on information sources.

tip News Index

Want to search newspapers from around the world for the latest information on something? Visit News Index (**www.newsindex.com**), an innovative site that maintains an up-to-date, minute-by-minute archive of current news from around the world. It gets better: you can set up personalized search profiles that are delivered to you daily by e-mail.

Conclusion

There are many other newsclipping services available in addition to the ones reviewed in this chapter. We have no doubt that this is an industry that is only beginning to gain attention. Sometimes you can also find newsclipping capabilities such as those outlined in this chapter on the Web pages of certain news organizations, such as CNN. Customized news is a growing and important field. What is important is that you discover the most useful of these services and learn how to best take advantage of these tools.

Enhancing Your Web Site

Ready to move into the future? Futuristic technology that is here now is the theme of

this section. In the two chapters in this theme we look at two leading-edge technologies

and show how you can add them to your Web site.

In Chapter 14, "Setting Up Electronic Shopping on the Internet," we show how you can easily add to your Web site the ability to sell products online. A new category of company called an e-commerce service provider is now available on the Internet, making it easy for anyone to set up an electronic store on his or her Web site. We take a tour of what is out there and provide an assessment of the issues you will encounter on the way.

As high-speed access to the Internet becomes a reality, so does the ability to distribute audio and video online. In Chapter 15, "Adding Audio and Video to Your Web Site," we take a look at how easy it is becoming to get involved with this leading-edge online opportunity.

Setting Up Electronic Shopping on the Internet

Setting up shop in cyberspace is easier than ever, thanks to a crop of new services that help merchants build Web storefronts quickly—without much computer knowhow.

Mark Halper, "Cyberstorefronts for Rookies," *Business Week*, June 9, 1997

Highlights

1. A new type of service is emerging on the Internet. Companies called "electronic commerce, or e-commerce, service providers" provide small and medium-sized businesses with tools that allow them to sell their products online. These services are easy to set up and use and require very little technical knowledge on the part of the vendor.

2. To be able to accept credit cards on your Web site, you need to establish one or more "merchant accounts." Depending on the e-commerce service provider you choose, you may have to obtain these merchant accounts yourself, or they may be obtained for you.

3. E-commerce service providers vary in terms of cost and the features they offer. As the market for these types of firms becomes more crowded, the quality of these services will vary widely. As a result, use caution when choosing one of these providers.

4. There are many costs associated with setting up an online storefront: you have to pay a fee to your Internet service provider and/or e-commerce service provider; you have to pay a per transaction fee to the credit card companies you deal with and/or a credit card processing firm such as InternetSecure. Depending on your sales volume, selling products online may not be economical.

5. Before establishing an online storefront, consider the following questions: how will you promote your site? Can you keep it up-to-date and functioning on a 24-hour, 7 days-a-week basis? Even when you are on holidays? Success will also depend on how well you address consumer concerns regarding security, privacy, and credibility issues.

For a long time, the buzz on the Internet has been that it will soon become a place where people will do a lot of online shopping. And it has long been the dream of many that the Internet become one of the primary venues to sell products and services to customers. But for all intents and purposes, the Internet has not emerged as a significant force in the retail sector, for a variety of reasons. As we wrote in the 1998 edition of the *Canadian Internet Handbook*:

> It will take time for a broad cross section of society to become comfortable with the concept of shopping online, to develop trust in the technology, to overcome their perceived fears about the Internet, and to come to appreciate the convenience of shopping online.

But throughout 1998 the buzz about online shopping became real in a few sectors of the economy. Companies such as Dell and Cisco now sell millions of dollars' worth of product each and every day online. Airlines such as Canadian and Air Canada report an increasing number of online transactions. Financial services report an increased willingness by the general public to commit to financial products online.

But for the average user of the Internet, whether a corporate organization or an individual, the opportunity to add online shopping to a Web site has long seemed out of reach. It has been an area that many have avoided because of real or perceived complexities, excessive cost, and the immaturity of many of the available technology solutions.

The Emergence of E-Commerce Service Providers

In many ways, these issues are very real barriers for those who wish to be able to add electronic commerce to their Web site.

There is no doubt that setting up real electronic commerce activities can be quite complex. After all, to do it on your own you have to install a Web server, find appropriate electronic commerce or "shopping basket" software, arrange for merchant accounts with several credit card companies, figure out what you need to do to link into a secure credit card processing network, and many more activities. Simply learning about what is required can be a complicated and exhausting experience, particularly given the rapid rate at which e-commerce is evolving and the ever-changing standards within the financial services industry.

You can remove yourself from a great deal of that complexity by taking advantage of a new type of service that is now emerging on the Internet: the do-it-yourself Web store, or what is known as an "e-commerce service provider."

Rather than you setting up all the infrastructure that is required to add e-commerce capability to your site, you simply use the infrastructure of an existing service that provides everything you need to set up a "store" on the Internet. Your "store" can be configured to accept payment by credit cards, cheque, or other methods.

What is involved in creating your own "store"? By using one of these services, for a fee that ranges from $50 to $100 per month or more, you simply:

- Create your Web pages, usually by using an online template. These Web pages include information about the product or service that you wish to sell online as well as information about your company, the sales process, and more. The capabilities range from the creation of a simple store with a few products to a complex and detailed store with thousands of products and multiple shipping options and rates.

- Provide information on the pricing, shipping, tax, and other charges that will be applied to any purchases that are made.

- Arrange to get your own credit card merchant accounts to be able to accept credit card transactions online.

- Arrange to have your credit card orders processed in real time.

- Link the new transaction site into your existing site, if you have one, or use your new store as your primary Web site.

There are a number of e-commerce service providers emerging, and no doubt there will be more. This is certainly an area that is set for substantial growth in 1999. In this chapter we take a look at three such services, not in an attempt to provide exhaustive coverage of the players in the marketplace, but to give you an idea of the types of service and flexibility now available in creating an online store.

How Do These Services Work?

Let's put into perspective how these services work by using the IBM Home Page Creator for e-Business as an example:

- IBM hosts the Web site, just as any other company might host a site.

- IBM has integrated sophisticated software into this Web site to help create an online store.

- IBM works with a company, Automated Transaction Services, or ATS (**www.atsbank.com**), which specializes in online transactions, to create the ability to process credit card transactions.

- ATS requires you to obtain a merchant account for each credit card that you plan to accept. If you already have merchant accounts, you can provide this information to ATS. If not, you must arrange for those separately.

- Once set up, anyone can go to your Web site and order a product. The combination of the IBM computers and the ATS computers processes the transaction and notifies you of the order. This is all transparent to the online customer; the integration of the IBM and ATS systems is seamless.

tip Where to Look For E-Commerce Advice

You can find many useful articles and lots of information about electronic commerce, in particular, setting up an online store, at Web Commerce Today (**www.wilsonweb.com/wct**). There is an annual fee of $49.95. While you may not be used to paying for information on the Internet, the site does offer one of the most comprehensive and detailed sources of information about the topic to be found on the Internet today.

Complexities of Online Commerce

We are extremely excited about the opportunity that is emerging here. We believe that setting up an online store on your Web site has become easier with the emergence of the e-commerce service provider.

But there are still some hurdles and complexities that must be faced if you decide to venture forth. Our experience has shown that most of the problems come from simply understanding what you need to do to get the proper credit card accounts set up and activated.

When setting up an online store, you must obtain a merchant account for each credit card that you plan to accept in your store. A merchant account is an arrangement between an organization and a bank that allows the organization to accept credit card payments from customers. If you already have merchant credit card status and accept credit card orders in a retail store or by some other means, it is quite likely that you will have to contact your credit card representatives and advise them that you plan on accepting orders over the Internet. They will then have to make some changes to your account so that these transactions do not cause a problem. You will probably run into challenges if your account representative is not familiar with the Internet.

If you do not have merchant accounts, you will have to arrange to get a VISA, MasterCard, and/or American Express merchant account. There is a setup fee for each account. We paid a little over $100 to set up our VISA account. There are two ways that you can set up merchant accounts:

- You can contact these organizations directly. This is the case with IBM's Home Page Creator for e-Business system and SunCommerce's SecureMerchant service, both of which we examine below.

- You can use an intermediary organization that works with the credit card companies to streamline the process of arranging for merchant accounts. DXShop is such a service, and we will look at this later in the chapter. DXShop works with InternetSecure, based in Oakville, Ontario. InternetSecure specializes in providing credit card transaction services to companies on the Web. The organization will arrange for all three credit card accounts and charge a $570 setup fee. You can sign up online.

Learning About Credit Card Merchant Accounts

Most of the major Canadian banks have some information about merchant accounts and point-of-sale equipment on their Web sites, but most of the information is targeted to retail stores. As a result, if you have never been involved with accepting credit cards at the retail level, you can use these sites to learn all about it. Simply visit your bank's Web site, where you can usually find some useful information:

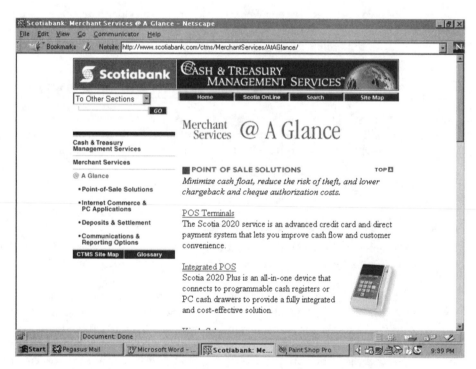

You will find that some banks offer specific information about Internet transaction services, although the quality and depth of the information that is available vary greatly:

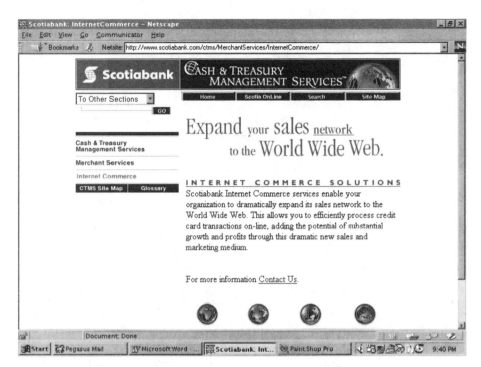

For example, we found that many such Web sites do not provide much more information on how to get a merchant account other than a page like this one, which tells you to go to your local branch and get a kit or contact name:

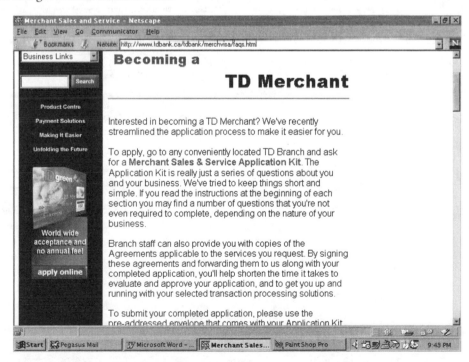

Unfortunately, the credit card companies are no different. Some will provide information on why you should choose their card, but in order to get a merchant account, you actually need to contact one of their offices. (This may change over time. When we looked, only American Express in the United States offered the ability to apply for a merchant account online, and only U.S. organizations could use the online application process. Furthermore, while all the major credit card companies have Web sites, there wasn't very much Canadian information available online.)

What should you do if you want to learn about merchant accounts? We suggest that you visit several bank Web sites as well as the credit card sites to get an idea of what is involved; then through your local bank, contact the appropriate representative.

The type of information you need to supply when setting up a merchant account includes banking information, company information, the projected number of monthly transactions, and the average dollar value of each of these transactions. You also need to submit a void cheque to verify banking information.

You can learn about the security issues involved in accepting credit card transactions online if you still have concerns. Most of the sites, whether banks or credit card companies, provide an overview of how they are addressing Internet security issues:

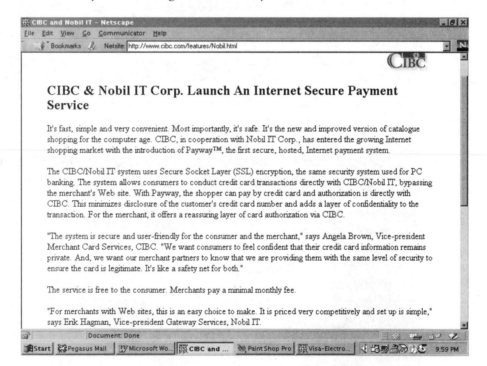

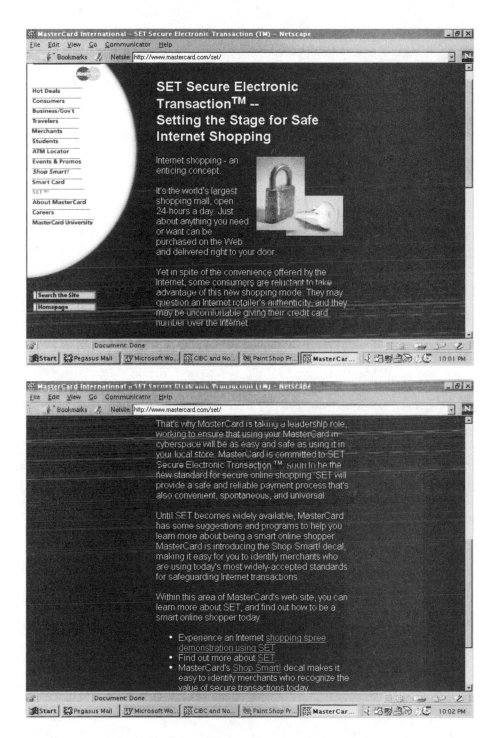

Finally, keep in mind that the field of merchant accounts and the Internet is very much a moving target in terms of cost. Don't forget that you have to pay the credit card company each time a purchase is made on your Web site. Find out what you will have to pay to each credit card company in terms of a setup fee, transaction charge, and the percentage of the sales that will be taken on the transaction in addition to or in excess of any transaction charge.

The process of actually getting a merchant account might not necessarily be a smooth one. Our own experience in setting up an electronic store brought home this fact. The reason? We think that while the various credit card companies are scrambling to put together an infrastructure and support system to handle transactions on the Internet, they have a long way to go in getting staff throughout their entire organization up to scratch.

Quite simply, the folks that you could end up dealing with at a credit card company may not know how to cope with the Internet, so you may have to take a deep breath when dealing with them.

When setting up our online store with the IBM Home Page Creator for e-Business system, we were responsible for getting our own merchant VISA account. For this, we first contacted our bank, a branch of the Royal Bank of Canada. They advised us that we would have to contact the local VISA account representative to arrange for our merchant VISA account.

We spoke with this individual to get the ball rolling and began filling out the appropriate forms. At one point, the individual queried what we planned on using the VISA account for; we replied for purposes of accepting credit card orders over the Internet. We explained how the IBM Home Page Creator system worked, how it linked into VISA, and the fact that VISA and IBM were working together to put this technology in place.

As soon as we mentioned the Internet, things started to go off the rails. It quickly became obvious that the VISA representative had little knowledge of the Internet, how the VISA organization had integrated itself into Internet electronic commerce, and was overly concerned about the risk of the Internet. Quite clearly, the head office of VISA hadn't made its account representatives aware that everything in terms of Internet electronic commerce was OK.

The result was that the process of arranging for our merchant accounts took an inordinately long period of time.

Why? We were the ones who had to educate this individual about the Internet, had to put her in touch with IBM, suggest she contact the VISA head office, and do several other things to ease the concern with respect to the technology. The Internet was something that was very new to this person, and because she didn't know how to deal with it, problems surfaced.

Your experience might echo our own, although we expect this type of problem to disappear over time. As a result, we suggest that if you start down this road, be prepared for complexities in getting new merchant accounts set up and in ensuring that your existing merchant accounts can be used through the Internet.

With this background information in mind, let's take a look at a few of the e-commerce service providers available in Canada today.

tip No-Hassle Internet Merchant Accounts

As we described, getting a merchant account for the purpose of selling products on the Internet can be a difficult task. Unless you have an excellent relationship with your bank and a history of steady income, it can be difficult for small organizations and home-based businesses to obtain merchant status from their local banks. Because banks view the Internet as a higher security risk than in-store (i.e., retail) transactions, they compensate by increasing the fee that merchants have to pay for each credit card transaction. In addition, your bank may also require a large deposit (often several thousand dollars) from you as collateral in the event that you accept a stolen credit card and the real cardholder later refuses to pay the charge. Fortunately, there's a Canadian company called InternetSecure that will act as an intermediary between you and the major credit card companies. Because InternetSecure already has established relationships with the major banks, they can obtain merchant accounts for you far more easily than if you had to go through the application process yourself. Once you have set up your online store, you can link it to InternetSecure, who will then process your credit card transactions in real time. InternetSecure can be reached at **www.internetsecure.com** or at 1-800-297-9482.

IBM Home Page Creator for E-Business

One of the authors of this book has set himself up online with the IBM Home Page Creator for e-Business (**www.can.ibm.com**), a service available from IBM Canada's Small Business Division, to be able to sell some of his books:

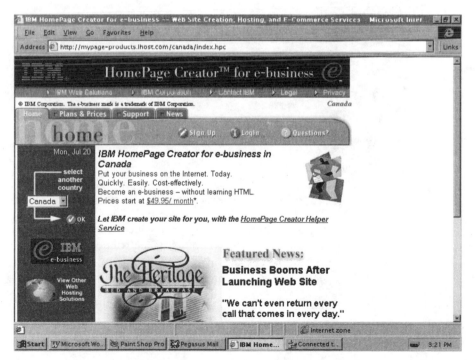

The Home Page Creator service wasn't designed primarily for the purpose of providing electronic commerce capabilities, although that is a key component of the service. IBM set up the service to make it easy for small businesses without a lot of technical skills to establish a Web site. IBM provides the program and the space on their computers for people to create and store their Web sites. They have also put in place a link to ATS Bank (**www.atsbank.com**), the company that processes the credit card transactions.

The Home Page Creator service excels as a solution for individuals and organizations looking for a basic electronic store online, and with prices starting at $49.95 a month, it is the lowest cost do-it-yourself electronic commerce service available.

Once you have signed up with the service, you are provided with an administrative account that you use to create your "store." Through this account you can create and edit your Web pages without having to know anything about HTML, the language used to build Web pages. In addition, you can register your site on various search engines, access sales reports, upload graphics to your site to be used as part of the design, and other tasks:

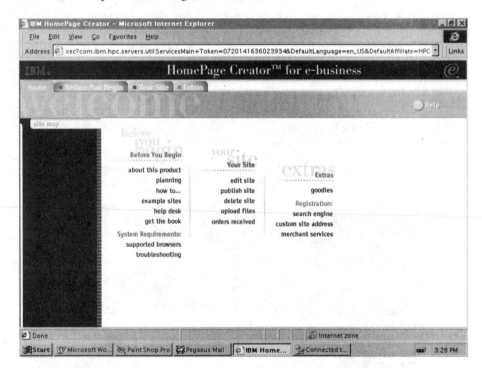

You can create your Web pages using a number of predesigned templates, or you can design your own using a blank template. At all times, you have a separate window, which IBM calls a "Control Panel," which details the elements (i.e., graphics and other content) that you have used on the Web page. The site also provides extensive help throughout on what is involved in creating your online Web site and store:

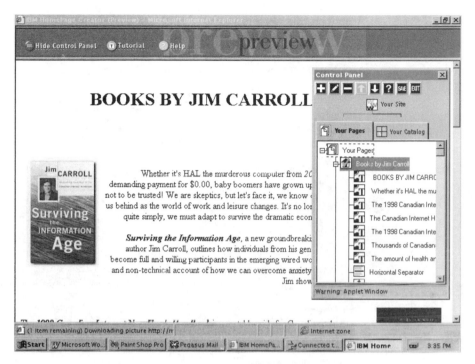

Through a series of boxes that open up within your Web browser, you can easily modify the details associated with any Web page. IBM has taken extensive advantage of Java technology to provide a sophisticated yet simple means of adding and modifying content within your site:

In setting up individual products within your catalogue, you specify the price, weight, tax status, description, and other information. Some of this will be used in the creation of the Web page for the product, and some will be used by the transaction system when an order is processed. You can also upload an image for the product:

Once you have established your online catalogue of products, you need to provide details of your merchant accounts. If you do not have merchant accounts already set up, you will have to arrange to get them from VISA, MasterCard, and/or American Express. Once you have your account(s), you provide details to ATS Bank through the IBM merchant services section:

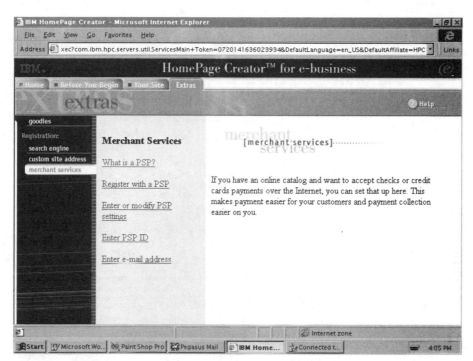

For example, you provide details on a particular merchant account that you have, indicate who should be notified when orders are placed on the site, and indicate the extent of verification that you want to apply to the online transaction (such as matching up the address provided on an order form to the address actually associated with a particular credit card):

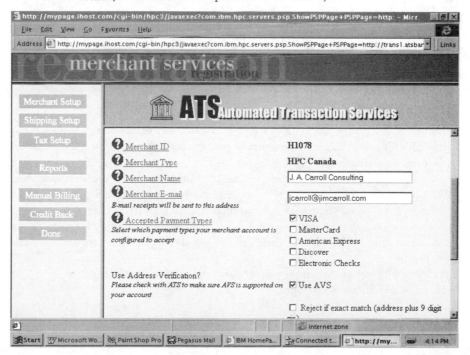

You also have extensive capabilities in terms of configuring tax and shipping information. Once you are finished, visitors to your site will be able to browse your electronic catalogue, add items to their shopping basket, and check out:

When a sale is made on your Web site, you will be notified by e-mail, and a credit will be applied to your merchant credit card account. You can also access a section of the Web site to obtain summary and detailed information about orders placed through the site.

For the price you pay and the sophistication you get, the Home Page Creator is definitely worth looking into if you want to add straightforward shopping capabilities to your site.

SunCommerce

Another alternative is SunCommerce (**www.suncommerce.com**), a Vancouver-based organization. This Canadian initiative promises to get you up and running with an online store in less than five minutes—and they're right!

They offer two online services: SecureMerchant Lite and SecureMerchant Pro. The two services differ in features, for example, the number of products you can handle and permitting suppliers to link into the system. You create the site, then you have 10 days of free service. If you do not wish to continue with SunCommerce after the 10 days, your site will be removed. If you like what you see and want to keep your site, then you can use the SecureMerchant Lite service at a cost of $99 per month.

It's easy to get going: simply visit the site and choose to create a new store. The first step is to set up an administrative account:

Then you provide the information that you would like to have appear on the first page of the store. At this point, you can upload a graphic image from your computer, perhaps using an image or company logo from an existing Web site, if you already have something suitable:

Then you add a product category. This is simply to get the store functioning; you can add other product categories later:

You then provide information for one sample product that you will sell through the site; again, you can add others later (up to 250 with the Lite version):

And voilà! Your store is in operation, ready to accept credit card orders immediately:

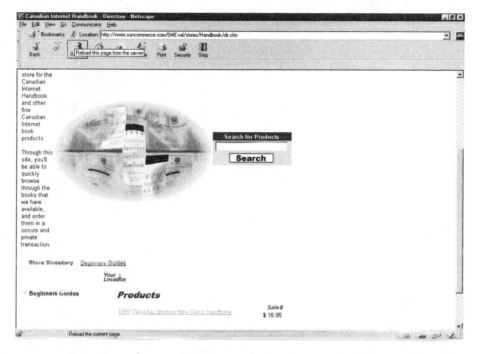

SunCommerce will notify you by e-mail when an order has been received. The e-mail message will include a secure Web address that you can link to and retrieve information about the purchase, including the customer's credit card number. SunCommerce does not obtain merchant numbers for you or process your credit card transactions in real time. However, if you wish to have your credit card transactions processed in real time, SunCommerce will assist you in linking your online storefront to a Canadian online credit card processing service like InternetSecure (**www.internetsecure.com**):

Assessing the Effectiveness
of Your Web Site

Protecting Yourself Online

Improving Your Productivity
on the Internet

Enhancing Your Web Site

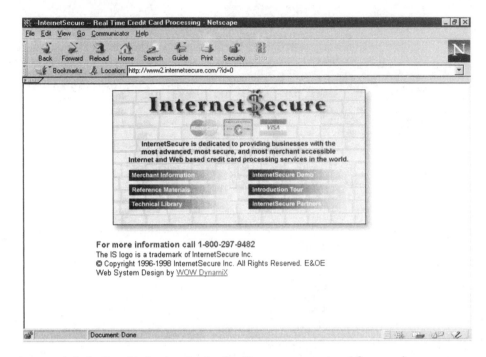

There is a good deal of sophistication in the SunCommerce service. After you have set up your store, you are sent an e-mail with details on where the starting page can be found as well as information on how to get into the administration account. If you want to create the store under your own domain name or with a new domain name, you can arrange for this when you first set up the site. Within the administration account, you can set up additional product categories, modify the appearance of the pages in the store, add inventory to the store, and perform other functions. For example, you can easily set up formats such as how tax will be charged in the store:

as well as provide information on various shipping methods and the amount to be charged. This lets the shopper choose from a variety of shipping methods, each of which bears a different rate:

At any time, you can retrieve reports on sales to date or sales for any particular period of time:

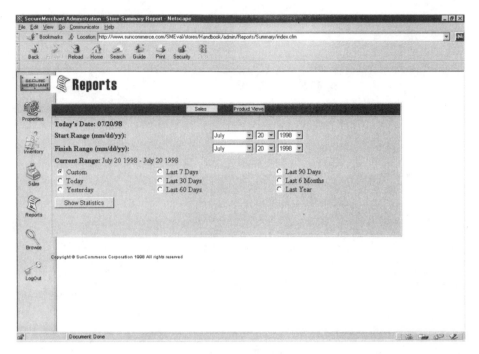

The folks behind the service aren't new to the e-commerce game. Indeed, they built the technology that supports MegaDepot (**www.megadepot.com**), one of the largest online computer stores in Canada; hence they have a keen eye with respect to the design and layout that make a successful online store. They have applied this technology and experience to the design of their service and have definitely come up with a winner.

Online Retailing

According to Forrester Research (**www.forrester.com**), online retailers will generate $17 billion in sales annually by the year 2001.

DXShop

Oakville, Ontario, is the home of DXShop (**www.dxshop.com**), one of the most sophisticated e-commerce service provider solutions that we have seen. Prices start at $125 per month for a storefront carrying up to 50 items. Like SunCommerce's SecureMerchant Lite service, you can sign up for a trial session and create a working store in a matter of minutes:

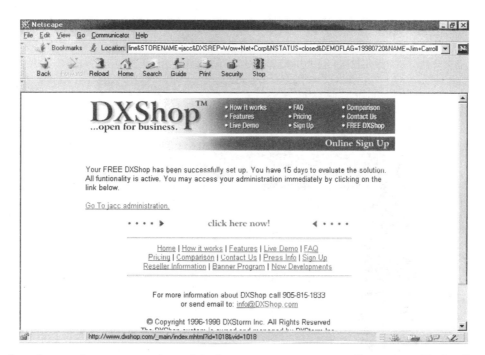

Like the other services, once you have signed on, you are sent an e-mail message with details on where to find your store as well as an administrative account.

The top of the administration screen features the choices that you have when designing your commerce site. From here, you can choose to access sections of DXShop that will help you to set up your pages, upload graphics to the site, configure shipping information and tax rates, establish product categories, and provide individual product information as well as other activities:

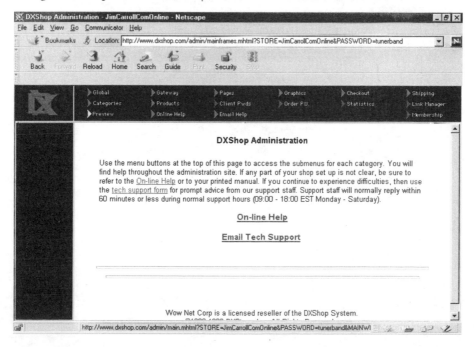

From the "global configuration screen" you can choose to add search facilities to your site and configure other aspects of the appearance of your site. There is a great deal of flexibility in terms of the overall design:

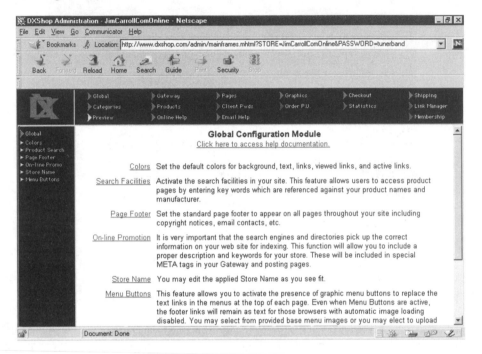

One of the best features about DXShop is the flexibility that it provides your site's layout. For example, on this screen you can choose from one of five different layouts for a Web page containing information about a particular product:

In terms of setting up credit cards, you simply choose which ones you want to accept:

Through their alliance with InternetSecure (**www.internetsecure.com**), DXShop allows you to have your credit card transactions processed in real time. If you go this route, InternetSecure will arrange merchant accounts for you from VISA, MasterCard, and American Express.

DXShop's shipping section is one of the most sophisticated we have seen; you can set up cus-tomized shipping rates for over 300 countries:

Once you have gone through the process of creating your site and establishing the catalogue items, you are in business. If you wish, you can choose to set up your online storefront under your own domain name. We certainly recommend this, since it looks a lot more professional to prospective customers.

DXShop provides a lot of sophistication in terms of what is possible. Company officials tell us that a number of their clients are actually Web developers who use the DXShop service to build electronic shopping capabilities into their own clients' sites. If you are a Web developer, you can explore this option as well.

tip Online Storefronts By Yahoo!

Another e-commerce service provider to consider is Yahoo! Store (**store.yahoo.com**). Like the other services described in this chapter, Yahoo! Store allows you to set up an Internet storefront quickly and easily at prices starting at U.S. $100 per month. As you can tell by its name, Yahoo! Store is operated by the same company that runs the popular Yahoo! Internet directory service.

Issues to Think About

If you haven't been in the retail business or haven't been involved in selling your products in other ways, then you may find setting up an online store to be more complicated than you thought, and it has little to do with the technology, which we found straightforward.

For example, you will find yourself dealing with taxation issues (GST/HST, PST, customs, etc.). You will have to find out the taxation rates that you must charge for each province, which can be a daunting experience.

Shipping will prove to be complex, particularly if you plan on shipping internationally. You will have to take the time to figure out how much to apply as a shipping charge for each country that you end up sending product to and figure out the different shipping rates to apply for different volumes of product. If you end up offering several different shipping methods, that is, regular mail or courier shipments, then you will have to factor those in as well.

There are many other issues you will have to deal with, which we review below.

Transaction Fees

When you accept credit cards on your Web site, credit card companies will keep a percentage of the transaction as their fee for handling the sale. This is called the "discount rate." The discount rate you receive will depend on your relationship with the bank, the volume of sales you receive, and other factors. Normally, merchants who are selling on the Internet have to pay a higher discount fee than retail stores, because banks view Internet sales as a higher security risk. In addition to the discount rate, if you decide to have your credit cards processed in real time using services such as ATS Bank (**www.atsbank.com**) and InternetSecure (**www.internetsecure.com**), you will have to pay these organizations a per-transaction fee as well. In some cases (e.g., InternetSecure), both charges are combined into a single fee. This is not the case with ATS Bank.

Economics

In addition to the fees just discussed, you will have to pay a monthly fee to your Internet service provider to host your Web site. If you choose to use an e-commerce service provider such as IBM, SunCommerce, or DXShop and integrate these services into your main Web site, you will have to pay for their services too. (If you choose to have your online storefront as your only Web site, you will only have to pay one fee, since you are only dealing with one organization.) Before you proceed, decide whether this makes economic sense. You could spend a lot of time and money setting up your Web site and then pay fairly hefty transaction fees on each transaction, only to discover that you aren't getting a lot of business online. When thinking about online commerce, be cautious in your expectations of just how many people might purchase something from you online. You should also do a breakeven analysis to figure out just how much you will have to sell in order to break even on your setup and monthly fees.

Staying Up-to-Date

Be sure to update your Web site on a regular basis for new products, changes in product pricing or descriptions, tax changes, shipping charges, and other details. There is nothing worse than permitting customers to undertake transactions online, only to advise them later that something has changed.

Delivery

Make sure that you have arrangements in place to quickly ship the product. This is particularly important for small business; for example, what happens when you go on vacation?

Promotion

You need to take time to promote your new online store, just as you would any Web site. In fact, you may be able to list your store in more places on the Internet than your regular Web site.

Ease of Use

Concentrate on design and layout when setting up your Web site. The services we looked at above provide a fair degree of flexibility with the design of your online store, so don't hesitate to experiment with the layout. Your site should be easy for customers to use.

Security, Privacy, and Credibility Concerns

You should be sensitive to the fact that many consumers are still afraid to use their credit cards on the Internet. Not only are consumers concerned about the risk of a hacker getting their credit card if they use it on the Web, they are worried about the credibility of the organizations that are selling products online. How do consumers know that your online storefront isn't a fake, designed solely to collect credit card numbers from online shoppers? How do customers know that you are actually going to ship the product to them once they have given you their credit card number? What happens if the product doesn't arrive, or the customer isn't satisfied with it? Will the customer be able to return the product without a hassle? Will you still be in business a week from now? How are you going to use the personal information that customers supply to you as part of an order? How do customers know that you won't sell their names and mailing addresses to organizations? These are the questions that go through the minds of shoppers when they are thinking of buying a product over the Internet. Unless you're a well-known company like Eaton's, customers are going to think twice about giving you their credit card number if they've never heard of your organization or have no way to assess your organization's reputation and credibility.

How do you alleviate these concerns? One way is to take advantage of some of the decal programs that have been established to boost consumer confidence in online shopping. These decal programs allow you to display a "seal" or logo on your Web site that certifies you have met the issuing organization's standards for electronic commerce. Many of the organizations administering these decal programs are well-known organizations, so displaying their decal on your site can give your site, and your organization, added credibility in the eyes of a potential customer. Here are examples of some of the programs we recommend you look at:

- MasterCard (**www.mastercard.com**) will allow you to display a "Shop Smart" decal on your Web site if you meet MasterCard's criteria for secure online shopping:

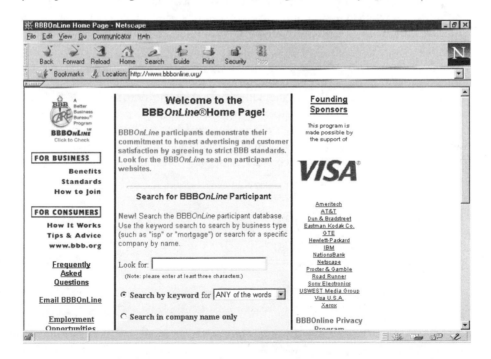

- The Better Business Bureau (**www.bbb.org**) has established a program called BBBOnLine, which allows participants to display a BBBOnLine seal on their Web site if they become members of the Better Business Bureau, agree to binding arbitration in the event of a customer dispute, have a satisfactory complaint-handling record with the BBB, and agree to other program requirements:

- There are two other organizations, The Canadian Institute of Chartered Accountants (**www.cica.ca**) and TRUSTe (**www.truste.org**), which we discussed in Chapter 6, "Protecting Your Privacy Online." The CICA initiative, called "WebTrust," allows an online vendor to display a seal from the CICA if the vendor's site meets CICA standards for processing online transactions and handling private customer information. And the TRUSTe organization has a privacy program that licences the use of its seal to Web sites that agree to display a privacy statement on their Web sites in accordance with TRUSTe's requirements.

ADDRESSES FOR DECAL PROGRAMS

MasterCard's Shop Smart!	**www.mastercard.com/shopsmart**
CICA's WebTrust	**www.cica.ca/webtrust**
Better Business Bureau's BBBOnLine	**www.bbbonline.org**
TRUSTe	**www.truste.org**

Bank Policies Concerning Online Fraud

When you obtain a merchant account from your bank, make sure you ask how cases of Internet fraud will be handled. For example, suppose someone purchases a product from your online store-front using a stolen credit card. Once you have shipped/delivered the product, are you on the hook for the charge if the real credit card owner refuses the charge?

The Future of E-Commerce Service Providers

We have no doubt that 1999 will see the emergence of many sophisticated services similar to the three we examined above. It can be expected that the e-commerce service provider business will quickly become as crowded as the Internet service provider and Web server businesses became. Naturally, many e-commerce service providers will not survive. That is why, when choosing a service provider, you should ensure that you assess the stability and viability of the company that will host your store, examine the support and service they provide, and obtain and check out references of other clients. In addition, you should examine the security they provide for credit card transactions, assess the ease of use and reliability of their service, and examine how they process credit card transactions. (One way to do this is to try out a transaction or two on a store that someone has already set up on his or her service.) In effect, you should use the same criteria you would use when choosing an Internet service provider or Web design company.

chapter fifteen

Adding Audio and Video to Your Web Site

According to Mark Sanders, president and CEO of Pinnacle Systems, there are 35 million households in North America that have a PC, camcorder, VCR, and "a closet full of tapes"—and only one-tenth of 1 percent of people in those households currently use their computers for video editing.

"PC Market Set for Boom In Desktop Video Editing," *Computer Shopper*, June 1, 1998

Highlights

1. Adding an audio or video file to your Web site is a five-step process: you have to transfer the audio/video from its source to your computer, edit it, convert the file into a format suitable for the Internet, place the file on a Web server, and then link the file to your Web site.

2. To create and edit audio/video files on your computer, you will need a lot of hard disk space and a computer with an extremely fast processor.

3. To capture audio from a source such as a VCR and turn it into a digital sound file, you can use the Windows Sound Recorder or download a third-party sound recorder from the Internet. To capture and edit video on your computer, you need a video capture card as well as video capture software. Two popular software programs that allow you to capture and edit video are Ulead MediaStudio Pro and MGI VideoWave.

4. To edit and assemble your video/audio presentation, you must decide on a story line as well as the transition effects you want to use.

5. When preparing your audio/video files for distribution on the Internet, you can create your files in native format or streaming format. Files in native format have to be downloaded to the user's computer before they can be played. Files in streaming format don't have to be downloaded and can be played immediately by a visitor to your Web site.

6. RealAudio, RealVideo, and Apple's QuickTime are the most popular types of streaming audio and video formats on the Web.

7. The company hosting your Web site may have to make some modifications to their Web server so that your Web site will be capable of playing streaming audio and video files. There may be an extra cost for this service, or the company may not allow it. In addition, if the company hosting your Web site charges you for disk space and/or data transfer, you could end up paying additional fees, depending on the size of your audio/video files and the number of times that Internet users access them.

The time is ripe for adding audio and video multimedia to your Web site, particularly since the emerging technologies such as cable modems and ADSL allow a greater number of Internet users to access the larger file sizes that are associated with audio and video. Add the growing number of companies that have high-speed connections to the Internet, and you expand your audience considerably.

You may find audio and video to be useful additions to your Web site for promotion, training, support, or countless other reasons. Imagine, for example, your business placing a video on your Web site providing detailed instructions on how to install a particular product in order to reduce support costs. Or you decide to produce and make available, simply for the fun of it, your own "movie." Whatever the case may be, technology is maturing to such a degree that such capabilities, which have long seemed far out of reach, are today practical and doable.

In this chapter we take a look at the steps needed to offer audio and video capabilities on your Web site. Given the complexity of the topic and the number of ways that you can approach such a task, we can only begin to scratch the surface of the field in terms of the many different file formats, options, and methods that can be used to do this.

Keep in mind that when we refer to a video file in the pages that follow, we are referring to a video that contains both the video (pictures) as well as the associated audio (sound) that goes with the video.

There are several steps involved in making audio/video files available on your Web site:

- **Transferring audio/video to your computer.** The first thing you need to do is get the audio or video that you want to make available on your Web site into your computer. If you have the right computer equipment, you can take audio or video from a CD, cassette player, VCR, or video camera and convert it into a format that your PC can understand. Always keep in mind copyright issues: if the file you wish to use is not your own original creation, be sure to get permission first from the copyright holder.

- **Editing the audio or video files.** Next, you may need to edit or rearrange the audio or video files that have been brought into your computer, so that they are in a layout and format that is acceptable to you. This is where you put your "producer" hat on, in that you are determining the nature of the audio or video content that you will provide online.

- **Converting the files to a format for the Internet.** Third, you need to convert or save the audio or video files to a format that can be used by people on the Internet. They include formats such as RealAudio, RealVideo, and QuickTime.

- **Placing the audio or video files on a Web server.** Next, you need to place the files on a Web server that can make these audio or video files available to the world.

- **Linking the audio or video files to a Web page.** Finally, you need to create a Web page that allows people to easily play the audio or video file by clicking on the audio or video button. In addition, you need to make it easy for people to get the proper "player" to listen to or view the audio/video file, if they don't already have such a program.

Before we walk you through these steps, we first need to review some of the general concepts and terms that you will need to know and understand when dealing with audio and video files.

The Complexity of Digital Audio and Video

While the above steps may seem straightforward, keep in mind that there are several things that you need to deal with along the way and concepts that you must become familiar with. The journey into the world of digital (computer-based) audio and video is complex; hence be prepared for a bit of a learning experience. You will have to come to grips with the following issues, in addition to many others:

Size of Files

When you bring audio or video into your computer and convert it to computer format, be prepared to deal with some pretty massive files.

For example, transfer a $3\frac{1}{2}$-minute song to your computer in a sound quality that is comparable to what you would hear from a CD, and you will find that you are dealing with a file that is 60 MB——that is 60,000,000 bytes——in size. Transfer 15 minutes of video to your PC in a quality that will replay on your television, and you are looking at a file of about 2.5 GB—that is—2,500,000,000 bytes.

These are pretty big files, far in excess of any type of computer file that you would normally be used to working with. A typical word processing document, for example, is probably only around 100,000 bytes in total.

So you must have large amounts of hard disk space available, often several times in excess of the anticipated size of the files that you might be working with, because there will be a lot of temporary storage and working space required as you edit the material.

Fortunately, the cost of upgrading your computer to a larger hard drive has decreased substantially in the last few years. You are looking at a cost of about $250 to $300 for 5 or 6 GB of storage. Expect that cost to continue to decrease. Hence, if you are serious about working with audio and video, be prepared to invest in some additional hard disk space.

Processing Power

Most computers today, ranging from basic Macintosh computers to PCs that contain an Intel 80486 processor or better, can handle any of the work needed to prepare an audio file for the Internet, as long as you have adequate disk storage. Obviously, the faster the computer you have, the better.

When it comes to video, however, it is a different matter altogether. To capture, edit, and output video on your computer, you need a video card that has the ability to input and output a digital video signal. These are often referred to as video capture cards. That is, it must have input jacks that can be used to feed in video from a video camera or VCR. If it has input jacks, it probably also will have output jacks that can be used to output a video to your VCR.

The manufacturers of video cards often specify a certain minimum configuration in terms of the type of computer you can use (usually something like a Windows 95 system or better running on at least a Pentium 166, or something like that). You shouldn't always expect stellar results on a slower computer, even though it might meet the minimum specifications provided by the card manufacturer.

The reason for this is that the process of capturing or transferring a video to your computer, editing it, and then producing a final video is extremely processor-intensive. If you don't have a computer that is powerful enough to properly handle video, even though it meets the minimum specifications, you'll find that you will lose information when capturing the video to your computer, you will become very frustrated at how slow the video editing process can be, and you will end up spending quite a bit of time waiting for the final video to be "produced" when trying to produce a version of the video suitable for the Internet.

So keep in mind that while your computer may meet the minimum specifications as indicated by the manufacturer of your video card, your capabilities may be minimal at best.

That's why the more power you have, the better. And if you are serious about the task, consider upgrading to the latest and greatest technology. To produce video for his video site, one of the authors bought himself a new computer with a 400 MHz Pentium II processor, 128 MB of main memory, and almost 21 GB of hard disk storage, for around $3,500. That was a configuration that worked the best for him.

Capturing Audio and Video

Capturing is the term used to describe the transferring or converting of audio/video material onto your computer. When you capture audio or video, you are transferring it from an analog format such as a VCR tape or cassette tape into the digital 1s and 0s that computers understand. You do so by linking a cable from your VCR, tape recorder, or other device into a device—the video or audio capture card—in your computer that can understand the audio or video signal.

Video capture software then converts the signal into computer format. When capturing, there are a lot of settings that you get involved with that affect the quality of the digital audio or video that you obtain, a topic we discuss in greater depth below.

Quality and Size Considerations

When dealing with audio and video on your computer, you'll quickly learn that there is a trade-off between the size of the computer file that contains your audio or video and the quality of what you get. The quality of what you capture and what you create is directly related to the size of the computer file that contains the audio or video. The smaller the file, the lower the quality. The better the quality, the larger the file. This is, of course, ignoring "compression" concepts, which we introduce below.

Let's put the quality/size trade-off into perspective. When you convert an audio signal into a computer file, you can choose from a number of different levels of quality, ranging from telephone quality all the way up to CD quality. The quality depends on how much of the audio is "captured" when transferred to your computer.

When dealing with the world of video, you can choose to capture and edit a video that is suitable to display on only a tiny window on your computer all the way up to something that is the equivalent quality of a television signal. The size of the video file will vary considerably, depending on the quality that you choose to work with.

This is an important point when it comes to the Internet, given that it is still a relatively slow method of distribution of multimedia information. After all, it is unlikely that anyone has an Internet link fast enough to receive $3\frac{1}{2}$ minutes of CD quality audio over the Internet that is found in a computer file that is 65 MB in size. And certainly, no one can easily deal with receiving a video file that is 2 GB in size.

That is why, when preparing your final audio or video file for distribution on the Internet, you must learn how to make the trade-off between quality and size. Reduce the quality of the video—in terms of the actual size of the video or in terms of how many frames per second it shows—and you will reduce the overall size of the file.

Compression Concepts

The size of the file that you create and make available on the Internet can also be directly related to the type of compression that you apply to the file when creating it.

Computer specialists involved in multimedia have long realized that one way to deal with the massive size of the files that are created by converting audio and video to a computer file is to compress some of the information. You will become familiar with compression concepts if you use programs like StuffIt and WinZip, which take a computer file and compress it to a smaller size using sophisticated mathematical concepts and algorithms. While compression of audio and video files works in somewhat the same way, it is far too complex to describe in this book. But think of it this way: in a video of someone standing on a stage speaking for 30 seconds, it is likely that the person is moving around, but the background is not. Video compression concepts will take that unchanging background and, rather than keeping each and every bit of information related to that background for the entire 30 seconds, figure out a way to store it but once and reuse it. This way, a substantial amount of storage space is saved.

There are many compression methods for all the different types of audio or video files that you might produce, and wading into the field can be a quagmire of confusion. Hence we suggest that you invest some time learning about compression concepts as you wade into the field of providing audio or video on the Internet. And as we will see below, when you create your audio or video, you can usually choose within the software program that you use the type of compression that should be used as well as various options related to how that compression method or scheme should work.

File Formats

Finally, you will discover that a voyage into the world of digital audio and video will involve you with a multitude of different file formats. For audio, you'll find that you will have to learn about WAV, AIF, and AU files; for video, you'll have to learn about MPG, AVI, MOV, and other video formats. There are so many different file types that it is impossible to cover them all. Suffice it to say, we'll stick to the major types of files that are used on the Internet today.

Step 1: Transferring Audio/Video to Your Computer

The first thing you need to do is get the audio or video that you want to make available to people on the Internet into your computer. This means converting your audio or video into a digital computer format from an analog format, that is, turning the information found on a cassette or VCR tape into the 1s and 0s that can be understood by a computer.

Audio

It can be pretty straightforward to transfer audio over to your computer. Why would you want to put only audio on your site instead of video? First, because it takes up much less room, so it might make sense to limit yourself to working with audio only. Second, perhaps the material you are using is only available in audio, such as a recording of a radio interview you might have done.

Over the last few years most of the Macintosh and Windows computers have come with built-in audio capabilities. If you have speakers linked to your computer, you'll probably discover that there is a jack that can be used to provide input to your computer. Plug a jack from the "audio output jack" on your source—a CD player, tape deck, or even television—into the audio port on your computer, and you are almost in business. If there isn't an output jack, you might be able to use the headset jack.

You need software that will take the audio input and convert it to a digital sound file. Most Windows and Macintosh computers sold in the last few years come with software that will do this. If you have an older computer that doesn't have an audio card, you'll have to purchase one. The necessary software to record audio comes with the card.

In Windows 95/98, you will find the program "Sound Recorder" located in the Programs/Accessories/Multimedia section within the Start menu. If it isn't there, you didn't install it when you set up the Windows program. You can install it at any time by choosing these menu options from the Start menu: Settings | Control Panel | Add/Remove Programs | Windows Setup | Multimedia. In there, click on the item Sound Recorder, and you'll be prompted to insert your Windows CD-ROM or installation disks.

Once you have your tape drive, CD player, or other source that you want to use to play the audio, you run the Sound Recorder program. Start your audio on the CD or tape recorder, then press the Record button (the red button) on the Sound Recorder. The Sound Recorder provides a straightforward way of saving an audio file to your computer that is captured from the audio port on your PC:

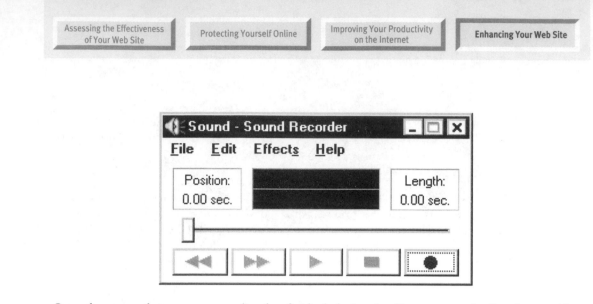

Once the source that you are recording has finished playing the file, you press the Stop button (the square button) on the Sound Recorder. Then save the audio to a file.

The basic audio recording programs that come with Windows 95/98 or Macintosh offer limited flexibility in terms of what you can do during the recording or input process and in terms of what you can do with the audio file once you have it on your computer. That's why you might consider using some third-party audio recorder/editor that allows you to not only capture an audio file, but manipulate it by adding special effects (such as fading at the end or amplification of quieter parts). You can find many such programs on the Internet. A good place to locate these types of programs is TUCOWS (**www.tucows.com**), which features an extensive list of software for both the Windows and Macintosh environment:

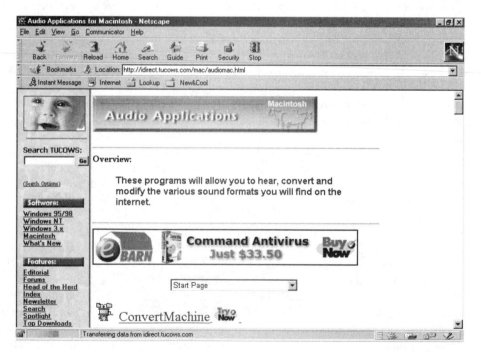

Finally, you will find that many of the video capturing programs that we describe below also include the capability to capture just audio.

Video

Capturing video is more complex. The first thing you need is a video card with "video capture" capability (commonly called a "video capture card") as well as video capture software.

Keep in mind that there are many video cards that don't have such capability. However, many of the newer PCs sold from 1998 on come installed with a video card as well as software that can be used to capture a video signal to your computer, so you may already have what is needed.

For example, the IBM ThinkPad 770 laptop that one of the authors uses came with a capture card as well as a video program, Assymetrix Digital Video Producer, which features digital video capture.

If you don't have a video card, you'll need to purchase one that includes capture capability. You are looking at $1,000 to $1,500, depending on how sophisticated you want to get.

Canadian Success Stories

Canada is a world leader when it comes to the manufacturing of video cards. ATI Technologies (**www.atitech.com**) of Markham, Ontario, and Matrox Graphics (**www.matrox.com**) of Montreal have both gained a significant international reputation for their video cards. In fact, many leading computer manufacturers bundle ATI or Matrox video cards with their new computers.

Let's walk through an example of what one of the authors did when adding video to his Web site. His project involved preparing a promotional video. His goal was to assemble various pieces of video and text onto a videotape. After completing that, he then wanted to put the video that he had prepared onto his Web site for others to access through the Internet. To do his digital video capturing and editing, he used a Windows 95 PC with a Matrox Millennium II video card. Attached to this is an add-on card called a Matrox Rainbow Runner card. (Matrox sells this particular configuration as two cards: a basic video card and a video capture card. Other products, such as their G100 and G200 video cards, include everything on one card.) The primary feature of the Rainbow Runner card is that it allows you to capture video, edit it, and then replay it to your television, without noticing any loss of quality. For an investment of a few hundred dollars it lets you do what would have cost tens of thousands of dollars just a few years ago.

When it comes to capturing video to your computer, the trick is figuring out whether your computer is up to the task at hand. When stored on a computer, video consists of a number of "frames." Each frame contains a "snapshot" of a digital image of the video plus the sound at a split-second moment in time. Assemble a number of frames together and replay them, and you'll reproduce the video plus audio.

The key to capturing and editing video is to get enough frames together in a short enough period of time to maintain the quality of the original video and audio. Television quality video plays 30 frames each and every second (or, to be precise, 29.97 frames per second). Squeeze that many frames playing together in the period of a second, and you get a smooth video. Do something with only 15 frames per second, and you'll get a video that, when played back, looks jerky.

Hence, if you want to capture television quality video, you'll need a computer, video card, and video capture software that can handle 30 frames per second. Of course, for the Internet, you can't play back anywhere even close to 30 frames per second, so the "frame rate" that you capture is less important when you create your video for distribution on the Internet.

The video capture software we used was the Ulead MediaStudio Pro 5.0 Video Capture program from Ulead Systems (**www.ulead.com**) that came with our Matrox Rainbow Runner video card.

(You'll find that most video capture cards come with software that can be used to capture and assemble a video. The software is usually a "lite" version with a limited set of features. If you want more features and options, you can often upgrade to the full version for an additional fee.)

Once you have your video hardware set up correctly, you simply tell the capture program how many frames you want to capture per second and the quality of the audio you want to capture. Start your VCR, and the program then works on converting your video to a digital file on your computer. You'll be advised if many frames are being dropped, so that you can try a capture again if necessary. (We'll discuss this issue below.)

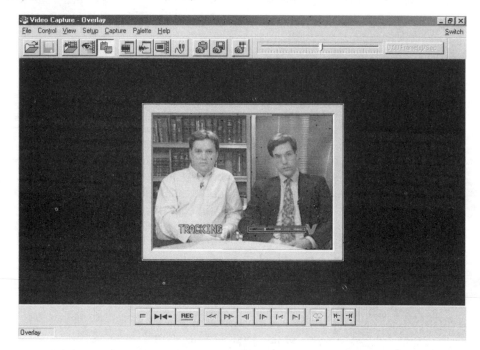

We also used the MGI VideoWave software to capture video. Made by a Toronto company, MGI Software Corp. (**www.mgisoft.com**), the program is a simple and straightforward tool that excels at helping the novice deal with video editing on a PC. We highly recommend it for those who are new to the field. It is also bundled with many leading video cards:

The speed of your computer is very important here. If you don't have a very fast computer and fast hard disks, you may not be able to adequately capture your video. If you tell your computer to capture 30 frames per second, it will try. But if the hard disk or the computer's processor can't keep up with the massive amount of data that this entails, it will do the only thing it can: it will drop frames. That is, for every 30 frames per second of video, it might drop a few.

You may find that if you try to capture a minute of video from your VCR (i.e., 30 frames × 60 seconds), you will be told that the capture process dropped 127 of 1,800 frames in that minute. The result will be a video that has a bunch of missing information and plays back in a jerky fashion, particularly if the dropped frames are spaced close together.

You'll have to experiment with the settings (i.e., frames per second, size of the video, compression methods, etc.) that you use to capture video. You may have to go with a lower number of frames per second, for example, to ensure the smoothest possible playback. This is a tricky area, but one which you will learn simply by working with the technology.

Finally, when capturing video, you'll probably want to capture not one large video file, but a bunch of different smaller files or segments of the video, which are called "clips," each anywhere from a few seconds to a few minutes long. You'll want to assemble these clips into a final video, which we discuss next.

Step 2: Editing Your Audio or Video Files

Once you have several digital audio or video clips in your computer, you can proceed to edit them to pull them into a finished format. We won't go into a lot of detail here about what you can do. Suffice it to say that with the sophisticated programs available for both the Windows and Macintosh environments today, you can prepare some pretty professional-looking video with a lot of very cool special effects. And with some of the audio editors that are available on sites such as TUCOWS, you can do some very interesting things to your audio files.

tip Your Video Story Line

Anyone who works in the video editing business will tell you that the first thing you must do when creating a video is develop a story line. In other words, before you begin assembling your video in a digital editing program, decide what you want your video to say. Determine what text to integrate into the story or what music to use as background. How do the various video clips fit together to tell the story? All of these issues are considerations that you should address before you actually start to bring your video together.

We have been using both Ulead MediaStudio Pro and MGI VideoWave to edit our video files. The latter is a straightforward tool suited to those who are new to the concept of video editing, while the former is more complex to learn but provides a greater degree of editing flexibility. Both programs are often bundled with popular video cards as we mentioned above, as are others, so you may have received a limited version of the program to try out. You can then pay an upgrade fee to obtain the full version. Another popular, albeit expensive, video editing program for high-end users is Adobe Premiere. This software is definitely not for casual users, but if you're interested, you can learn more at **www.adobe.com/prodindex/premiere/main.html**.

The MGI VideoWave program is a good example of the straightforward, easy-to-learn video editing programs that have become available. Once you have captured the clips you want to use in your video, you place them in the filmstrip at the top of the screen in the order in which you would like them to appear, keeping in mind that you want your video to tell a story:

You can then add "transition effects." At the bottom of the screen above you can see the two film clips that we are working with. In the middle of the two clips are two strips of film overlaying each other. This indicates that we have chosen to "fade" from one clip into the other. We have defined that the fade should take one second in total from the first clip to the second. This will, when the final video is produced, give us a very clean and professional-looking fade from one scene into another. You can also introduce title slides (e.g., titles for opening or closing your video or title segments throughout your video) or place words (e.g., someone's name) on certain sections of the video.

For more sophisticated work, we have been using Ulead MediaStudio Pro. This program is more complex than the MGI software we described above. In this program you bring in the various video clips that you have captured and place them on a "track." (Think of this as being comparable to the way that movies were assembled years ago. Clips of actual physical film were placed in sequential order on a board and were taped together to assemble a final movie. Now, with software, you simply place your video and audio clips in sequence on the program "track." In the screen below we have three video tracks and three audio tracks.)

You can then place title slides throughout the video and add an audio soundtrack that fades in and out as might be required. You can also provide sophisticated transitions from one scene to the next. Overall, you can do quite a bit of sophisticated stuff to prepare a reasonable quality professional-looking video:

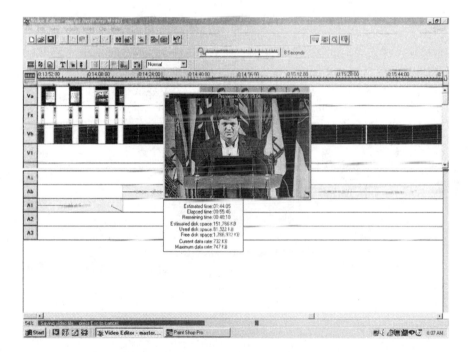

While you can learn the fundamentals of video editing fairly quickly with either program and any others of the many available, keep in mind that the skill of preparing a truly professional-looking video is not easily learned. If we can suggest anything, it's this: don't go overboard with all the features and special effects that are available to you during the editing process. The reaction of some people to the first cut of one of the authors' video was that it looked amateurish, simply because it used every special effect we could get our hands on.

It's a good point. Our experience with video editing made it clear to us that this new application will probably have results much like those of the early era of desktop publishing or the early days of Web site design. At the time when each of these technologies first arrived, a lot of people with very little in the way of artistic skills found themselves creating brochures or Web sites that used a wide variety of fonts and far too much information. Web sites and desktop published brochures were cluttered with images, suffered from poor design and layout, and looked far too amateurish. So, too, will it be as people avail themselves of the sophistication found with video editing programs.

To properly edit a video, be prepared to learn a lot about video production; it helps if you have at least some artistic talent. The alternative is a video that looks like it has been produced by an amateur.

tip Product Reviews

For detailed reviews of the latest video editing software and video capture cards, visit the following Web sites:

ZDNet's Video Software Web page: **www.zdnet.com/products/videouser/software.html**

ZDNet's Video Hardware Web page: **www.zdnet.com/products/videouser/hardware.html**

Step 3: Converting the Files to a Format Suitable For the Internet

Now comes the tricky part, converting the final audio or video file that you have edited into a format that can be used for listening or viewing on the Internet. Why do we say tricky? Because now you have to figure out how you want to distribute your audio and video files on your Web site. You can choose to make your audio and/or video files available to people in one of two file formats: native file format and streaming file format.

- **Native file format.** If you use this format, visitors to your Web site must download the entire audio or video file before they can play it. This can be impractical, given the often massive size of files that are associated with audio and video.

- **Streaming file format.** If you make your audio or video available in a streaming format, then visitors just click on a link or icon on your Web site and immediately begin hearing/seeing the audio/video clip. Internet users prefer streaming file formats because they don't have to wait for a large file to download. One of the most popular formats for streaming audio and video on the Web is RealAudio/RealVideo (**www.real.com**).

You can actually choose to make your files available in both formats. We'll take a look at both approaches below.

If you provide your audio/video files in native file format, one thing that you must do, when preparing your files, is test how long they take to download using a regular modem. Otherwise, you might discover that while you have created a great audio or video, you haven't prepared something that is usable by the vast majority of people on the Internet.

Native File Formats

There are a number of common native audio formats for the Internet. They include files with the extensions **.wav, .au, .aiff**, and others. If you place these files on your Web site and link them to a Web page, visitors using Netscape or Microsoft browsers (version 3 or higher) will be able to access them easily, since these browsers have audio "player" programs built in to them. However, as discussed above, the disadvantage of using a native file format is that the user has to wait for the file to download to her computer before she can begin hearing it. When it comes to audio, be sure to look into MP3, a rapidly evolving standard on the Internet that allows you to distribute CD quality audio through your Web site. MP3 promises to revolutionize the field of audio distribution on the Internet. You can learn more about this audio standard at **www.mp3.com**. In addition to keeping you up-to-date on MP3 technology, this site has lots of programs that let you take an audio file and convert it into MP3 format.

There are countless native video file formats as well, including MPG and AVI. You can create video files in these formats and make them available for downloading. Users have to download the entire file; then they can view it using the capabilities built into their Web browser, provided they are using version 3 or higher of either Netscape or Internet Explorer, which have the capability to automatically view these video file formats.

The key thing is creating your native format audio or video files in a way such that they are not too massive to use through the Internet. This is usually straightforward with audio files, since normally they are not too big. For video, most of the video editing programs will also allow you to output it in a variety of formats suitable for purposes of distributing over the Internet.

MGI VideoWave, for example, handles the Internet issue quite easily. When you first set out to create your video, you are asked if it will be output to videotape, CD-ROM, or to the Internet. If you choose the Internet, it will automatically choose the best settings in terms of number of frames, size of the video, audio, and other parameters that are best for Internet distribution. In addition, should these automatic settings not be good enough, you can go into a screen and manually specify the size of the video, the type of compression that should be used when it is prepared, the sound quality, and many other options:

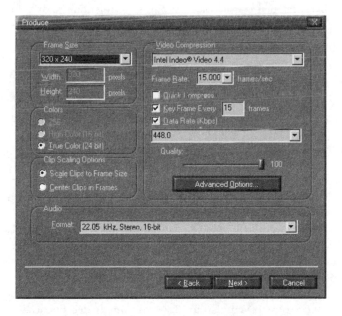

But you don't have to mess with these settings if you want to keep things simple; simply indicate to the program that you want to output to the Internet when creating your final video, and it will choose the best settings for you.

Similarly, in Ulead MediaStudio Pro there is a lot of flexibility in specifying the options that should be used when saving your file, such as the compression scheme, number of frames, and audio quality. You can choose from a number of predefined options as well to make it easier to create a file for the Internet:

Video Save Options

Video Editor | General | Advanced | Compression | Cropping

Compression:

None

Quality: 100%

Key frame for every 1 Frames

Data type: 8 Bits RGB

☑ Use common palette 3-3-2 (bits)

About...

Configure...

Preview...

Load...

Audio...

Format: PCM

Attributes: 44,100 Hz, 16 Bit, Mono

OK | Cancel | Help

What will likely happen is that you'll end up experimenting with these settings to figure out what works best for the video file that you are hoping to make available on the Internet.

tip MPEG Resources

One of the most popular native file formats for video files is MPEG. For a comprehensive index of MPEG resources and programs on the Internet, visit **www.mpeg.org**.

Streaming File Formats

The problem with making audio or video available in a native file format is that visitors to your Web site must download the entire file before they can listen to it or view it. Given the large size of many audio and video files, this is often impractical.

This reality led to the emergence of streaming files, the most popular of which are RealAudio/RealVideo from RealNetworks (**www.real.com**) and QuickTime (**www.quicktime. com**) from Apple. Streaming allows someone to see or hear the audio or video immediately, rather than having to wait for the entire file to download first.

Although there are a large number of streaming file formats available, certainly the two above are the most common. If you plan to make streaming video files available on your Web site, you should at least include the above two formats, in addition to any other special streaming format(s) that you want to offer.

RealAudio/RealVideo (audio and video)	**www.real.com**
QuickTime (audio and video)	**www.quicktime.com**
VDOLive (video)	**www.vdolive.com**
Windows Media (audio and video)	**www.microsoft.com/netshow**

RealAudio/RealVideo

RealAudio/RealVideo is a special format for audio and video files that uses a special compression scheme to provide a variety of file sizes used for streaming. The compression that is applied can vary, depending on who you want to make the audio or video available to.

In our case, our high-quality video, which in final form was 2 GB in size, was compressed all the way down to 4 MB (or about 0.0002 of the original file) so that people with slow modem connections could access it. The quality? Marginal...very jerky screens and rather fuzzy sound. But at least it makes the video available to the lowest common denominator user of the Internet in terms of speed.

To create a RealAudio or RealVideo file, you can use the free RealEncoder, available from the RealNetworks Web site (**www.real.com**). The RealEncoder program is straightforward and fairly easy to use. Your source of the audio or video which is encoded in the RealEncoder can be from several sources:

- You can use an audio or video file that you have on your computer. This would be the file that you created from your audio or video editing program, such as MGI VideoWave or Ulead MediaStudio Pro.

- You can record a Real file directly from your microphone, from a CD player, or from another device attached to your computer.

- You can do a live broadcast that you would make available if you had the RealAudio server, an issue we discuss below. Most of us wouldn't choose this option; this is the type of thing used by the CBC to broadcast its radio signal live on the Internet:

New Session - Choose Recording Wizard

Select a Recording Wizard for the media clip that you want to create.

○ Record From File

This option allows you to create a media clip from existing audio or video files located on your hard drive.

○ Record From Media Device

This option allows you to capture a media clip from a media device such as a Microphone, PC Camera, CD Player, or VCR connected to your computer.

○ Live Broadcast

This option allows you to broadcast a live media stream from your computer to a RealNetworks RealServer.

☐ Don't use Wizards on start.

[OK]   [Cancel]

The next thing you need to do is indicate the type of file that you want to prepare. There are two choices. You could choose the "single rate" option. This would allow you to create one file for 28.8 Kbps modem users, another file for users of 56 Kbps modems, and still another file for cable modem users. Your Web pages would advise visitors which of these files they should download, depending on the speed of their connection to the Internet. In essence, you would create three RealAudio/RealVideo files, each aimed at someone with a different speed of connection to the Internet. There are differences in the quality of each, that is, those with a slower connection to the Internet get a lower quality audio or video. And keep in mind that if you make available three different files, you'll be using more hard disk space.

The second choice is to use the new Stream Smart technology introduced by RealNetworks in 1998 with the G2 version of its software. This allows you to create a single file that can be accessed by anyone, regardless of modem speed:

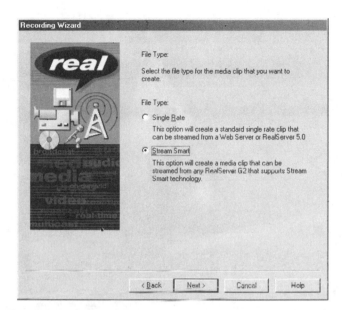

If you choose the Stream Smart approach, you need to provide some information on the types of connections that you are willing to support. This information is used to adjust the quality of the audio/video provided to each type of user:

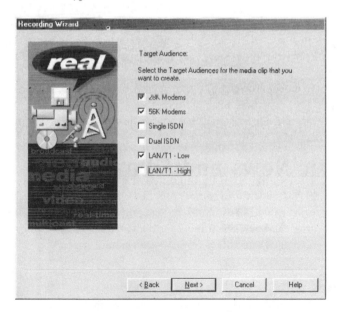

Once you have done that, you are in business. The RealEncoder program proceeds to prepare an encoded RealAudio/RealVideo file based upon the preferences that you have selected:

If you want to get more sophisticated, consider purchasing the RealPublisher program. It does the same thing as RealEncoder, in that it will let you prepare a RealAudio/RealVideo file, but also provides a greater number of options and more flexibility in terms of what you can do. For example, it gives you a "wizard driven" Web page creator, which makes it very easy to create Web pages containing all your audio or video files. It also allows more flexibility in the way you make your audio or video files available to visitors. In addition, you can record in real time from microphones, video recorders, or other sources.

Once you have processed your audio or video file in the encoder program, you have a RealAudio or RealVideo streaming file format that you are ready to make available on the Internet.

tip Historic News and Film Clips

FOOTAGE.NET (**www.footage.net**) provides a free searchable database of hundreds of stock footage sources worldwide. Search the video archives of CNN, ABCNEWS, Paramount Pictures, and other leading databases. You'll be using the database that the pros use! FOOTAGE.NET also lets you screen QuickTime videos from several archival sources.

QuickTime

QuickTime is the other format that you should definitely use if you want to make audio or video files available on your Web site. With the release of QuickTime in the 1980s, Apple established itself as a preeminent leader in the field of computer-based video. It is estimated that at least half the multimedia video content on the Internet today is in QuickTime format.

Apple released, in 1998, QuickTime 3, a program that serves as both a player and a creator/encoder. You can download the program at **www.quicktime.com**.

Install the program, and you can use it to play QuickTime audio and videos. But purchase the upgrade online for U.S. $29.95, and you'll get a special registration code that will unlock the capability to use the program to create your own audio and video in QuickTime and other formats such as AVI, a common file format for Windows systems.

In our case, we took the video that we created in Ulead MediaStudio Pro (which was created in AVI format) and imported it into QuickTime.

(Note that MediaStudio Pro can also generate a QuickTime movie directly, but since we already had an AVI file, we decided to take this route.) We then chose to export it to QuickTime format. When doing so, we were able to specify the video and sound settings that we wanted to use. QuickTime makes this an easy decision; your quality of video, for example, ranges from low to high. Each of these settings has a different impact on the size of your video:

In addition, we indicated that we wanted the QuickTime movie to be set up for a "fast start on the Internet." This allows a QuickTime movie to stream. In other words, people accessing the video through the Internet should begin seeing the video as soon as they click on the appropriate link on your Web site, rather than having to wait for the entire file to download. (If you don't select this item, then people will have to download the entire file first.)

Assessing the Effectiveness
of Your Web Site

Protecting Yourself Online

Improving Your Productivity
on the Internet

Enhancing Your Web Site

Movie Settings

☑ Video

[Settings...]
[Filter...]

Compression: Video
Quality: Medium
Key frame rate: 24

☑ Sound

[Settings...]

Format: Uncompressed
Sample rate: 22.05 kHz
Sample size: 16
Channels: 1

☑ Fast Start for the Internet

☐ Compress Movie Header

[OK]   [Cancel]

One of the most exciting features of the QuickTime program is that it allows you to create a QuickTime movie with "Sorenson" video compression. Sorenson Vision Inc. (**www.s-vision.com**) is a company that has long been involved in digital video and has come up with a compression method that achieves a remarkable reduction in the size of the video file while maintaining the high quality of the video:

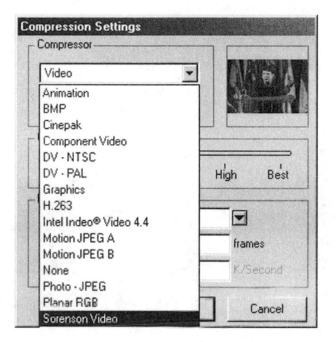

If you'd like to see a professional-looking video that has been compressed with Sorenson video compression, visit **www.theforce.net/troops**. There, you will find a hilarious spoof of *Star Wars* and the TV show *COPS* combined into a production called *Troops*. The production was filmed on a regular video camera, digitally edited, and made available on the Internet in a variety of formats, including QuickTime. The quality of the video, about 10 minutes in length, is excellent. It has gained the attention of CNN and other media:

Assessing the Effectiveness
of Your Web Site

Protecting Yourself Online

Improving Your Productivity
on the Internet

Enhancing Your Web Site

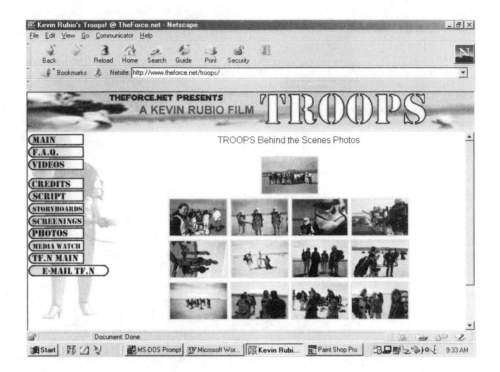

One of the authors used Sorenson compression on his own video. It reduced his 2 GB file to
180 MB for a very high quality video and 30 MB for a smaller one.

Other Formats

There are many other streaming audio and video formats on the Internet as we noted above, many
of which make claims regarding their popularity, superior qualities, etc. You might consider using
some of these other streaming options to reach the widest possible audience. It doesn't hurt to
offer other formats if you have the time to make files available in those formats, but be careful not
to confuse visitors to your Web site with too many different options.

Step 4: Placing the Audio or Video Files on a Web Server

Now that you have an audio or video file that is ready to be distributed on the Internet, the next
step is to get the file(s) onto your Web site. There are many issues that you need to consider. Cost
and Web server requirements are two of the most important.

Cost

Before you place any audio or video files on your Web site, figure out what your Internet service
provider or Web hosting company will charge you. Keep in mind that, as we have previously discussed, the audio and video files that you create can be very large, and you will likely exceed the
maximum amount of disk space that your ISP/Web hosting company has allocated you. As a result,
you will have to pay for any additional disk space you require.

In addition, the company that hosts your Web site may charge you for "data transfer"; that is, they will charge you if the amount of traffic generated by your Web site exceeds a certain minimum volume. For example, the first 100 MB of traffic on your Web site may be free each month, after which you will have to pay a fee for each additional megabyte of traffic. Under this scenario, if you have a video file that is 5 MB in size, and 100 people access it, you'll be 400 MB in excess of your limit (and we haven't included the traffic that all your other Web pages are generating). As you can see, it's important to find out what charges you may be subject to if your Web site starts to generate a lot of traffic. After all, you don't want a surprise on your next bill.

An alternative to putting these files onto someone else's computer is to set up your own Web server to deal with the video/audio files. One of the authors did this for his promotional video by taking an old 486 PC that was no longer being used and installing the Linux operating system on it (we discuss Linux in the Conclusion, "The Future of the Internet: Linux and Open Source"). When he installed Linux, he had it include installation of the free Apache Web server. Next, he linked the 486 computer to his home office network, which is connected to the Internet on a full-time basis through a cable modem. He then transferred his video file to the 486 machine. Next, he created a link from his regular Web site to the audio/video files located on the 486 machine. The end result? When visitors to his regular Web site click on the link, they are automatically connected to the 486 computer with the video files on it. By doing this, he was able to keep within the maximum storage space allocated to him by his Internet service provider because the video file was being served off his own Web server rather than his regular Web site, which is hosted by a Toronto-based Internet service provider.

Web Server Requirements

If you are using streaming file formats for your audio or video files, the computer that the files are stored on (i.e., the Web server) may need some additional programs to run your video/audio files, particularly if you plan on having a lot of people access one or more of your files simultaneously.

If you make a streaming QuickTime video or audio file available, there is no special configuration required on the Web server that holds your Web site. Simply indicate, when creating the video or audio, that you want a "fast start on the Internet" as seen above, and the file will stream.

RealAudio/RealVideo is another matter. To be able to run a RealAudio/RealVideo file, the Web server that stores these files needs to be configured in a certain way. There are two routes you can take:

- You will have to ensure that the company that hosts your Web site makes a change to their configuration to support the RealAudio/RealVideo files. Details on what is involved are on the RealNetworks Web site (**www.realstore.com/source/source.html**). On this page they note that "although this technique is not well-suited for high-volume sites serving numerous simultaneous streams, many smaller Web sites can benefit tremendously from this simple and inexpensive approach. Actually, it's better than inexpensive, it's free." In essence, you need to convince the company that hosts your Web site to add two small lines to their Web server configuration file, if they haven't already done so, that look like this:

        audio/x-pn-realaudio
        audio/x-pn-realaudio-plugin

It is so easy to do; in fact, on the Web page above where RealNetworks describes what is involved, they actually provide a form that you can fill out and e-mail to your ISP or Web hosting company asking them to make the appropriate change.

Assessing the Effectiveness
of Your Web Site

Protecting Yourself Online

Improving Your Productivity
on the Internet

Enhancing Your Web Site

- Alternatively, you can do what one of the authors has done and set up your own RealAudio/Video server on your own Web server machine. Or find a Web hosting company with a RealAudio/Video server that can host your files for a fee. A basic server is available for free online for Windows 95, Windows NT, Linux, and other systems, but you will have to pay for a version that supports more than a few concurrent users. The reason for this is, if a lot of people are trying to access your audio or video file at once, your Web server may not be able to handle it. Hence the fee-based RealAudio/Video servers are designed for situations where there are many people accessing the file at once. (The CBC and many other leading media organizations use RealAudio servers.)

If you choose to use a different file format other than the ones above, they too may have restrictions on how they are made available on the Internet. For example, to make available Microsoft Windows Media files in a streaming format, you must have a NetShow server components running on a Windows NT server.

Step 5: Linking the Audio or Video Files to a Web Page

The final step? Design a Web page on your Web site that provides a link to your audio/video files, wherever they may be stored. For users to view these files, they must have the necessary video/audio player installed on their computer as well. You should, therefore, also provide a link to the sites where they can download the necessary RealAudio/Video, QuickTime, or other audio/video player.

There's not much we can tell you here, except that the process of linking to your RealAudio/RealVideo file can actually be a little tricky, in that you don't link directly to the file, but to a file that contains a pointer to your file. We won't go into depth on what this involves; suffice it to say that the RealAudio documentation will describe to you precisely what you need to do.

Summary

The PC-based audio and video editing market is expected to boom over the next several years as computer processors become more powerful, the cost of editing software decreases, and high-speed Internet access technologies like cable modems and ADSL become more commonplace. Although the underlying technology can seem complex, it's getting easier to use, and the end result is very satisfying: a homemade video that you can use for promotional purposes or just to entertain your family and friends.

The Future of the Internet: Linux and Open Source

The explosive growth of the Internet is not a fad or a fluke, but the result of a digital free market unleashed.

"The Accidental Superhighway," *The Economist*, July 1, 1995

If we can learn anything about the Internet, it is this: in our past we find our future.

In 1994, in the original edition of the *Canadian Internet Handbook*, we commented on the hype and hysteria beginning to surround the Internet:

> *Information highways are currently a very hot topic! Politicians, the media, and senior business executives are very excited about the concept of the information highway. We are told that the highway will offer everything from online shopping and banking at home services, to interactive television, video games and instant video libraries. Hotels, car rentals, and brokerage services will be just a keyboard command away. New "information appliances" will appear which will bring together televisions and computers. Telephone, cable and satellite networks will merge, creating huge pipelines through which all this information will flow.*

Examine that paragraph today, and you will realize that most of it has come true. The Internet has solidified its role as the foundation of the economy of the 21st century and will certainly emerge as the most significant technology invented by humankind. It promises upheaval in our economic systems as the transactions that drive our economy move away from a paper-based system to an electronic system.

But what is fascinating about the above quote is that at the time, leading companies, government, and telecommunication organizations believed that the Information Highway of the future would be based on television technology and would be accessed through TV remote controls. We pointed out how wrong they were, that the Highway would be accessed using computers and through computer keyboards.

Why is this significant? Because there are many predictions made about the Internet today, involving its future, that we suspect may not come true. The reason? Because in our past we find our future.

Learning From the Past

In the 1995 edition of this book we wrote with scorn about the UBI Initiative, a project based in Quebec, sponsored by some major telecommunication organizations and consumer product companies.

The reason for our scorn was perhaps best found in the grand plan and premise of UBI as captured in its promotional video, which at one point showed a typical family ordering fried chicken through their television set.

This was it! This was the Information Superhighway. It was to be a television-based monstrosity through which the masses would order fried chicken. It was to be a giant global shopping mall, with consumers eagerly and quickly departing with their hard-earned dollars through online shopping. It was to be a robotic future, in which we the consumers would do very little online except shop.

We could barely contain our skepticism, while we pointed out that the Internet was emerging as the true Information Highway. We ridiculed with glee the plans of major telephone and cable companies of the time to build the ultimate home-shopping network, with their belief that the average user of the technology of the future would want nothing more than to order fried chicken online.

UBI died a well-deserved and quiet death a few years later, at the same time that global and national telecommunication giants came to realize that the Information Highway was not to be found in some television-based network, but in the global Internet.

The well-laid plans of the corporate sector to build a television-based information Superhighway were stolen by the geeks who had built the Internet.

The Geeks Who Stole Cyberspace, Revisited

The reality of the emergence of the Internet, and its impact on the corporate sector, was best put into perspective in a ground-breaking article, "The Geeks Who Stole Cyberspace," which appeared in the *New York Times* in 1995. In it, author Stephen Levy outlined how the Internet stole the vision of a television-based Information Highway from the corporate sector. He said that the Internet succeeded here because it was rooted in a global cooperative effort, that it was not controlled by anyone.

The theme was picked up elsewhere as other publications made similar observations. *The Economist* noted in a series of articles printed in its July 1, 1995 issue ("The Accidental Superhighway") that, while cable and telephone companies were busy running around creating an Information Superhighway that revolved around television, a technology that they could and would control, "they have been too busy to notice the unruly bunch of computer hackers, engineers and students scurrying about at their feet. They should have paid more attention. For while the giants have just been talking about an information superhighway, the ants have actually been building one: the Internet."

The ants are busy again. This time, they are building the future of the Internet, and it is to be found in two initiatives: Linux, a Unix-based operating system for personal computers, and open source software, software for which the source code is publicly available and does not have any licencing restrictions on its use, modification, or redistribution.

To understand the future of the Internet, you need to appreciate that the geeks are stealing cyberspace again. The impact will be dramatic, in terms of the future direction of the Internet, in terms of how you and I will use it, and in terms of who will control it.

The geeks are stealing control of cyberspace to keep it from being controlled.

The Significance of Linux and Open Source

Many of today's computers run an operating system such as DOS, Windows, or Macintosh and have software programs that are "closed"; this means that only the company that created the program can modify it. Linux, on the other hand, like many Unix systems, is "open," meaning that computer programmers can modify the very heart of their computer systems. And the global momentum behind Linux, combined with this ability to modify the operating system, promises to shake the foundation of computing to the core.

The open source concept is based on the philosophy that the best software comes not from closed programs such as those from Microsoft and other software companies, but from a global sharing of computer programming time, where anyone is free to develop, modify, and redistribute the computer code.

The development of Linux itself is based on this open source concept. It is being developed with a global cooperative approach that is truly stunning in both its breadth and acceptance.

Linux is significant, because its rapid rise and massive rate of adoption are eerily parallel to the emergence of the Internet. Linux is being developed at a furious pace, the result of a huge global effort. It is intrinsically and intimately linked to the Internet. Install it, and you have a Web server and all the other tools that are part of the global Internet.

In mid-1998, Linux made the covers of *Forbes Magazine*, the *Globe and Mail Report on Business*, most leading computer publications, and *Business Week* in rapid succession. The world began to notice that something big was happening in the same way that it noticed that something big was happening with the Internet in 1993.

Open source computing, of which Linux is but a part, picked up its own steam in 1998. The two most noteworthy developments? Netscape gave away the source code of its Web browser to the global computing community. Anyone who wanted to work with it, improve it, develop it was free to do so. And IBM adopted, for purposes of its electronic commerce initiatives, the Apache Web server, an open source software program.

Netscape bought into the open source philosophy because it believed that the best hope for the future development of its browser would come from giving away the source code—the basic computer instructions that make it work—for free. Netscape was convinced that its other revenue-generating products would benefit as a result.

IBM? It simply made sense to go with Apache. It may surprise you to know that more than half the Web servers in the world are built on top of Apache, a program that is not owned by any company or person. Apache, like Linux, is being developed at a furious and rapid pace by individuals and companies worldwide.

Both Netscape and Apache are part of the open source philosophy, which is stated on the Open Source Web site (**www.opensource.org**): "When programmers on the Internet can read, redistribute, and modify the source for a piece of software, it evolves. People improve it, people adapt it, people fix bugs. And this can happen at a speed that, if one is used to the slow pace of conventional software development, seems astonishing."

Learning From the Past

We would do well to remember that what is happening with Linux and open source today is a repeat of what happened with the Internet in the past. The geeks are stealing cyberspace again, and they intend to ensure that control of the network does not fall into the wrong hands.

Remember where the Internet came from:

- **The Internet emerged from the university and research sector.** The Internet was not hatched in the research lab of some massive global software company. It emerged in the university and research sectors, where leading-edge computer experts toiled away to define the most significant computer protocols in the history of computing.

- **The Internet emerged from a global, cooperative effort rooted in the hacker culture.** The Internet did not emerge aided and abetted by steroid-like corporate marketing budgets. The technology that drives the Internet emerged from the globally linked minds of leading computer programmers of the day. The honourable hacker culture—not the hacker community that seeks to break into computers and destroy things—was at work with the Internet. Early open source concepts are what drove the Internet forward. It was developed and enhanced by a global computing culture driven to explore, expand, and enrich the potential of computing worldwide. It evolved in a climate where programmers freely shared their ideas, opinions, and beliefs in order to create a computer technology that could be used by all.

Consider what is happening with Linux and open source computing, as history repeats itself:

- **Linux is emerging from the university and research sector.** Visit a university computing lab today, and you'll discover that the leading-edge computer pioneers of tomorrow are not working with Windows and Macintosh systems, but with Linux. On the university campuses of the world, Linux is the thing to do. Windows and Macintosh are not cool; Linux and open source are. The global commitment to Linux and open source concepts, particularly among younger generations, is stunning.

- **Linux is a global, cooperative effort rooted in the open source culture.** Linux is not being developed by one person, or one company, or even one organization. It is controlled by no one, but by everyone. It is a system that is being developed by tens of thousands of computer programmers and computer users, many of whom could be considered the brightest and best of their generation. The brain power coming together is unrivalled.

The 1995 article, "The Accidental Superhighway," in *The Economist* noted that "the growth of the Net is not a fluke or a fad, but the consequence of unleashing the power of individual creativity." So too is Linux, and so too is open source computing. And for that reason, we think that history is about to repeat itself again.

There is a massive amount of human creativity being poured into the Internet by thousands of people. The development cycle does not result in new versions of software every few months, but every few *days*. It is that type of momentum that we must respect and appreciate.

Control of the Internet

In essence, what is at stake here is control of the Internet. It is undeniable that the government wants to control and regulate the Internet, for whatever reasons. And it is undeniable that companies like Microsoft are trying to own and control as much of the Internet as they can.

It is also undeniable that both Linux and the open source movement are being fed by a "let's stop Bill Gates" philosophy, driven by the desire to prevent the Internet from being controlled and regulated by any person, company, or government authority. Control is prevented by distributing control.

There are many worldwide who are passionate in their opinion that the future of computing should not be controlled by any one organization or government. There are tens of thousands, if not hundreds of thousands, in the global computer fraternity who believe that Microsoft has gone too far and that government authority will never prevail.

Rightly or wrongly, they are dedicated to combining their intellectual capital and programming prowess to stop Microsoft dead in its tracks and to destroying any attempts by government to control the future.

If you devote the best and the brightest computer minds worldwide to achieving these goals, the results are obvious.

What Does It Mean to You?

What does the impact of Linux and open source software really mean? What impact will it have on you? What should you be doing?

We think it is this: respect the past as an indication of the future. We have no doubt that "the geeks who stole cyberspace" are stealing it again. We believe that Linux and the open source concept have achieved such a global critical mass that their impact on the future of the Internet will become undeniable. If you want to best understand the Internet of the future, then get involved today, appreciate what is going on. We think this is the best advice we can give you today.

We're not sure exactly what is happening, but we think you should be prepared to pay attention and to become involved. We certainly are. We think that you should take the time to:

- **Install and learn Linux.** Pioneers of the Internet, those who jumped onboard in 1993 or 1994, had to work with technologies such as FTP, Telnet, Veronica, Archie, and Gopher. Such technologies often involved the use of archaic strings of text and very difficult commands. Mastering the Internet was an exercise—a difficult and challenging one. But many jumped onboard because they were convinced this was the future.

  The World Wide Web, of course, changed all of that. Suddenly, here was a technology that anyone could use, that anyone could learn. The Internet emerged from the global collective programmers' mind and came into the mainstream. Those who got involved in the early days were richer for it.

  The state of Linux today is like the Internet of 1993. When we installed it in mid-1998, the installation process was horrendously complex. Indeed, it is the most complex and difficult technology that we have had to work with. But when we finally mastered the installation process, a Windows-like system emerged. The world of Linux opened up to us, much as the World Wide Web opened up the Internet to millions in 1994. There is promise in Linux, just as there was promise in the Internet. It is like a butterfly emerging from a cocoon, just as the Web emerged in 1994.

  Today, one of the authors has a full-fledged Web server running on his Linux system. We can serve audio and video up to the world for a fraction of a penny. We can run Netscape in a window much like we might on a Macintosh or Windows system; there is no difference in terms of the features that you get. We can avail ourselves of the fascinating software that is becoming available for the platform, including a full, Windows-like version of WordPerfect. We anticipate being able to do much more in the future. And we do this for a fraction of the cost of competing technologies.

  We think this is where the future is headed, and we plan to be part of it.

- **Understand open source, and monitor its development.** Spend some time at **www.opensource.org**, the home for the open source movement. Read what it says, and understand what it means. And track what is going on. Listen to the news, and watch for announcements by computer companies. We anticipate absolutely fascinating developments throughout 1999.

Learn and Respect What Is Going On

In our first *Canadian Internet Handbook*, published in 1994, we closed with the comment that you should "be a pioneer." We stated that:

> As you approach the Internet, treat it with some awe, apprehension, respect, but approach it. It's too valuable a resource to ignore. Yet, as you begin to work with the Internet, recognize it for what it is: a new territory. Treat the Internet as though you are a pioneer, because if you begin using it now, you are. Today, the Internet is a vast unexplored territory. There are only crude maps and few signposts, and those that do exist are quickly replaced by others. If you manage to carve out a place for yourself in this new and strange land, you must be prepared for some frustration along the way. Understand that you are going to have to put in some effort to access the Internet, to explore it, and to learn how to use it to your benefit.

Assessing the Effectiveness
of Your Web Site

Protecting Yourself Online

Improving Your Productivity
on the Internet

Enhancing Your Web Site

We think the same sentiment holds true for Linux and open source today. Yet, even as these visions come true, we look back at another comment that we made in the 1994 edition, what the Internet meant to people at the time:

> ...*many people are indicating that they see a different vision of the information highway. Through the highway, they want to be able to communicate with people, to explore new electronic frontiers, to enhance their working and professional skills, to debate topics in global conferences or to seek information.*

It was our belief at the time, and it remains true to this day, that the Internet is about far more than a consumer- and business-oriented network. It is far more than a place where we can undertake some type of electronic transaction, but a place of personal interaction and personal communication. It is a place for the little guy. And in that way, it is not a place that should be controlled by anyone or anything.

We think the future of the Internet and, indeed, the future of our world, is found in Linux and open source computing.

Index

Diagnostic software, 215-218
Did-it detective, 57-58, 76
Direct Hit, 83
Disability symbol, 26
Discussion groups. *See* Mailing list; USENET
Disney, 258
Dissident communities, 138
DocFather Applet Edition, 18-19
Doctor HTML, 34
Dogpile, 268
Domain name
    hijacking of, 170
    Web store, 332
Dow Jones, 305
Download
    audio/video players, 360
    incomplete, 195
    protecting, 181
    search results, 256-258
    software, 103
    time, 7-11, 50
    Web site, 232, 283
Download Butler, 181
DOWNLOAD.COM, 202
Dr. Solomon's, 101, 102, 110
Dreamweaver, 97, 98
Dropit, 193
DU Meter, 215
DXShop, 312, 328-333
    see also Electronic commerce; Web store
Dynamic Submission 2000, 64
DynamIP, 235

E

E-commerce service providers, 310-311
E-mail
    address, 135
    address book, 128
    anonymity, 134, 138-139, 140, 141
    archiving, 223-229
    attachments, 111, 113
    backup of messages, 128
    finding an address, 225, 267
    non-encrypted, 135
    reliability, 226
    security of program, 167
The Economist, 362, 365
Effective Web sites, 86-94
Elections Canada, 135
Electronic Advertising and Marketplace Report, 54
Electronic commerce

complexities of, 311-312
future sales, 328
setting up, 310
see also E-commerce service providers; Web store
Electronic Frontier Canada, 148
Electronic Frontier Foundation, 148
Electronic Messaging Association, 223
Electronic Privacy Information Center, 148
Electronic shopping. *See* Electronic commerce
EmailFerret, 266
Encrypted
    backup files, 129
    data, 130
    e-mail message, 135
    passwords, 107
Engage, 145
eSafe Protect, 111, 112, 113-114, 115
eSafe Protect Technologies, 112, 113
Eudora, 167
Excite, 57
    meta-tags, 72
    NewsTracker service, 177
    personalization features, 176-177
Expectations, 90

F

Face-recognition technology, 157
FarCast, 293
FBI's National Computer Crime Squad, 164
Feedback, 90
FerretSoft, 266
Fetch, 97
File and printer sharing, 158
FileFerretPRO, 267
FileHound, 195
Files
    backup, 115
    validity of, 30-37
Filtering programs, 218-221
Financial Post, 279
Finjan Software, 112
Firewall, 164-166, 169, 244, 251
First Place Software, 76
5Star Shareware, 202
Flypage Web Backup, 119-20
Focus groups, 44
FOOTAGE.NET, 354

Forbes, 363
Form browser, 191-193
FormBot, 191, 193
Forrester Research, 173, 328
Frames, 7
Fraud
    bank policies, 336
    fraudulent services, 64
Freedom of speech, 135, 138
Freeware, 103
Frustration, assessment of sources of, 43
FTP Software, 124
Fyodor's Playhouse, 152, 157

G

Gamay, David, 170, 173
Gates, Bill, 364
"The Geeks Who Stole Cyberspace," 362
General Motors of Canada Internet Marketing Organization, 86, 88, 92, 97, 98
Geocities, 141-142
GetRight, 195
GIF Construction Set, 98
GIF Lube, 11
GIFbot, 9, 11
GIFWizard, 11
Global Internet Liberty Campaign, 138
The Globe and Mail, 6, 166, 303, 305, 363
GlobeFund, 6
Google, 83
goto.com, 260
Grab-a-Site, 232
Graphics
    optimization, 11
    resizing, 20
    turning off, 221

H

Hacking, 150-157
    ethical, 170-172
    exploration of culture, 153
    honourable, 154-155
    security exploits, 153
Hader, Thomas, 85, 91, 93, 95, 96, 98
Halper, Mark, 309
Hard drive, 222
Harmon, Amy, 134
Headliner, 285
Here, 235

Assessing the Effectiveness
of Your Web Site

Protecting Yourself Online

Improving Your Productivity
on the Internet

Enhancing Your Web Site

Notification service, 41
NSClean, 147
Nymserver, 139

O

Objectives, 87-88, 93
Online catalogue, 320
Online commerce. *See*
  Electronic commerce
Online focus groups. *See* Focus
  groups
Online forms, 191-193
Online marketing resources, 59
Online Privacy Alliance, 148
Ontario Corn Producers
  Association, 46-47
OnTrack! OnTrack!, 221
Open source software, 3, 362
  development of, 365
  origins of, 364
  significance of, 362-363
Open Source Web site, 363
Opera, 98, 214-215
Organization, assessment of, 43
Orphan pages, 46

P

Pacific Coast Feather Company,
  74
Paint Shop Pro, 9, 97
PaperMaster, 232
PassMan, 168
Password Keeper, 168
Password Manager, 168
Passwords
  backup of, 128
  encrypted, 107, 156
  management programs, 168
  variety of, 167-168
  see also User IDs and pass-
    words
PBS, 150
PC Computing, 33
PC firewalls. *See* Firewall
PC Magazine, 33, 202
PC Magazine Utility Guide 98,
  253
pcANYWHERE, 233-234, 236,
  237
  cable modem connection,
    239-241
  corporate network, 244
  dial-up connection, 243-244
  firewalls, 165
  Internet connection, 238-239
  methods of using, 238

security options, 241-243
PCSecure, 166
PeakJet, 209, 210
People with disabilities, 24-28
Performance, 37-41
Philip Environmental, 137
PhoneFerret, 267
Ping programs, 37
Pinnacle Systems, 337
PointCast, 285, 294
Pop-up survey software, 42
Popularity, 83
PositionAgent, 80-81
Press release services, 286, 287
Privacy
  analysis of, 135
  as hot issue, 134
  Internet backup services, 129
  of Internet connection, 135
  IP address, 135
  issues, 148
  legislation, 142
  Philip Environmental situa-
    tion, 137
  tools, 135
  Web sites' policies, 141-144
  Web store, 334
  see also Anonymity
Privacy Commissioner of
  Canada, 148
Product information, 93
Product usability, 52
Productivity tools
  bookmark file synchroniza-
    tion, 194
  capturing Web pages, 197-200
  default Web page, 181-186
  form browsers, 191-193
  incomplete downloads, 195
  monitoring Web pages for
    changes, 193-194
  multiple sites, 195-196
  redialing busy sites, 186-187
  search engine personalization
    features, 176-181
  sharing Web pages, 200-201
  tracking previously viewed
    sites, 187-191
  unzipping Web files, 194-195
Programming fundamentals, 94
Promotion
  with Internet service
    provider, 91
  marketing techniques, 89
  Web site address, 88
  Web store, 334

Prompt Software, 268
Protection
  firewalls, 164-166
  from Internet vandals,
    111-116
  from viruses, 111-116
  proxy servers, 164
Pullam, John, 85, 88, 94, 97
Push services, 285

Q

QueryN Metasearch, 253
Quickscape, 212
QuickTime, 338, 350, 351, 354-
  358, 359, 360

R

RAM, 221
Rankin, Bob, 117
Ranking, 64-83
  assessment of, 65-66
  improvement techniques, 72
  individual algorithms, 73
  for key words and phrases, 65
  keywords, 71
  meta-tags, 71
  optimizing position, 65
  popularity as factor, 83
RankThis, 81-82
Reader's Digest Canada, 85, 87,
  88, 89, 90, 91, 94, 95, 97
RealAudio/RealVideo, 338,
  348, 350, 351-354, 359, 360
RealEncoder, 351, 353
RealNetworks, 350, 359
RealPublisher, 354
Reference.COM, 147
Registration, 56-57
  services, 64
Reliability, assessment of, 37-41
Remote access, programs,
  236-238
Repeat visits, 21
Research
  Canadian-specific informa-
    tion resources, 265
  competitive, 81
  culture-specific, 259
  geographic-specific, 259
Resolution, 19-21, 251
Reuters, 149
REX, 128
Rice, Marshall, 21
Rogers, 238
Rootshell, 150-152, 158, 166
Royal Bank, 108, 316

Also Available from Jim Carroll and Rick Broadhead

Canada's Most Comprehensive Guide to Researching Online

1999 Canadian Internet Directory and Research Guide

Really two books for the price of one, the 1999 *Canadian Internet Directory and Research Guide* gives you the tools you need to maximize your enjoyment and efficiency online.

Written by Canada's bestselling Internet authors, this indispensable guide is essential reading for anyone who's ever tried to find something on the Internet.

You'll learn time-saving techniques and strategies to help you access the information you need in a fraction of the time it currently takes. Of course, part of the challenge in searching the Internet is finding the best places to start. This book highlights and recommends dozens of online search tools that you probably didn't know existed!

The second part of this book contains annotated listings of thousands of Canada's top Internet resources—hand-picked for their content, quality, and usefulness.

$29.95

Available at bookstores across Canada

Small Business Online:
A Strategic Guide
for Canadian Entrepreneurs

If you own or work for a small business, have a home office, or dream of becoming self-employed, this book is for you. *Small Business Online* is the first book of its kind to help Canadian small businesses prosper in this new world of opportunity.

From advice on how to market your Web site to strategies for tackling the Year 2000 problem, *Small Business Online* will show you how to harness the power of the Net to both establish and expand your company. You'll learn how to skilfully use the Internet to:

- assess your entreprencurial skills
- research a business idea
- formulate a business plan
- obtain financing for your company
- set up your home office
- choose a Web design firm
- gain credibility in the global marketplace
- promote your organization internationally

Loaded with practical, up-to-date advice, this is a book that no small business owner can afford to be without!

$18.95

Available at bookstores across Canada

Mutual Funds and RRSPs Online:
A Personal Finance Guide for Every Canadian

The Internet is opening up fabulous opportunities for savvy investors who want to save money, conduct research, and share advice on money matters. With *Mutual Funds and RRSPs Online* readers will discover the best investment Web sites in Canada (and the ones to avoid!), helpful advice to create a strong investment portfolio and some great wealth-building tips and techniques. With a myriad of mutual fund and RRSP choices now available, many Canadians want to know how to use the Internet to sort out the "best from the rest" and make their choices without unnecessary sales pressure. With the guidance of this timely new title, Canadians will learn how to get the Internet working for them!

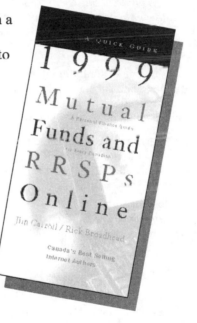

$16.95

Available at bookstores across Canada

Workshops and Presentations
by Rick Broadhead

"Have you ever experienced a presentation that moved so fast and so stretched your picture of how life operates that you knew you'd seen something important, but could barely say what? That happened to me while listening to Internet expert Rick Broadhead.... Rick has co-authored 19 books, including the Canadian Internet Handbook, and he knows his stuff."

Newsletter of the Canadian Association of Professional Speakers, June 1998

Rick Broadhead is acknowledged as one of Canada's leading authorities and public commentators on the Internet. Widely recognized for his extensive industry knowledge and non-technical approach to the Internet, Rick has been retained as a keynote speaker and workshop facilitator by organizations and professional associations across North America.

Rick's expertise has been sought by thousands of professionals in all areas of management, and his consulting services have been used by Fortune 500 companies and other organizations seeking strategic and policy guidance with respect to the Internet and corporate Web site development/management.

His clients include prominent businesses across a wide range of industries, including McDonald's, EMI Music Canada, PolyGram, Manulife Financial, the Royal Bank of Canada, Imperial Oil, Sprint Canada, Mackenzie Financial Services, BC TEL, CTV Television, Microsoft, and VISA International, where he was commissioned to prepare an overview of the strategic implications of the Internet for VISA's member financial institutions worldwide. In addition, his services have been used by a wide variety of associations and membership organizations, including the Canadian Real Estate Association, the Canadian Paint and Coatings Association, the National Utility Contractors Association, the Canadian Wood Council, the Canadian Association of Insurance and Financial Advisors, the Canadian Meat Council, Credit Union Central of Canada, and the Municipal Electric Association.

Rick is also an instructor at York University's Division of Executive Development in Toronto, where he has advised executives and senior managers from hundreds of leading North American firms and helped them to integrate the Internet into all facets of their businesses.

For further information about Rick Broadhead's consulting and speaking services, you may contact him directly by telephone at **(416) 487-5220** or by e-mail at **rickb@sympatico.ca**. Alternatively, for speaking engagements, you may contact his representatives at CanSpeak Presentations using the numbers listed below. They will be pleased to assist you!

1-800-561-3591 (Central and Eastern Canada)
1-800-665-7376 (Western Canada)

For more detailed information about Rick Broadhead, please visit his Web site:
http://www.rickbroadhead.com

Tucows Licence Agreement

IMPORTANT This is an agreement between you and TUCOWS Interactive Ltd. Please read it carefully before proceeding. This agreement provides you with rights described below to use the software programs contained on the "Tucows Top 100" CD-ROM (the "Software"). Proceed only if you agree to all terms.

BY OPENING, YOU ARE CONSENTING TO BE BOUND BY THIS AGREEMENT. IF YOU DO NOT AGREE TO ALL OF THE TERMS OF THIS AGREEMENT, DO NOT CONTINUE.

1. PERMITTED USE. The Licensor hereby grants to you a personal, non-transferable and non-exclusive right to use the Software solely in object code format, solely for your own internal business or personal purposes and solely on a single computer at any one time. If you wish to use The Software on additional computers, you must obtain a separate licence for each.

2. RESTRICTIONS ON USE. You agree that you will not: (a) copy the Software except that you may make one copy of The Software solely for backup purposes; (b) assign this Agreement of transfer, lease, export or grant a sublicence of The Software or the licence contained herein to any other party unless authorized by the Licensor in writing; (c) network The Software or otherwise use it on more than one computer system at any one time; (d) reverse engineer, demcompile or disassemble The Software; (e) use the Software except as authorized herein; and, (f) permit third parties to use The Software in any way that would constitute breach of this Agreement.

3. OWNERSHIP AND COPYRIGHT. The Licensor and its suppliers are the owners of all intellectual property rights in The Software, related written materials, logos, names and other support materials furnished in this package. No title to the intellectual property in The Software, magnetic media or any other material provided therewith is transferred to you by this Agreement.

4. NETSCAPE NAVIGATOR SOFTWARE. Contrary to the license agreement that will be displayed when installing all versions of Netscape Navigator software that forms part of the Software, the versions of Netscape Navigator contained herein are fully licensed, not trial licensed, and all distributions of Netscape Navigator are being made with the permission and agreement of Netscape Communications Corporation.

5. LIMITED WARRANTY. The Licensor warrants to you that the media on which the Software is recorded is free from defects in materials and workmanship under normal use for a period of ninety (90) days from the date of delivery assumed to be seven days from the date of shipping.

THE SOFTWARE AND RELATED MATERIAL IS PROVIDED "AS IS" WITHOUT WARRANTY OR CONDITION OF ANY KIND, INCLUDING BUT NOT LIMITED TO THE IMPLIED WARRANTIES OR CONDITIONS OF MERCHANTABLE QUALITY AND FITNESS FOR A PARTICULAR PURPOSE. THE LICENSOR DOWS NOT WARRANT THAT THE SOFTWARE WILL MEET YOUR REQUIREMENTS OR THAT ITS OPERATION WILL BE ERROR-FREE.

IN NO EVENT SHALL THE LICENSOR BE LIABLE TO YOU OR ANY THIRD PARTY FOR ANY DIRECT, INDIRECT, SPECIAL OR CONSEQUENTIAL DAMAGES EVEN IF ADVISED OF THE POSSIBILITY THEREOF.

6. LIMITATION OF REMEDIES. The Licensor's entire liability and your exclusive remedy shall be:
(a) refund of the purchase price, less any shipping costs if The Software package is unopened and the package is returned to the Licensor within ten (10) days with proof of the purchase;
(b) the replacement of any media not meeting the Limited Warranty herein which is returned to the Licensor within thirty (30) days with proof of purchase; or,
(c) termination of this Licence Agreement.

7. TERMINATION. This Agreement is effective until terminated. You may terminate this Agreement at any time by destroying all copies of The Software and related materials. The Licensor may terminate this licence without notice to you if you fail to comply with any of its terms. Any such termination by the Licensor shall be in addition to and without prejudice to such rights and remedies as may be available, including injunction and other equitable remedies. Upon receipt by you written notice of termination from the Licensor or termination by you, you shall immediately (a) cease using The Software; (b) return to TUCOWS International Ltd. Or the Licensor The Software and all written documentation and all magnetic media provided to you (or destroy all copies thereof in your possession); and (c) within five (5) days thereafter, provide the Licensor with a written confirmation that you have complied with the foregoing. The provisions of Sections 2, 4 and 6 herein shall survive termination of this Agreement.

8. MISCELLANEOUS. This is the entire agreement between you and the Licensor pertaining to your right to use The Software, and supersedes all prior or collateral oral or written representations or agreements related thereto. In the event that one or more of the provisions if found to be illegal or unenforecable, this Agreement shall not be rendered inoperative but the remaining provisions shall continue in full force and effect. This Agreement shall be governed by the laws of the Province of Ontario, Canada.

NETSCAPE CLIENT SOFTWARE END USER LICENSE AGREEMENT REDISTRIBUTION OR RENTAL NOT PERMITTED

This Agreement sets forth the terms and conditions of your use of the accompanying Netscape client software product(s) (the "Software"). Any third party software that is provided with the Software with such third party's license agreement (in either electronic or printed form) is included for use at your option. If you choose to use such software, then such use shall be governed by such third party's license and not by this Agreement. This Agreement has 3 parts. Part I applies if you have a free of charge license to the Software. Part II applies if you have purchased a license to the Software. Part III applies to all license grants. If you initially acquired a copy of the Software free of charge and you wish to purchase a license, contact Netscape Communications Corporation ("Netscape") on the Internet at http://home.netscape.com. As used in this Agreement, for residents of Europe, the Middle East and Africa, "Netscape" shall refer to Netscape Communications Ireland Limited; for residents of Japan, "Netscape" shall refer to Netscape Communications (Japan), Ltd.; for residents of all other countries, "Netscape" shall refer to Netscape Communications Corporation. For purposes of this Agreement, "Licensor" shall be defined as follows: If you have acquired a third party product or service and such product or service included the Software, then such third party shall be the Licensor. Otherwise, Netscape shall be the Licensor.

PART I — TERMS APPLICABLE WHEN LICENSE FEES NOT (YET) PAID

(LIMITED TO EVALUATION, EDUCATIONAL AND NON-PROFIT USE)

LICENSE GRANT. Licensor grants you a non exclusive license to use the Software free of charge if (a) you are a student, faculty member or staff member of an educational institution (K-12, junior college, college or university, or the international equivalent, or a library), a staff member of a religious organization or an employee of an organization which meets Licensor's criteria for a charitable non-profit organization; or (b) your use of the Software is for the purpose of evaluating whether to purchase an ongoing license to the Software. The evaluation period for use by or on behalf of a commercial entity is limited to ninety (90) days; evaluation use by others is not subject to this ninety (90) day limit. Government agencies (other than public libraries) are not considered educational, religious or charitable non-profit organizations for purposes of this Agreement. If you are using the Software free of charge, you are not entitled to hard-copy documentation, support or telephone assistance. If you fit within the description above, you may use the Software in the manner described in Part III below under "Scope of Grant."

DISCLAIMER OF WARRANTY. Free of charge Software is provided on an "AS IS" basis, without warranty of any kind, including without limitation the warranties that the Software is free of defects, merchantable, fit for a particular purpose or non-infringing. The entire risk as to the quality and performance of the Software is borne by you. Should the Software prove defective in any respect, you and not Licensor or its suppliers assume the entire cost of any service and repair. In addition, the security mechanisms implemented by the Software have inherent limitations, and you must determine that the Software sufficiently meets your requirements. This disclaimer of warranty constitutes an essential part of this Agreement. No use of the Software without payment of license fees to Licensor is authorized hereunder except under this Disclaimer.

PART II — TERMS APPLICABLE WHEN LICENSE FEES PAID

LICENSE GRANT. Subject to payment of applicable license fees, Licensor grants to you a non-exclusive license to use the Software and accompanying documentation ("Documentation") in the manner described in Part III below under "Scope of Grant."

LIMITED WARRANTY. Licensor warrants that for a period of ninety (90) days from the date of acquisition, the Software, if operated as directed, will substantially achieve the functionality described in the Documentation. Licensor does not warrant, however, that your use of the Software will be uninterrupted or that the operation of the Software will be error-free or secure. In addition, the security mechanisms implemented by the Software have inherent limitations, and you must determine that the Software sufficiently meets your requirements. Licensor also warrants that the media containing the Software, if provided by Licensor, is free from defects in material and workmanship and will so remain for ninety (90) days from the date you acquired the Software. Licensor's sole liability for any breach of this warranty shall be, in Licensor's sole discretion: (i) to replace your defective media or Software; or (ii) to advise you how to achieve substantially the same functionality with the Software as described in the Documentation through a procedure different from that set forth in the Documentation; or (iii) if the above remedies are impracticable, to refund the license fee you paid for the Software. Repaired, corrected, or replaced Software and Documentation shall be covered by this limited warranty for the period remaining under the warranty that covered the original Software, or if longer, for thirty (30) days after the date (a) of delivery to you of the repaired or replaced Software, or (b) Licensor advised you how to operate the Software so as to achieve substantially the same functionality described in the Documentation.

Only if you inform Licensor of your problem with the Software during the applicable warranty period and provide evidence of the date you purchased a license to the Software will Licensor be obligated to honor this warranty.

Licensor will use reasonable commercial efforts to repair, replace, advise or, for individual consumers, refund pursuant to the foregoing warranty within thirty (30) days of being so notified.

If any modifications are made to the Software by you during the warranty period; if the media is subjected to accident, abuse, or improper use; or if you violate the terms of this Agreement, then this warranty shall immediately terminate. Moreover, this warranty shall not apply if the Software is used on or in conjunction with hardware or software other than the unmodified version of hardware and software with which the Software was designed to be used as described in the Documentation.

THIS IS A LIMITED WARRANTY, AND IT IS THE ONLY WARRANTY MADE BY LICENSOR OR ITS SUPPLIERS. LICENSOR MAKES NO OTHER WARRANTIES, EXPRESS OR IMPLIED, INCLUDING BUT NOT LIMITED TO WARRANTIES OF MERCHANTABILITY, FITNESS FOR A PARTICULAR PURPOSE, AND NONINFRINGEMENT OF THIRD PARTIES' RIGHTS. YOU MAY HAVE OTHER STATUTORY RIGHTS. HOWEVER, TO THE FULL EXTENT PERMITTED BY LAW, THE DURATION OF STATUTORILY REQUIRED WARRANTIES, IF ANY, SHALL BE LIMITED TO THE ABOVE LIMITED WARRANTY PERIOD. MOREOVER, IN NO EVENT WILL WARRANTIES PROVIDED BY LAW, IF ANY, APPLY UNLESS THEY ARE REQUIRED TO APPLY BY STATUTE NOTWITHSTANDING THEIR EXCLUSION BY CONTRACT. NO DEALER, AGENT, OR EMPLOYEE OF LICENSOR IS AUTHORIZED TO MAKE ANY MODIFICATIONS, EXTENSIONS, OR ADDITIONS TO THIS LIMITED WARRANTY.

PART III — TERMS APPLICABLE TO ALL LICENSE GRANTS

SCOPE OF LICENSE GRANT.

You may:
* use the Software on any single computer;
* use the Software on a second computer so long as only one (1) copy is used at a time;
* use the Software on a network, provided that a licensed copy of the Software has been acquired for each person permitted to access the Software through the network;
* make a single copy the Software for archival purposes, provided the copy contains all of the original Software's proprietary notices; or
* if you have purchased a license for multiple copies of the Software, make the total number of copies of Software (but not the Documentation) stated on the packing slip(s), invoice(s), or Certificate(s) of Authenticity, provided any copy must contain all of the original Software's proprietary notices. The number of copies on the packing slip(s), invoice(s), or Certificate(s) of Authenticity is the total number of copies that may be made for all platforms. Additional copies of Documentation may be purchased from Licensor.

You may not:
* permit other individuals to use the Software except under the terms listed above;
* permit concurrent use of the Software;
* modify, translate, reverse engineer, decompile, disassemble (except and solely to the extent an applicable statute expressly and specifically prohibits such restrictions), or create derivative works based on the Software;
* copy the Software other than as specified above;
* rent, lease, grant a security interest in, or otherwise transfer rights to the Software; or
* remove any proprietary notices or labels on the Software.

ENCRYPTION. If the Software contains cryptographic features, then you may wish to obtain a signed digital certificate from a certificate authority or a certificate server in order to utilize certain of the cryptographic features. You may be charged additional fees for certification services. You are

responsible for maintaining the security of the environment in which the Software is used and the integrity of the private key file used with the Software. In addition, the use of digital certificates is subject to the terms specified by the certificate provider, and there are inherent limitations in the capabilities of digital certificates. If you are sending or receiving digital certificates, you are responsible for familiarizing yourself with and evaluating such terms and limitations. If the Software is a Netscape product with Fortezza, you will also need to obtain PC Card Readers and Fortezza Crypto Cards to enable the Fortezza features.

TITLE. Title, ownership rights, and intellectual property rights in the Software shall remain in Netscape and/or its suppliers. The Software is protected by copyright and other intellectual property laws and by international treaties. Title and related rights in the content accessed through the Software is the property of the applicable content owner and is protected by applicable law. The license granted under this Agreement gives you no rights to such content.

TERMINATION. This Agreement and the license granted hereunder will terminate automatically if you fail to comply with the limitations described herein. Upon termination, you must destroy all copies of the Software and Documentation.

EXPORT CONTROLS. None of the Software or underlying information or technology may be downloaded or otherwise exported or reexported (i) into (or to a national or resident of) Cuba, Iraq, Libya, Sudan, North Korea, Iran, Syria or any other country to which the U.S. has embargoed goods; or (ii) to anyone on the U.S. Treasury Department's list of Specially Designated Nationals or the U.S. Commerce Department's Table of Denial Orders. By downloading or using the Software, you are agreeing to the foregoing and you are representing and warranting that you are not located in, under the control of, or a national or resident of any such country or on any such list. In addition, you are responsible for complying with any local laws in your jurisdiction which may impact your right to import, export or use the Software.

If the Software is identified as a not-for-export product (for example, on the box, media or in the installation process), then, unless you have an exemption from the United States Department of State, the following applies: EXCEPT FOR EXPORT TO CANADA FOR USE IN CANADA BY CANADIAN CITIZENS, THE SOFT-WARE AND ANY UNDERLYING TECHNOLOGY MAY NOT BE EXPORTED OUTSIDE THE UNITED STATES OR TO ANY FOREIGN ENTITY OR "FOREIGN PERSON" AS DEFINED BY U.S. GOVERN-MENT REGULATIONS, INCLUDING WITHOUT LIMITATION, ANYONE WHO IS NOT A CITIZEN, NATIONAL OR LAWFUL PERMANENT RESIDENT OF THE UNITED STATES. BY DOWNLOADING OR USING THE SOFTWARE, YOU ARE AGREEING TO THE FOREGOING AND YOU ARE WAR-RANTING THAT YOU ARE NOT A "FOREIGN PERSON" OR UNDER THE CONTROL OF A "FOR-EIGN PERSON."

LIMITATION OF LIABILITY. UNDER NO CIRCUMSTANCES AND UNDER NO LEGAL THEORY, TORT, CONTRACT, OR OTHERWISE, SHALL LICENSOR OR ITS SUPPLIERS OR RESELLERS BE LIABLE TO YOU OR ANY OTHER PERSON FOR ANY INDIRECT, SPECIAL, INCIDENTAL, OR CON-SEQUENTIAL DAMAGES OF ANY CHARACTER INCLUDING, WITHOUT LIMITATION, DAMAGES FOR LOSS OF GOODWILL, WORK STOPPAGE, COMPUTER FAILURE OR MALFUNCTION, OR ANY AND ALL OTHER COMMERCIAL DAMAGES OR LOSSES. IN NO EVENT WILL LICENSOR BE LIABLE FOR ANY DAMAGES IN EXCESS OF THE AMOUNT LICENSOR RECEIVED FROM YOU FOR A LICENSE TO THE SOFTWARE, EVEN IF LICENSOR SHALL HAVE BEEN INFORMED OF THE POS-SIBILITY OF SUCH DAMAGES, OR FOR ANY CLAIM BY ANY THIRD PARTY THIS LIMITATION OF LIABILITY SHALL NOT APPLY TO LIABILITY FOR DEATH OR PERSONAL INJURY RESULTING FROM LICENSOR'S NEGLIGENCE TO THE EXTENT APPLICABLE LAW PROHIBITS SUCH LIMITA-TION. SOME JURISDICTIONS DO NOT ALLOW THE EXCLUSION OR LIMITATION OF INCIDEN-TAL OR CONSEQUENTIAL DAMAGES, SO THIS EXCLUSION AND LIMITATION MAY NOT APPLY TO YOU.

HIGH RISK ACTIVITIES. The Software is not fault-tolerant and is not designed, manufactured or intended for use or resale as on-line control equipment in hazardous environments requiring fail-safe performance, such as in the operation of nuclear facilities, aircraft navigation or communication systems, air traffic control, direct life support machines, or weapons systems, in which the failure of the Software could lead directly to death, personal injury, or severe physical or environmental damage ("High Risk Activities"). Accordingly, Licensor and its suppliers specifically disclaim any express or implied warranty of fitness for High Risk Activities.

MISCELLANEOUS. This Agreement represents the complete agreement concerning the license granted hereunder and may be amended only by a writing executed by both parties. THE ACCEPTANCE OF ANY PURCHASE ORDER PLACED BY YOU IS EXPRESSLY MADE CONDITIONAL ON YOUR ASSENT TO THE TERMS SET FORTH HEREIN, AND NOT THOSE IN YOUR PURCHASE ORDER. If any provision of this Agreement is held to be unenforceable, such provision shall be reformed only to the extent necessary to make it enforceable. This Agreement shall be governed by California law, excluding conflict of law provisions (except to the extent applicable law, if any, provides otherwise). The application of the United Nations Convention on Contracts for the International Sale of Goods is expressly excluded.

U.S. GOVERNMENT END USERS. The Software is a "commercial item," as that term is defined in 48 C.F.R. 2.101 (Oct. 1995), consisting of "commercial computer software" and "commercial computer software documenta-tion," as such terms are used in 48 C.F.R. 12.212 (Sept. 1995). Consistent with 48 C.F.R. 12.212 and 48 C.F.R. 227.7202-1 through 227.7202-4 (June 1995), all U.S. Government End Users acquire the Software with only those rights set forth herein.

Netscape Client Software EULA   Rev. 072197

Instructions for Installing the "1999 Canadian Internet Handbook Productivity Toolkit" CD-ROM

1. Insert the CD-ROM into your computer's CD-ROM drive.

2. After a few seconds, a window will appear on your screen. If it's the first time you've accessed the CD-ROM the licensing agreement window will appear; otherwise the "Welcome to Setup" window will appear. If neither of these windows appear you'll need to start the CD-ROM using Windows Explorer. (From the "Start" menu on your Windows 95/98 taskbar, select "Programs" and then "Windows Explorer." Double-click the letter corresponding to your CD-ROM drive (usually "D:") from the listing of "All Folders" on the left. From the "Contents" listing that appears on the right, double-click on the file called "install." This will bring you to either the licensing agreement window or the "Welcome to Setup" window.)

3. Many of the programs contained on the CD-ROM are compressed in "zip" format. If you don't have an unzip utility on your computer (such as Winzip), click on "Install Winzip" (found within the "Welcome to Setup" window) to begin the process of installing Winzip on your computer. Winzip will allow you to quickly install many of the programs on the CD-ROM.

4. If you already have a Web browser (such as Netscape or Microsoft's Internet Explorer) installed on your computer, proceed to Step 6. If you don't have a Web browser installed on your computer, continue to Step 5.

5. Click on "Install TUCOWS" to begin the process of installing Microsoft's Internet Explorer browser on your computer. This will take several minutes.

6. Click on "Browse CD" (found within the "Welcome to Setup" window) to begin browsing the programs on the CD-ROM.

7. The main screen for the CD-ROM will appear. You can:
   • click on the "WIN95/NT CONTENT" link to browse through a listing of all the programs on the CD-ROM, organized by category and subcategory, or
   • click on the "Windows 95" link that appears near the centre of the screen to view the list of program categories and subcategories.

   Regardless of which method you use, you can click on a subcategory name to see a description of each of the programs within that subcategory.

8. To download any of the programs from the CD-ROM, click on the blue and yellow "Download" button that appears beside the program name. Follow the instructions on the windows that appear. Be sure to save the program to a directory on your computer that you can easily locate. Once the download is complete, use Windows Explorer to locate the program in the directory that you previously chose. Double-click on the program name to install it on your computer. Again, follow the instructions on the windows that appear. If the file is a zip file, double-clicking on the program name will automatically start the unzip program (see Step 3 above—if necessary, consult the help files for your unzip program). Those files that aren't in a zip format will start to install as soon as you double-click on the program name.

9. If you encounter any problems, e-mail TUCOWS Support at **helpdesk@tucows.com**.